# MISSING

## in

## ACTION

*Resting in Peace?*

# MISSING
## in
# ACTION

*Resting in Peace?*

Dilip Sarkar

Ramrod Publications

**Other books by Dilip Sarkar: -**

SPITFIRE SQUADRON: *19 Squadron at War 1939-41*
THE INVISIBLE THREAD: *A Spitfire's Tale*
THROUGH PERIL TO THE STARS: *RAF fighter pilots failed to return 1939-45*
ANGRIFF WESTLAND: *Three Battle of Britain Air Raids*
A FEW OF THE MANY: *Air War 1939-45, A Kaleidoscope of Memories*
BADER'S TANGMERE SPITFIRES: *1941, The Untold Story*
BADER'S DUXFORD FIGHTERS: *The Big Wing Controversy*
MISSING IN ACTION: *Resting in Peace?*
GUARDS VC: *Blitzkrieg 1940*
BATTLE OF BRITAIN: *The Photographic Kaleidoscopes Vols I - IV*
FIGHTER PILOT: *The Photographic Kaleidoscope*
SIR DOUGLAS BADER: *An Inspiration in Photographs*
JOHNNIE JOHNSON: *Spitfire Top Gun, Parts 1 & 2*
BATTLE OF BRITAIN: *Last Look Back*
SPITFIRE!: *Courage & Sacrifice*
Dilip also contributed a chapter on historical accuracy to the late Robert Rudhall's best-selling BATTLE OF BRITAIN: *The Movie* (being re-printed 2006).

Most of Dilip's books have been out of print since shortly after their release dates. **Victory Books** will be re-printing the majority of these works so that, for the first time, all will be concurrently available from May 2006 onwards. To receive early notification of our publications and signed limited editions, join the Victory Books privileged customer mailing list.

**Missing in Action: Resting in Peace?**
© Dilip Sarkar MBE, 2006
ISBN 10: 1-905768-00-1
ISBN 13: 978-1-905768-00-4

Second Edition: Victory Books International, 2006.

For further information regarding further books by Dilip sarkar MBE, and or other titles, please contact: Victory Books International, PO Box 573, Worcester WR5 3WU, UK. Tel: 07921 503105. Fax: 01905 767735. www.victorybooks.co.uk

Design & layout by Victory Books, printed and bound in the UK.

# Contents

# Dedication

I am honoured to dedicate this book to:-

The Servicemen, of all nations, reported 'Missing' during the various conflicts of the 20th Century and have no known grave, and indeed their families, left behind to suffer in silence.

Amongst those who gave their lives in the Great War, for example, was my great-grandfather: Private 21307 Herbert Smith, reported Missing in Action at Gallipoli on July 27th, 1915 (4th Battalion, The Worcestershire Regiment). Herein lies an appropriate tale, however. The 4th Worcesters were taken out of the line on July 16th, 1915, to rest on the Isle of Lemnos; they did not return to the peninsula until July *29th*. Someone, somewhere obviously made a mistake when recording Private Smith's date of death. Private Smith is remembered on the Helles Memorial, on which the names of 20,000 soldiers with no known grave appear. As there are 13,000 Allied soldiers buried as 'unknown' on Gallipoli, however, there is a chance that he could be amongst them. It was my intention, therefore, to search the cemeteries for an unknown soldier with the same date of death (perhaps even finding one specifically of the Worcestershire Regiment); symbolically at least, such a grave could have been my great-grandfather's. Unfortunately, due to what is obviously a contemporary clerical error, I am denied this exercise. This rather sets the scene, in fact, for the rest of this book.

# Introduction

The very nature of being reported 'Missing', either in action or on active service, I find tremendously moving; the pain suffered by families with no headstone to visit, no tangible full stop upon which to focus their grief, is unimaginable. It is a sad fact, however, often due to administrative errors, that this need not have been the case in respect of a number of casualties; we can only feel especially deeply for their families. My friend Larry McHale, an aviation poet of growing repute, perfectly encapsulates our feelings in the following poignant verses:-

*The limitless void holds many souls,*
*Those young boys will never grow old.*
*In flush of youth, their lives cut short*
*Be they ever bright in daily thought.*

*Missing in Action: Resting in Peace?*
*Are there those who know no earthly release?*
*They have no grave to mark the place*
*Where death began its cold embrace.*

*Almighty God allay their fears,*
*And wipe away their lonely tears,*
*His Tender Love on them bestow,*
*Rewards for deeds so long ago.*

*So many souls entwined with Death,*
*For us they gave life's final breath,*
*We'll not forget, their names shall shine,*
*Never dulled within the mists of time.*

On May 21st, 1972, aviation archaeologists excavated the crash site of a WW2 fighter aircraft on Romney Marsh in Kent. Parts discovered soon indicated it to be a Hurricane, but there was a disturbing surprise in store: a parachute pack followed by the pilot's mortal remains. Surprisingly enough, this incident is not unique: during the next 14 years, 13 airmen reported missing in 1940 would be recovered in similar circumstances. On September 9th, 1986, however, the Protection of Military Remains Act (PMA) became a part of the law of this land and thus amateur civilian recoveries became illegal. The policy of the Ministry of Defence (MOD) was (and remains) one of non-disturbance, and so the Act should have maintained the *status quo* in respect of any further sites. Nevertheless, further airmen have been recovered, and for some time feelings have been running high within both our enthusiast sub-culture and the MOD. For several years I have been convinced that the whole emotive subject was moving towards a final showdown; it seems, however, that the public relations exercise which this project also represents may have averted potential disaster for all concerned.

The reason for writing this book has been to place the evidence and facts regarding this complex subject into the public domain, to thus allow, for the first time, the general public and enthusiast alike to formulate an *informed* opinion. I hope that the contents will be of help to anyone who finds themselves involved with the subject on an official basis, and complimentary copies have therefore been sent to various HM Coroners, Chief Constables, the Crown Prosecution Service and the MOD. Whilst some of my previous books have been intended to be as definitive an account of certain subjects as these times now permit, this book is more a comprehensive report regarding a subject yet to be concluded. I have no doubt that this book will stimulate further debate and research into the subject which will, I hope, serve to further assist the history of these tumultuous times. A fascinating read, I believe, is guaranteed.

**Dilip Sarkar,**
Bayhouse,
Worcester,
March 1998.

*Dilip Sarkar, French eye-witnesses and the team he took to France in
May 1996 to recover what was hoped to be Wg Cdr Douglas Bader's
Spitfire near St Omer. As a recovery the dig was a huge success,
yielding an enormous amount of Spitfire. Subsequent research, however,
indicated that it was not W3185 but actually LZ996.
The full and acurate account of this epic operation appears in Dilip Sarkar's*
Bader's Tangmere Spitfires: The Untold Story, 1941.
*(Author)*

PROLOGUE

# Missing in Action

Every Remembrance Sunday since 1987 has seen a unique and intensely personal gathering at a small roadside memorial, commemorating a Polish Spitfire pilot, near Malvern in Worcestershire. A scientist, a road safety officer, a gardener, a warehouseman and a policeman, all members of the (now former) Malvern Spitfire Team (MST); uniquely, none are of the wartime generation. Nevertheless, over a decade ago, all were sufficiently moved by the story of Flying Officer Franciszek Surma for their lives to become fused together, to some extent, and never be quite the same again.

Franek Surma was born on July 1st, 1916, in Galcowice, Poland. On September 1st, 1936, three years before the German invasion of his homeland, Surma volunteered for service in the Polish Air Force. By July 18th, 1939, his training was complete and Lieutenant Surma joined No 2 Air Force Regiment. Six weeks later came the *Blitzkrieg*, and although we suspect that Surma participated in the brief fighting, detail is scant. Fortunately he escaped the Polish defeat and, via Roumania, Syria and France, eventually arrived in England to fight with the

*A suitably solemn looking James Sarkar (then aged four) at the Surma Memorial, Remembrance Sunday, 1996.*
*(Author)*

RAF. In July 1940, Pilot Officer Surma received tuition on Hurricanes at No 6 Operational Training Unit (OTU), and was consequently amongst the first foreign nationals posted to swell the numbers of Fighter Command's squadrons. On August 20th, he joined 151 Squadron at North Weald, with whom he destroyed an He 111 over the Thames Estuary just 10 days later. No 151 had been in action throughout the French campaign and first half of the Battle of Britain, but as Surma had joined the unit fairly recently, when it was withdrawn he was posted, on September 11th, to another unit in southern England's No 11 Group: No 607 Squadron at Tangmere. Again Surma was frequently in action, on September 26th claiming an Me 109 destroyed off St Catherine's Point. When 607 was pulled out, he was again moved on to another squadron, No 46 at Stapleford, on October 18th, but strangely, just four days later was posted to Squadron Leader RRS Tuck's No 257 'Burma' Squadron at North Weald. Six days later the Pole destroyed an He 111 over Ashford, but the following day survived being shot down himself, by the *Gruppenkommandeur* of III/JG26, *Oberleutnant* Gerhard Schoepfel, during a surprise low-level fighter-bomber attack on North Weald.

After the Battle of Britain, Pilot Officer Surma served with Squadron Leader Douglas Bader's 242 Squadron, flying Hurricanes on endless convoy protection sorties out of Suffolk's Martlesham

*Plt Off Franek Surma at Readiness, Tangmere, September 1940.*
*(Author)*

Heath. By early 1941, however, in addition to the two Polish and one Czech fighter squadrons operational during the Battle of Britain, various foreign squadrons had been formed. Combat experienced pilots like Surma, who had knowledge of RAF operating procedures, provided these squadrons' backbone. On March 14th, 1941, therefore, Pilot Officer Surma reported for duty with No 308 'City of Krakow' (Polish) Squadron based at Baginton, near Coventry. On March 26th he was in action again, with two less experienced Poles, damaging a Ju 88 intercepted in the vicinity of their airfield. Around this time, the Poles began exchanging their Hurricanes for Spitfires, the latter being received from No 65 'East India' Squadron which was completing a rest period at Kirton-in-Lindsey. They were Mk Is, and obsolete in terms of operational efficiency.

On May 11th, 1941, Pilot Officer Surma scrambled from Baginton in Spitfire R6644, ZF-H, to intercept a 'bogey' reported in the Kidderminster area of Worcestershire. This unidentified radar plot was later confirmed as a Blenheim, so Surma and his No 2, Sergeant Widlarz, merely undertook a general patrol of the Worcestershire area. When high above the Malvern Hills, however, R6644, an aircraft with a substantial number of flying hours, developed an engine fire. Surma slowly lost height, steering the aircraft away from the built up areas of Malvern below, strung out along 11 miles of hills, and eastwards over the rural River Severn flood plain. It is possible that his first intention was to undertake a forced-landing, but when the cockpit suddenly filled with smoke he was unable to maintain control and baled out. The Spitfire impacted harmlessly in a field near Madresfield Court, a stately home near Malvern, and the pilot landed safely nearby. Although less dramatic than a pilot wrestling with controls at low-level in such circumstances, Pilot Officer Surma's actions had undoubtedly avoided a potential tragedy in Malvern that far-off Sunday morning.

A month after Surma's crash, No 308 Squadron joined No 1 Polish Fighter Wing at RAF Northolt, an established station on the north-western approaches to London (more recently newsworthy for receiving the body of the tragic late Diana, Princess of Wales). By the spring of 1941, Fighter Command had opened the Non-Stop Offensive, 'reaching out' across the Channel in a war of attrition against the *Jagdwaffe*. The Poles were soon embroiled in this new strategy, and Surma enjoyed success against the enemy both on the ground and in the air. On September 1st, he was promoted to Flying Officer and awarded the Cross of Valour. October 28th saw him receive the squadron's first *Virtuti Militari*, Poland's highest gallantry award (in various classes), from General Sikorski himself, the leader of the Polish people in exile.

On November 8th, 1941, many Fighter Command squadrons participated in the last Circus operation of the year, No 110, a daylight attack by a small number of Blenheim bombers against the power station at Lille. For a variety of reasons the operation was not a success, not least for 308 Squadron. The Polish Fighter Wing was tasked with escorting the bombers, 308 being top cover squadron, 303 close, and 315 medium. Unfortunately, due to the position of the sun, 308 Squadron missed the rendezvous with the bombers over Manston. Unable to communicate due to strict radio silence, the Wing Leader, Wing Commander Tadeuz Rolski, flying with No 303 Squadron, rocked his wings violently in a forlorn attempt to alert 308 Squadron to the fact that their Spitfires were turning in the wrong direction. Dazzled, by the bright sun, the 'City of Krakow' squadron continued onwards. Unable to wait, the rest of the 'beehive' set course for enemy occupied France. Eventually Squadron Leader Pisarek, 308's CO, had no alternative but to break radio silence and seek advice from the Ground Controller. Pisarek was instructed to patrol the Dunkirk to Calais area between 16,000 - 25,000 feet. Towards the end of their endurance, when low on fuel and with little to spare for combat, the Polish Spitfires were 'bounced' by Me 109s in a diving attack from above. The Spitfires immediately broke, rapidly seeking to disengage and return safely over the Channel.

Whilst hurtling back over the sea at 20,000 feet that grey November day, Pilot Officer Poplawski paired up with Pilot Officer Stabrowski. Both pilots saw an Me 109F attacking a lone Spitfire, to the aid of which they hurried. From 200 yards range, Poplawski fired at the enemy, observing 'explosions' on the right wing. After two more bursts, the 109 went down, 'smoking from underneath the fuselage'. Upon the appearance of four more enemy fighters, Poplawski made good his own escape, not witnessing, therefore, the fate of either the Spitfire or 109. Stabrowski also claimed to have hit the 109, having delivered a long burst of both cannon and machine-gun fire from 300 yards. Short of fuel, although he saw the enemy aircraft 'dive towards the sea near the French coast', 'being short of ammunition and petrol', Stabrowski was 'unable to chase the 109 and returned to England'.

Back at Northolt, the Poles were to wait in vain for the return of Flying Officer Surma. The squadron's Operations Record Book describes the day as 'depressing', adding that the 25-year-old Surma had been lost in 'unknown circumstances'. He was officially posted 'Missing in Action'.

There the story would have ended if not for the common fascination in the crash of R6644 at Madresfield shared by a group of people, from various walks of life, who became the Malvern Spitfire Team in 1986. Having researched the 'life' of Spitfire R6644, the crash and Flying Officer Surma's service record, I became determined to discover his fate. It seemed a possibility that the 'lone Spitfire' assisted by Poplawski and Stabrowski could have been his; I traced Wing Commander Poplawski in Buenos Aires:-

It is wonderful to know that someone like yourself is so interested in the events of a time during which you were not even born. I must congratulate you for the high standard of this work. It is an extremely interesting experience to read the story of one's own life, researched and written by a 25-year-old. It really makes me feel that what we fought for was worthwhile when your generation remembers and feels for our sacrifices in such a tangible way.

I believe that it was Franek Surma's Spitfire being attacked by a least one Me 109. The German attack that day was so sudden that its intensity overwhelmed us. We tried to assist the Spitfire under attack, but I was warned by Squadron Leader Pisarek to 'Break left!', which I did immediately. There were more 109s diving to attack me, and being short of fuel I was unable to hang around.

An analysis of German casualty records indicate no aircraft lost in circumstances attributable to No 308 Squadron. Regarding the enemy combat claims, just one stands out, a Spitfire destroyed near Dunkirk by *Hauptmann* Johannes Seifert, *Gruppenkommandeur* of I/JG26. As no other Fighter Command losses cross-reference with that claim, it is reasonable to conclude that Flying Officer Surma was actually killed by *Hauptmann* Seifert; ultimately, the victor of that combat, however, was to be killed by American fighters in 1943.

To the MST, the fact that Flying Officer Surma was missing in action somehow amplified the poignancy of his story; although his name is inscribed, together with hundreds of other Polish airmen, on the reverse of the Polish Air Force Memorial beside the A40 at Northolt (see Chapter Two), we had no grave to visit. As the project had virtually consumed our lives, we all felt this most keenly. Unanimously we decided that it was appropriate to remember this gallant young Pole near the crash site of R6644; we felt that, due to his actions on May 11th, 1941, the people of Malvern owed him something.

On Saturday, September 12th, 1987, the MST recovered the remains of R6644 at a public event organised to raise money for the 'Wings Appeal'. That afternoon a Tornado of 229 Operational Conversion Unit roared low over the site in tribute, and our roadside memorial to Flying Officer Surma was unveiled by two of his former comrades, Squadron Leaders Ludwik Martel and Boleslaw 'Gandy' Drobinski. At the televised service, the Rev. Eric Knowles moved us all: 'his was an example of how to serve our country and our God'.

This experience also made me consider very early on that if we of the MST felt most keenly the fact that Flying Officer Surma was missing, how must his family feel, grieving on the other side of Europe? The answer to that question was provided in February 1989, in the form of the most moving letter I have ever received, from Flying Officer Surma's very elderly sisters: Mrs Elzbiete Morcinek and Mrs Otylia Paszek; to quote selectively therefrom:-

> During the war we received just one letter, via Holland. He told us that he had written two other letters and had sent some money home. Only one of these letters was ever received. Via Portugal we received tins of sardines, which we knew to be a sign that he was still alive. Can you imagine our great joy? These were the only moments of happiness in those cruel days. After the war ended, we received another parcel; we were overjoyed as we believed, therefore, that Franek had survived. We waited for a very long time but he did not come home. Eventually we enlisted the aid of the Red Cross, which told us that our brother had probably been killed the in the cold

waters of the English Channel. In the fullness of time we received his medals and some photographs. The loss of our dear brother drove us all to the utmost depths of dispair.

Since that tragic time, nearly 50 years have passed and we are now incredibly happy that the memory of Franek is still alive, not just with us, but with you in far away England who have not forgotten him. We are so proud that he is our brother and are astonished at your achievements as such a young man, your efforts are really heart-warming. Please express our sincerest gratitude to everyone who has contributed to the commemoration of Franek Surma. It is hard for us to express our thanks in words, as none adequately express the feelings of two old ladies keeping alive the memory of their dear brother.

Your letter has evoked our reminiscences and shows how wonderful people can be. Many special thanks go to you and we will be praying for your success in life, prayers for a person who is now very close to us. May God take care of you and the organisation which you have created. We are so happy that there is still someone to light a candle for Franek on All Souls Day.

We are delighted because the memorial erected to him now acts as his spiritual grave, a symbol which he can look down upon from Heaven. We are always worried that, having no known grave, Franek could never be a peace; now we are all at peace, thanks to you.

The memory of Franek Surma has also been perpetuated through publication of his story in my second book, *The Invisible Thread: A Spitfire's Tale* (Ramrod Publications, 1992, out of print since 1993), and the Surma Memorial Trust for Youth. The latter was a registered charity which we founded in 1992, offering financial assistance to projects working for youth in Malvern. Some £10,000 was raised through the sale of prints, from a painting by Mark Postlethwaite G.Av.A., depicting R6644 over the Malvern Hills. The money having been appropriately distributed, 10 years after R6644 was recovered, both the MST and the Trust were dissolved. We all felt that life had moved on, and to mark this significant event, on December 10th, 1997, a plaque commemorating Flying Officer Surma was dedicated at Malvern Youth Centre. Unveiled by Mrs Barbara Sykes, niece of Flying Officer Franek Gruszka, reported Missing in Action on August 18th, 1940 (see Chapter Three), we hope that the plaque will ensure that the Surma story is brought to the attention of many generations of local youngsters. As I said that evening, both Mrs Morcinek and Mrs Paszek are now deceased; at least we know that they are indeed 'all at peace' now. No doubt their spirits too joined that of their brother at Malvern Youth Centre for this moving occasion.

The story of Flying Officer Surma has both an appropriate and extremely poignant ending. There are other 'missing' pilots, however, whose stories are actually disturbing, from various viewpoints, as the remainder of this book seeks to explain.

CHAPTER ONE

# Their Finest Hour

On May 10th, 1940, Hitler's *panzers* crashed across Germany's western border and commenced an unprecedented advance towards the Channel coast. Unable to stem the field-grey tide, the Allies were soon in full retreat towards the port of Dunkirk, from where 350,000 troops were ultimately evacuated. As Winston Churchill said, 'What General Weygand called the Battle of France is over; the Battle of Britain is about to begin'.

The Battle of Britain was fought to deny Hitler aerial supremacy over Great Britain as a prelude to a seaborne invasion. His Directive No 16 stated that:-

> As England, in spite of her hopeless military position, has so far shown herself unwilling to come to any compromise, I have decided to begin preparations for, and if necessary, to carry out the invasion of England.

> This operation is dictated by the necessity to eliminate Great Britain as a base from which war against Germany can be fought. If necessary the island will be occupied.

Having conquered Poland, Norway, Denmark, Holland, Belgium, Luxembourg and France, the German *Wehrmacht* stood on the Calais cliffs sublimely confident; *Reichsmarschall* Herman Goering, Commander-in-Chief of the Luftwaffe:-

> My Luftwaffe is invincible.... And so now we turn to England. How long will this one last - two, three weeks?

Air Chief Marshal Sir Hugh Dowding, Air Officer Commanding-in-Chief RAF Fighter Command felt somewhat differently, despite the overwhelming odds he faced:-

> My strength has now been reduced to the equivalent of 36 squadrons .... we should be able to carry on the war single-handed for some time if not indefinitely.

To place Fighter Command's daunting task into context, this is what the British Prime Minister considered to be at stake:-

> The whole fury and might of the enemy must very soon be turned upon us. Hitler knows that he will have to break us in this island or lose the war. If we can stand up to him, all Europe may be free and the life of the world may move forward into broad sunlit uplands. But if we fail, then the whole world, including the United States, including all that we have known and cared for, will sink into the abyss of a new Dark Age made more sinister, and perhaps more protracted, by the lights of perverted science. Let us therefore brace ourselves to our duties, and so bear ourselves that, if the British Empire and Commonwealth last for a thousand years, men will still say 'This was their finest hour'.

For official purposes the conflict began on July 10th, 1940, and opened with attacks on Channel bound convoys and coastal radar stations. Then Fighter Command's airfields were hammered, but just when the situation became critical for the hard pressed defenders, on September 7th, the Germans switched to attacking London. Their intention was two-fold: firstly London was considered the only target capable of forcing Fighter Command to commit all of its fighters to battle, for destruction *en masse* by the waiting Me 109s, and secondly it was considered that heavy bombing would crush the civilian population's morale. The enemy was wrong on both counts. The change in targets gave Fighter Command the chance to make good damage at its vital Sector Stations, and Londoners declared 'we can take it', winning the admiration of the free world. Contrary to the *Ober Kommando der Wehrmact's* (OKW) belief, however, RAF fighter squadrons were not concentrated in South-Eastern England alone, but distributed throughout the country, some in the front line, others in reserve. Wherever the *Luftwaffe* attacked, even in the north, there were always plenty of Spitfires and Hurricanes waiting to meet them throughout the entire Battle of Britain.

On September 30th, due to mounting losses the OKW called a halt to using massed formations of bombers during daylight hours (although the *Kampfgeschwadern* were then to dominate the night sky for the next eight months). The day battle's final stages saw attacks on the British aircraft industry, by Ju 88s operating in mere *Gruppe* strength (around 30 aircraft) escorted by many fighters, or lone 88s engaged on harassing attacks. The Me 109 fighters continually swept over southern England, the *Jabos* (fighter-bombers) within their formation dictating that Fighter Command could not ignore these otherwise relatively harmless intrusions. Consequently Fighter Command was forced to mount almost constant standing patrols during daylight hours and many survivors remember this as the most exhausting phase. Officially the 16 week aerial conflict ended on October 31st, Hitler's invasion plans having been postponed indefinitely. Fighter Command remained very much in existence, however, and Great Britain's defiance and resolve, therefore, remained unchecked.

German historians, and some academics attempting to place the Battle of Britain into 'perspective', argue that there was never a victory as such, certainly not by the end of October 1940. It is true that the *Luftwaffe* did not give up sustained air attacks on England until May 1941, when Hitler transferred his forces eastwards to invade Russia, and indeed both sides remained forces to be reckoned with. In 1940, however, Britain had stood alone, its army in tatters after the Battle of France, and Fighter Command was equipped with 33 squadrons of Hurricanes compared to just 19 of Spitfires. By 1941, much re-building had already taken place in England, and many more Spitfires had reached operational squadrons. By 1941, it is equally arguable that the circumstances had greatly changed, and invasion was no longer even a pipe dream. The fact remains, therefore, that Hitler was unable to invade England in 1940 due to the efforts of RAF Fighter Command; if that is not a victory, then show me one! To suggest otherwise reflects a great misunderstanding of the Battle of Britain, not to mention enormous disrespect to the memory of the 544 aircrew who lost their lives in the defence of this realm.

Collectively, Winston Churchill paid homage to the 2,927 men of Fighter Command whose courage made victory possible:-

> The gratitude of every home in our island, in our Empire, and indeed throughout the world, except in the abodes of the guilty, goes out to the British airmen, who, undaunted by odds, unwearied in their constant challenge and mortal danger, are turning the tide of world war by their prowess and devotion. Never in the field of human conflict was so much owed by so many to so few.

Without a doubt, RAF victory in the Battle of Britain was the first turning point for the Allies in the Second World War. With Britain in German hands, Hitler could have concentrated on waging war against Russia, whilst the USA, if indeed ever forced into a war with Germany, would have had no base from which to launch a European liberation campaign. Without the 'Few', democracy would have suffered a mortal blow from which it may *never* have recovered. This should not be forgotten, *ever*.

Throughout the Battle of Britain, the aircraft of both sides crashed in droves throughout southern England. As most combats took place between 15-25,000 feet, when a pilot or crew baled out at such an altitude, the doomed aircraft was capable of making a deep impression in the ground upon impact. In the case of a single-engined fighter, for example, momentum would often carry the front-half of the fuselage up to 15 feet, or even deeper, into the ground. The fate of many Hurricanes abandoned in such circumstances are prime examples, although Spitfires had a habit of losing one wing on the way down, causing the aircraft to thereafter flutter, rather than plunge vertically at full speed. At sites where aircraft had 'gone in', however, the first on the scene were often greeted by nothing more than surface fragments and a smouldering crater. Often, due to the limitations of both equipment and resources, aircraft defied recovery, and in such circumstances the sites were tidied up and craters levelled.

When an RAF aircraft failed to return, its unit would notify the Air Ministry, which then contacted HQ No 43 Maintenance Group at Cowley, the responsibility of which was to task the local Maintenance Unit (MU) with recovering the aircraft concerned. The responsibility for clearing wrecks in Kent, Sussex, Surrey and Hampshire - the principle battlefield - was that of Squadron Leader Goodman's No 49 MU located at Faygate, near Horsham, Sussex. The unit operated a number of crash parties, each of eight - 10 men commanded by a senior NCO. There were, in addition, a number of crash inspectors, Pilot Officers who surveyed every site and decided upon the method of recovery and resources required.

Naturally, as the tempo of battle increased, 49 MU became overwhelmed with an ever increasing work load. In addition, the unit itself suffered casualties: on August 12th it lost a staff car and Commer low-loader during a raid on Hawkinge, and four days later, at Tangmere, two drivers were killed and both a Coles crane and one Bedford three-tonner were destroyed.

To assist 49 MU, the Air Ministry commissioned a number of civilian firms, largely from the road haulage business. To give some idea of the amount of work involved, on September 15th, 31 aircraft of Fighter Command crashed in southern England, 14 of their pilots being killed and 11 wounded. On the same day, some 37 *Luftwaffe* aircraft were also brought down, 28 of their crewmen being killed. When one considers that the Battle of Britain lasted for 16 weeks, and that August and September were particularly bitterly contested months, the quantity of aircraft requiring salvage can be appreciated.

One of the civilian contractors concerned was AV Nicholls & Co., located at 100 North Road, Brighton. This firm worked under the direct control of 49 MU, but it must be remembered that, unlike the RAF recovery teams, these men were untrained in such work. Generally only two civilians were despatched to each job, they being expected to dismantle or dig up a wreck as appropriate. It must also appreciated that in 1940 these men did not enjoy the high-tech mechanical diggers of today, their equipment comprising just a pair of sheerlegs, cutting equipment, and literally buckets and spades. Both in terms of manpower and equipment, these pitiful resources can only be described as woefully inadequate.

Damage to RAF aircraft was given three categories: Category '3' represented a total loss, '2' an aircraft requiring extensive overall back at a repair depot, and '1' minor work on station. Relatively undamaged RAF aircraft were obviously a precious commodity, as they could either be repaired and put back into service, or at least cannibalised to keep other fighters in the air. Such downed machines, therefore, had to be considered a priority.

*A forced-landed Spitfire of 234 Squadron. Such aircraft were a priority for salvage.*
*(Via Andrew Long)*

Not all forced-landings went smoothly, however. On October 17th, the Hurricanes of Tangmere's 213 Squadron were bounced over Kent by the Me 109s of I/JG77 based at Marquise; Flight Lieutenant Geoffrey Stevens, at the time a Sergeant pilot, remembers:-

*Sgt Geoffrey Stevens.*
*(Author via Stevens)*

213 Squadron was scrambled late in the afternoon, getting on for 1700 hrs as I recall, and as we climbed away from Tangmere I remember thinking that I wished Jackie Sing ('A' Flight commander) was leading us, as in my opinion he was the best. Neither did we have a tail end Charlie for reasons which escaped me.

We climbed to about 17,000' when I noticed anti-aircraft shells bursting ahead and below. I reported this and at about the same time we had a course correction starboard. As we turned I saw strikes on Red 2, just ahead of me. We were flying the stupid close formation 'vic' of three aircraft in line astern (I was Yellow 2). Simultaneously I was hit in the engine by three or four cannon shells. The rev counter went off the clock and smoke and flames enveloped outside. The standard practise if hit was to get out of the action as quickly as one could. I shoved the stick over and went into a spiral dive. Flames, smoke and glycol fumes were everywhere, and I went down switching off everything I could think of.

I entered cloud at about 10,000', coming out at 5,000 whilst preparing to bale out. The flames appeared to have stopped, I lifted up my goggles to have a look round and saw that I was over a town. I knew that if I baled out my aircraft would cause some severe damage, possibly loss of life. A field containing an anti-aircraft gun was within gliding distance and so I opted for a forced-landing.

I did not appear to be in any immediate danger at this stage and so settled into a straight glide towards the field. Having sorted everything out in my mind, knowing exactly what I was going to do, I was dismayed to see what I have since described as electric light bulbs, but what were in fact tracer shells, going past my cockpit. Looking in my rear view mirror I saw a yellow-nosed 109 on my tail. Without power, evasive action is limited, especially with so little height to play with. I used rudder to skid out of the German's sights, and am told that fortunately he was chased off by another Hurricane, but I'd lost a lot of height.

The effect of this on my carefully planned approach was disastrous. I opened the hood and blinded myself with glycol fumes. I put my goggles on again, but by this time I was very low, about 100', travelling much too fast and in the wrong position for an approach to the field. Everything was wrong! I did a steep left-handed turn towards the field and slammed the Hurricane onto the ground, it was all I could do. It was unfortunate that I had been forced to choose the one approach which ended up with my wing root against a four-feet thick tree stump. The aircraft shot into the air over on its back into a sort of marsh. With all that had gone on leading up to this, I had omitted to lock the sliding cockpit hood open, and my harness back. The hood consequently slammed shut and I was propelled forward upon impact with some force, cutting my face on the reflector gunsight.

I was hanging upside down with blood running Down my face. I could smell the petrol leaking out everywhere and hear the hissing of the cooling engine in the wet marsh. Otherwise everything seemed dead quiet, I tried to open the hood but it was useless. I was expecting the aircraft to go up in flames at any time and seemed powerless to effect an escape. I carefully released my straps and let myself down so that I lay on my back on top of the cockpit hood. I think this was more to do something than hang upside down doing nowt!

Although it seemed like an age, assistance actually came very quickly. People seemed to come from nowhere, including the army. One helpful farmer got himself a corner post with a pointed metal end and rammed it through the perspex hood. Had I been hanging upside down it would have gone straight through my head, as it was it went just past my nose! To cut a long story short, one wing was lifted enough to allow the hood to slide back. The small clearance from the ground was sufficient for me, I was out of the wrecked aircraft like a bullet from a gun, I'd never moved so fast in my life!

When I got out I could not stand up because the stick had come back and whacked my knee and I was somewhat shaken. However, with two men supporting me on each arm we made it to HQ and I can remember being amazed at the number of people who were there. As we walked up the field it was a crescent of people all looking to the centre. I only mention this because shaken though I was it made an impression on me which I can still see to this day.

I was taken to hospital in Ashford, and later the soldiers came out to see me and asked if I would join them for a drink that night. I was willing but the doctor was having none of it!

Amongst the seven JG77 pilots who claimed Hurricanes destroyed in this action (although Fighter Command actually lost but three) was *Gefrieter* Karl Raisinger of the 3rd *Staffel*; in his *Flugzugbuch* (flying log book) he wrote 'London, *Abschuss* (aerial victory) - Hurricane'. Just eight days later, however, Raisinger fell to the guns of Fighter Command. His Me 109E-4, '13+', was hit in both the engine and radiator, the pilot safely forced landing near Saltdean where he was captured. Of course processing prisoners of war created even more work; the civil police stations of southern England were well used as clearing houses for the multitude of German airmen captured throughout the 16 week conflict in addition to shot down RAF pilots attempting to return to their units. To give some idea regarding the volume of prisoners of war, on September 15th alone there were some 61 German aircrew captured in the UK. Prisoners had to be handed over to the nearest military unit for interrogation by A1 1(k) at Trent Park, Cockfosters, North London. Downed enemy aircraft were inspected by the RAF technical intelligence branch, 1 (g), which had to report on and officially release the aircraft prior to removal.

Gfr *Karl Raisinger, who possibly shot down Sgt Stevens, en route to captivity. (Via Chris Goss)*

Naturally the aerial knights of Fighter Command were the rightful heroes of their time. On August 26th, 'A' Flight of Kenley's 616 Squadron was bounced over Dungeness by JG51. Four Spitfires were shot down, Pilot Officer William Walker falling to the guns of the *Geschwaderkommodore*, the *Luftwaffe's Oberkanone* (Top Gun), Major Werner Moelders himself. Fortunately Walker baled out, albeit with the remains of a cannon shell in his foot, and was rescued from the English Channel; he recalls his reception at Ramsgate harbour:-

Quite a crowd had gathered, who must have watched the whole incident and rescue from the shore, and gave me a right rousing cheer as I was put in the ambulance. A kind old lady handed me a packet of cigarettes and so I started thinking that being shot down was not such a bad experience after all!

On September 30th, 19-year-old Sergeant Peter Fox scrambled for the first time with 56 Squadron, from Boscombe Down, intercepting KG55's Westland bound raiders over Lyme Bay; upon first sighting the enemy *Valhalla*, Peter 'just couldn't believe it'. Whilst absorbed in attacking an He 111, his Hurricane was bounced by an Me 110 escort fighter:-

I broke to starboard, pulling upwards and away, with all controls apparently working correctly. I got over land at 3,000' and was wondering whether I could make Warmwell airfield when I saw flames coming up between my legs. I don't think that I even thought of my next action but instinctively rolled the kite upside down, released my harness and saw my feet above me and the plane above my feet, presumably staled. Where was the ripcord? I told myself to calm down, and pulled the 'D' ring straight away! I had never before pulled a ripcord, never seen one pulled, never seen a parachute packed, and never had any instruction. The 'D' ring was flung into the air, followed by some wire. Obviously I had broken it. Then I felt the small tug of the pilot 'chute followed almost immediately by the full wrench of the main parachute. I was safe! The next second I was aware o an 'enemy' which I assumed was going to shoot me. It was, however, my flaming Hurricane which literally missed me by inches. The kite slowly screwed round, going into a steeper and steeper dive until almost vertical, aimed directly at the cross-hedges of four fields to the NE of a wood towards which I was drifting. It hit the cross-hedges spot on, a short pause and then a huge explosion followed by another pause before flames shot up to a great height. I'm glad I wasn't in it!

How astonishing that no parachute training was given! It may also surprise some readers to know that for many OTU fresh pilots, the first time they actually experienced air-to-air firing was in anger.

*Peter Fox and (the sadly now late) Hans 'Peter' Wulff consider a piece of the former's Hurricane during the MST recovery, 1995. (Author)*

On September 11th, Sergeants Tony Pickering and Eddie Egan of 501 Squadron undertook a local patrol of the Kenley area, as the former Hurricane pilot remembers:-

We were flying along, just the two of us, looking about all the time for trouble. I saw four 'Spitfires' behind us. We were talking to each other on the R/T, constantly monitoring the movements of the 'Spitfires'. Suddenly one of them zoomed forward and shot Eddie down. I turned towards the attack but the old Hurricane was just too slow and the Hun who had got Eddie just flew off with the others at top speed. I looked over the side and could see Eddie going down, the aircraft in flames. I saw it crash into a wood just outside Ashford in Kent. After I landed I naturally reported on the incident, giving the location of where I saw Eddie crash. Six months later I had to see the Air Ministry and pin-point the site as Eddie could not be found.

The location of some crash sites in remote areas was a problem. As we shall see, it was many years later that Tony was to hear the name of Eddie Egan (see Chapter Four).

*Tony Pickering whilst serving
with the Desert Air Force.
(Author via Pickering)*

*Sqn Ldr Jack Stokoe DFC pictured
after the Battle of Britain.
(Author via Stokoe)*

Squadron Leader Jack Stokoe has an interesting story to contribute, which raises important issues:-

Only a year before the Battle of Britain, my contemporaries and I were pursuing our civilian occupations whilst learning to fly with the RAF Volunteer Reserve in our spare time. The majority of us were only 18-19 years-old. Being aircrew, when called up, we were automatically given the rank of Sergeant, which at first caused some dismay in the ranks of professional Sergeants, many of whom had taken 20 years to reach that exulted rank!

Most of us had only 50-60 hours flying on elementary types like Magisters and Tiger Moths before being called up in September 1939. After a brief spell at Initial Training Wing (ITW) to instil some discipline into us, we had about 100 hours on Harvards at Flying training School (FTS), including a few trips actually firing guns. We were then posted to an OTU to fly Spitfires, in my case No 5 at Aston Down in Gloucestershire. With between 10 - 15 hours on Spits we would then be posted to an operational fighter squadron. I eventually joined 603 'City of Edinburgh' Squadron, an Auxiliary Air Force unit based at Dyce in Scotland. There were only three of us NCO pilots, the remainder being officers. By August 27th, 1940, the squadron had moved to Hornchurch in Essex, just north of the Thames Estuary, by which time I had about 70 hours on Spitfires and therefore most fortunate; I could have gone straight to a front line fighter squadron direct from OTU, as indeed so many young pilots did, and in which case I would not have rated my chances of survival very highly. I had even seen, but not engaged, two German aircraft, He 111s on reconnaissance over northern Scotland.

On August 29th we flew four patrols, intercepting Me 109s on two of them. I claimed one damaged but the trimming wires on my aircraft were shot away. On August 30th we made four more interceptions, during the course of which I was credited with an Me 109 confirmed destroyed and another damaged. Again, however, my own aircraft was damaged, by a cannon shell in the windscreen, and in fact my hand was slightly cut by splinters. On September 3rd came three more interceptions of 20 plus enemy aircraft, one of which I shot down in flames over Canterbury. On September 2nd I was involved in two interceptions during the course of which I damaged two enemy aircraft but was myself shot down in flames, fortunately baling out.

On that occasion, as I was attacking an enemy aircraft I remember machine-gun bullets, or maybe cannon shells, hitting my Spitfire followed by flames in the cockpit as the petrol tanks, situated in front of me, ignited. I thought 'Christ, I've got to get out of here quick!' I undid the straps and opened the hood, but this turned the flames into a blow-torch. I was not wearing gloves, as during our hurried scramble I had forgotten them, and had to put my hands back into the flames to invert the aircraft so that I could drop out (no ejector seats in those days!). I remember seeing sheets of skin peeling off the backs of my hands before I fell out of the aeroplane. I was then concerned regarding whether the parachute would function or whether it had been damaged by fire, but I pulled the ripcord and fortunately it opened perfectly.

I landed in a field, but the Home Guard queried whether I was an enemy agent! A few choice words in English soon convinced them I was genuine and thereafter I was rushed into the emergency hospital at Leeds Castle suffering from shock and severe burns to my hands, neck and face.

I was in hospital for six weeks before returning to operational duties on October 22nd, with further combat successes. A second tour of duty with 54 Squadron followed, which included a second bale out. I was then seconded to a training unit but returned to Ops, flying night-fighters, later in the war.

The point about the incident when I was shot down over Kent on September 2nd, 1940, is that at the time 603 Squadron itself was suffering such heavy casualties that things got pretty chaotic; for four days after baling out, although quite safe in hospital, I was officially posted 'Missing in Action'!

With the administrative system choked by the huge amount of work concerning RAF, *Luftwaffe* and civilian casualties, prisoners of war, not to mention damage to property, military installations, and lost aircraft, it is not surprising that such clerical errors occurred under pressure. The problem did not just affect the living, as indicated by the story of 21-year-old Sergeant Geoffrey Wilberforce Pearson.

Pearson joined 501 Squadron at Gravesend, on the Thames Estuary's south bank, straight from OTU in late August 1940. As Squadron Leader Peter Morfill recalls, 'I was a Flight Sergeant in those days which were busy times. We used to start Ops at about 0600 hrs, and it was usually still busy at 1600'. Squadron Leader Peter Hairs remembers that 'I was a Pilot Officer then and I certainly was very busy, we used to fly up to eight patrols or scrambles a day'. Tony Pickering was amongst Geoffrey Pearson's fellow NCO pilots: 'We used to play a card game together, to while away the time spent at Readiness, but I put a stop to it as I was taking too much money off Geoffrey and I'm no gambler!'

Although times stated in official records are contradictory, as is so often found to be the case, during the morning of Friday, September 6th, 11 Hurricanes of 501 Squadron were scrambled to intercept an incoming raid. The Hurricanes flew first to Dymchurch, on the Kentish coast near Lympne. Over Dungeness the raiders, comprising 20 bombers and '100 plus Me 109s at an altitude of 20,000 feet and upwards', could be seen crossing the English coastline near Rye. The enemy fighters belonged to Major Adolf Galland's JG26 *Schlageter*, and in the ensuing combat the outnumbered Hurricanes (odds being at least 10:1 against) not surprisingly came off second best. Three of 501's pilots were shot down, Pilot Officer HC Adams, killed when his parachute failed to open, Sergeant OV Houghton killed at the controls of his fighter; Sergeant Pearson was reported Missing. Peter Hairs recalls 'a pilot falling through the air trailing an unopened parachute and have always since assumed this to have been Adams. There was certainly much activity during this combat with aircraft all over the place and a large number of parachutes'.

The following day, No 49 MU inspected the wreckage of Hurricane P3516, Sergeant Pearson's aircraft, at Cowleas Farm, Hothfield, just NW of Ashford in Kent. Indeed, the dead pilot had already been recovered from the aircraft, but somehow identification details were lost between there and the local mortuary. Consquently the airman was buried four days later at St Stephen's,

*Survivor: Plt Off Peter Hairs.*
*(Author via Hairs)*

*Casualty: Sgt Geoffrey Pearson.*
*(Author)*

Lympne, as 'Unknown'. Many years after the war, Sergeant Pearson's brother-in-law, Richard Griffiths, himself a former fighter pilot, undertook his own research into the events of September 6th, 1940. A simple analysis of Fighter Command casualties on the day in question indicated that Sergeant Pearson was the only pilot outstanding. This process of elimination proved that the airman at St Stephen's was Geoffrey Pearson, a fact accepted by the Commonwealth War Graves Commission at Easter 1982; appropriately a named headstone was erected soon afterwards.

Two particular stories, however, set the scene for the remainder of this book.

At 1405 hrs on October 1st, 1940, Hurricane L1946 crashed in a pond at Villa Farm, Aust, Gloucestershire. The pilot, Sergeant Dennis Hayter, was a pupil at No 5 OTU, based at Aston Down (also in Gloucestershire), and had been engaged on aerobatics practice. Eye-witnesses recollect watching the Hurricane start a dive at 5,000 feet, levelling out at 3,000 feet. Immediately afterwards the pilot, for some reason, lost control, his aircraft plunging vertically into the ground at high speed. According to the Accident Record Card, the aircraft 'dived into quick mud' and defied salvage by 50 MU (based at the Morris Works, Cowley, Oxford); the pilot was presumed killed although his remains were not recovered.

Mr LJ Hawkins was Superintendent of the Civil Defence Rescue Service (ARP) for the Thornbury Division and in charge of 10 men. In 1984, he wrote that:-

It was a matter of some concern to the people of Aust that the RAF had made so little attempt to recover the pilot's body. Consequently I volunteered my force to undertake the recovery, and we started in mid-November, some weeks after the crash. A ditch was dug to drain away the pond water and what remained was baled out with buckets. The site was dug by hand, the recovery taking five weeks to complete; the pilot's body and engine was eventually recovered at a depth of 25 feet.

On December 20th, 1940, 50 MU's 'Superintendent' (name illegible, but an unusual title for an RAF unit) wrote to Mr Hawkins:-

As requested by you I have given instructions for a gang to proceed to Villa Farm to collect the engine and portions of fuselage which you have salvaged from Villa Farm, near Aust.

I have also given instructions for the gang to tidy up the site to the satisfaction of the farmer.

I must congratulate you and your men on your perseverance in reaching the body of the pilot of this machine.

As a result of the efforts of Mr Hawkins and his team, 22-year-old Sergeant Hayter was buried at High Wycombe Cemetery. If not for the feelings and efforts of these local people, this pilot would doubtless have remained 'Missing'. This story also emphasises the sad fact that many airmen were lost in such training accidents before having the opportunity to meet the enemy; at the time of his death, Sergeant Hayter had recorded just two solo hours on the Hawker Hurricane.

Our second story concerns another casualty of October 1940: Peter Roy Charles McIntosh who was born on August 9th, 1920, at Crofton Park, Brockley. Two years later the family moved to 220 Lower Addiscombe Road, Croydon, where the young Peter was to spend his formative years. His sister, now Mrs Mary Cooper, recalls those happy days:-

Like his friends, many of whom also sadly perished during the war, he had a happy growing up. At school he enjoyed being a cadet, especially on field days - getting lost but if lucky being on the winning side, summer camps and tattoo days at Whitgift Middle School in Wellesley Road, Croydon. In the long summer holidays we had the choice of three airfields to visit by cycle - Croydon, Kenley or Biggin Hill. Biggin was a long way to go but from the road the planes could be seen on the ground. Kenley was closer but although we lay for hours in the long grass, often not one plane was espied. Croydon even offered real cream ices on the roof of an airport building but we hadn't much pocket-money so rarely enjoyed this delicacy. I actually had very little interest in aviation so stopped going after a while, but Peter was always able to sufficiently enthuse some friend or other to accompany him.

Peter later became a clerk with the Eagle Star Insurance Company, joining the RAFVR, as AC2 No 745004, on February 7th, 1939. An aircrew volunteer, the following day he was promoted to Sergeant and commenced 'square bashing' at ITW. Between January 1st and May 21st, 1940, he completed his basic and advanced flying training before learning to fly Hurricanes at 6 OTU. On July 6th, the 19-year-old pilot was posted to No 151 Squadron, at the North Weald Sector Station in Essex. Sergeant McIntosh remained with 151 for over two months, during which time he flew numerous patrols and convoy protection sorties. On September 13th, he joined No 605 'County of Warwick' Squadron at Croydon, where the pilots lived in two-bedroom houses adjacent to the airfield. No doubt the young pilot welcomed this opportunity to serve close to his family and at the very airfield which he had found so inspiring as a youth.

On October 12th, the *Jabo Staffel* of *Lehrgeschwader* 2 undertook a 'tip n'run' raid on London. At least three of these fighter-bombers reached the capital, over which bombs were dropped from 20,000' and at random. Consequently five civilians were killed in Piccadilly Circus by a single SC250 bomb which there found its mark. In return, a number of Me 109s were shot down by defending fighters, but 605 Squadron had a casualty: Sergeant McIntosh who was reported Missing. Again, Mrs Cooper remembers:-

Peter telephoned home at about mid-day, telling us that he would be on Ops during the afternoon but would 'phone again later. When he neither telephoned or came home to see us, our father called the squadron and received the devastating news that Peter was missing. There was no other official news throughout the next day, but we knew from other pilots that there had been a combat over the Kentish coast. Our father and elder brother then travelled by car to tour the country area over which the combat had been fought. They stopped and questioned people regarding whether they had seen a British fighter crash on the day in question, and were eventually directed to Littlestone Golf Course, near New Romney, by a farmer who had seen a plane come down there. They subsequently returned home with a piece of fuselage bearing the number P3022, which identified the aircraft concerned as being Peter's Hurricane. When approached by my father, the Air Ministry had said that it had no personnel available to search for missing aircraft, and so, needless to say, in our house there was much bad feeling against the authorities. In the event, father still had difficulty convincing them that he had found Peter's crash site. Eventually my brother's remains were recovered by the RAF and brought home. Ten days after his death in action, our dear Peter was buried in Shirley churchyard.

*Sgt Peter McIntosh.*
*(Via Colin Brown)*

Young Sergeant McIntosh was undoubtedly hacked down by an Me 109 over Dungeness that fateful day, but how disturbing that his crash site should be discovered by his family; a lack of resources seems to have been the authorities' excuse in respect of such matters for a very long time. The reader may be surprised to learn that, nearly 60 years on, other 'Missing' pilots *still* lie at *known* crash sites in Southern England and are now the subject of bitter controversy. Before moving on to examine this problem in detail, however, the reader needs to be familiar with further background details, which the next chapter seeks to provide.

*Littlestone Golf Course, Romney Marsh, Kent: this spot would have been Sgt McIntosh's last resting place if not for his family's efforts in 1940.*
*(Via Colin Brown)*

CHAPTER TWO

# Lest We Forget

The war in Europe finally ended on May 8th, 1945, an auspicious date celebrated everafter as 'Victory in Europe Day'. By then, Hitler was dead amidst the ruins of Berlin, his Third Reich completely destroyed. For nearly six long years the world had been aflame, the cost of human life running into millions. As the Allied advance had progressed across Germany, prisoners of war had been liberated in their hundreds of thousands. These men were rapidly repatriated, returning home anxious to get on with their lives. With no war to fight, slowly the armed forces were demobilised; these servicemen too, upon 'demob', faced a return to and the responsibilities of civilian life. Also, the civilian population of Great Britain had also endured both danger and hardship; understandably, therefore, the prevalent attitude was one of 'getting on with it' and trying to forget the war, so far as was possible.

It was only after VE Day that the true scale of the conflict, particularly in respect of loss of life, became known. The Holocaust, which defies both description and condemnation through mere words alone, was discovered along with numerous other atrocities against humanity in the former Nazi occupied lands. The world demanded vengeance, and to some extent this was satisfied during the International Tribunal at Nuremberg which called the guilty to account.

Due to the common dangers from Germany and Japan, during the war the two worlds of Capitalism and Communism had been forced together. Once victory had been achieved, the rival ideologies resumed the mutual suspicions harboured since the Bolshevic Revolution of 1917. The war had also redefined Europe's boundaries and so down slammed the Iron Curtain, protecting Stalin's territorial advances; the world was now locked into the Second World War's political aftermath: the Cold War.

Against such a backdrop, the dead were collected from battlefield graves in all theatres of war and buried collectively in official military cemeteries. This work had actually commenced during the Great War when a Red Cross Mobile Ambulance Unit decided to search for, locate, identify and register many thousands of graves. By 1917 the work was officially conducted by the Imperial War Graves Commission (IWGC), the duties of which were marking and maintaining the graves of all those who died in the service of the Empire during the Great War. Also, the Commission was to construct cemeteries and memorials, and publish records pertaining. In 1960, the Commission changed its name to the Commonwealth War Graves Commission (CWGC), under which name it still operates. The Commission's intention is:-

> That each of the dead should be commemorated individually by name either on the headstone of the grave, or by an inscription on a memorial; that the headstone and memorials should be permanent; that the headstone should be uniform and that there should be no distinction made on account of military or civil rank.

Each headstone measures 2ft 8in in height and 1ft 3in wide, bearing the badge of the service, name, rank and number together with decorations, if appropriate, and an inscription chosen by relatives. Some of the latter can be particularly moving; buried at Esquelmes, Belgium, is Grenadier Guardsman EJ Portsmouth, killed in action on May 21st, 1940: *We think of him in silence but all we have are memories and a photo in a frame*. The headstones were originally made of Hopton

Wood or Portland stone, but Botticino limestone is now used which requires less maintenance. In the cemeteries the headstones stand in narrow borders planted, wherever possible, with roses and perennials offset with lawns, shrubs and trees.

If doubt exists regarding the exact location of a grave within a cemetery, the headstones are inscribed 'Buried near this spot', or similar. Those of the unidentified bear the inscription chosen by Rudyard Kipling: 'Known unto God'. He also suggested the wording for the Stone of Remembrance, found in all but the smallest cemeteries: 'Their Name Liveth for Evermore' (Ecclesiasticus, Apocrypha 44:14). Sir Edward Lutyens designed the Stone, and Sir Reginald Blomfield created the Cross of Sacrifice, found in all cemeteries.

Other countries also had war graves work to undertake. Naturally Germany had to give consideration to her many war dead, which were also largely gathered together at communal cemeteries. For example, German casualties suffered in Belgium were virtually all interred at Lommel, where some 39,000 German soldiers now lie. In England, during the war, German servicemen were often buried in the appropriate local churchyard or cemetery, but afterwards the *Volksbund Deutsche Kriegsgräberfürsorge* (German War Graves Commission, VDK) arranged communal burial in the *Soldatenfriedhof* on a lonely hillside at Cannock Chase in Staffordshire. The headstones there are a direct contrast to those of the CWGC, being roughly hewn from a granite like stone; details recorded are scant: name, dates of birth and death.

*The headstone at Cannock Chase of three German airmen all recovered during the 1970s (see chapters 3 & 4).*
*(Andy Saunders)*

*Willi Schocke's headstone at Gosport; note incorrect date of death.*
*(Miss M Balfour)*

As previously discussed, on September 30th, 1940, KG55's He 111s mounted what was to be the last major daylight bombing raid of the Battle of Britain, directed against the Westland aircraft factory at Yeovil. Due to a covering of cloud, a tragic, but perfectly understandable, navigational error saw not Westlands obliterated but the neighbouring Dorset beauty spot of Sherborne. The old biscuit-coloured town, an inspiration to Thomas Hardy, was of no military significance but 18 civilians lost their lives. The raiders themselves had been harried by Fighter Command since before reaching the English coastline to virtually their return landfall over France; four Heinkels were lost, all of which came down in the sea. Three of the enemy aircrew concerned were rescued by the *Seenotdienst*, including Major Dr Ernst Kuhl, the *Geschwader* Operations Officer who had planned the raid; 12 were *Vermisst* (Missing). The bodies of four were later washed ashore and their deaths confirmed. One of these men was a 21-year-old air gunner, *Obergefrieter* Willi Schocke, whose body was washed ashore on October 14th at Horsesand Fort in the Solent. Schocke was buried at Gosport cemetery where he lies to this day. In fact, despite the general policy of gathering their dead at Cannock Chase, a surprising number of German casualties can still be found buried at their original locations around the UK. Their headstones, however, are different to those at the *Soldatfriedhof*, being more in keeping with those of the CWGC. National markers are based upon the style of the Iron Cross (a non-political but national military symbol).

Of course the question of identifying casualties, as bodies were washed ashore on the south coast sometimes many days after the date of death, was often a problem. For example, in Folkestone New Cemetery in Kent, near Hawkinge, a number of German graves can be found, like that of *Obergefrieter* Schocke at Gosport, which have remained at their original burial place; one there records simply *Ein Deutscher Soldat* (A German Soldier). Problems of identification also arose due to the violent nature of air crashes. On September 2nd, 1940, a I/JG53 Me 109 crashed at Bridge Farm, Bilsington, but was completely burnt out. The charred remains of the pilot defied identification and so were buried as *Unbekanst* (unknown) in Aylesham Cemetery. German records apparently indicate that this *Jagdflieger* is either *Leutnant* Riegel or *Oberfeldwebel* Kuehlmann, both of whom were *Vermisst* after this sortie over England.

In the wake of the Second World War, much effort went in to identifying certain Allied casualties, particularly those who had fallen overseas. In an attempt to trace the last resting places of thousands of RAF airmen missing after raids over occupied territory, the Missing Research & Enquiry Service (MR&ES) was established. By 1950, 20,000 of the 40,000 missing aircrew had been located, either buried by the enemy or recovered from the crash sites of their aircraft. Amongst those cases dealt with by the MR&ES was that of Squadron Leader THD Drinkwater DFC.

On May 18th, 1944, 'Drink' led 122 Squadron's Mustangs on a Ranger to the Tours - Nantes area of Occupied France. East of Tours, the CO was hit by flak, at low-level, and crashed near the River Loire. At the time he was buried at St Symhorien cemetery at La Salle as 'An Unknown English Soldier'. On June 22nd, 1946, Mrs Drinkwater received a letter from the Air Ministry:-

> I am reluctant to distress you by referring after so long an interval to the loss of your husband, but I am compelled to ask for your assistance. Some information has now been received which may enable us, with your help, to trace his burial place. We have received an exhumation report concerning a grave in St Symhorien Cemetery. The cemetery records contain an entry: Unknown British Soldier buried June 1st, 1944. The exhumation found that the body was that of a Squadron Leader with the DFC, wearing RAF battledress and a dark pullover. He had straight light brown hair. No means of identification could be found, but a cuff-link was taken from the

grave and has been forwarded here. The decorations and locality seem to indicate that this grave may be that of your husband, and if you could identify the cuff-link that would be conclusive. Unfortunately it is in a very bad condition but has marks of diagonal coloured stripes on a background of pale blue enamel. I am sorry to cause you distress, but I should be most grateful if you could say whether you recognise the link from this description. I hesitate to send it to you because of its condition, but should you wish to see it then I will send it to you.

The cuff-link was identified as having been a present from the Squadron Leader's younger brother, and so a named headstone was erected at the Nantes (Pont-de-Cens) Cemetery at Loire Sinfereure: Plot L, Row B, Grave 21. In more recent times, the grateful French have erected a memorial to this gallant airman, who rose from Aircraftsman to Squadron Leader DFC. In 1997, this was appropriately unveiled by his brother, Dunkirk veteran and former Grenadier Guardsman Les Drinkwater.

*Sqn Ldr THD Drinkwater DFC.*
*(Author via Drinkwater)*

*The original IWGC marker.*
*(Author via Drinkwater)*

Like German war dead in the UK, however, not all Allied casualties on the European sub-continent were gathered in communal military cemeteries. A particularly moving story of one such serviceman concerns Sergeant Peter Garratt Rose.

Peter Rose was born on May 17th, 1916, at Burton-on-Trent. Educated at the town's grammar school, he later maintained his family's tradition by working at the Bass, Ratcliff and Gretton Brewery. In 1936, Peter enlisted in the RAFVR and learned to fly at Burnaston airport near Derby. Called up in June 1939, Sergeant Rose eventually joined No 65 'East India' Squadron at Turnhouse in Scotland. He remained with the unit for its subsequent front line tour at Tangmere, but when 65 was withdrawn for rest at Kirton he became 'bored with uneventfully patrolling the east coast'. Consequently he transferred to No 1 Photographic reconnaissance Unit (PRU) at Benson. However, flying unarmed photographic reconnaissance deep within enemy occupied territory was a hazardous business. On May 3rd, 1941, the pilots of No 1 PRU flew a number of successful sorties, but two Spitfires failed to return: Flying Officer W Panton in X4495, and Sergeant PG Rose in R6805.

At 1300 hrs that fateful day, a Spitfire had appeared high over the village of Soumagne, near Liege, in Belgium. Villagers immediately realised that the aircraft was in some difficulty due to its rough-running engine. Suddenly the aircraft became uncontrollable, and a small bundle was seen to leave the cockpit. A white silk parachute then blossomed and commenced a gentle downward descent until a wing became detached from the doomed Spitfire. Tragically the debris hit the fragile parachute, damaging its shroud lines and deflating the canopy. The unfortunate Sergeant Rose then plunged to earth, being killed on land owned by the Spronck family near Maireux.

*Sgt Peter Rose.*
*(Author via the late Mr J Rose)*

The local policeman, Leonard Melon, had made his way to the scene where he was tasked by the Germans with guarding the wrecked aircraft. Later, with the assistance of German soldiers, he loaded the pilot's body onto a cart and drove to the local mortuary. Sergeant Rose's funeral service took place in Fecher's village church on May 5th. The underground Belgian newspaper *Le Courier due Soir* (Messenger of the Night) reported that nearly 2,000 patriots attended, including 300 students from Liege University, all carrying flowers in the national colours of Great Britain and Belgium. The German authorities had forbidden Sergeant Rose's proposed burial at Soumagne Cemetery, so the cortège made its way to the crash site itself. En route, the Germans broke up the gathering, no doubt anxious regarding the public order implications, and seized the body which was returned to the villagers for burial after the crowd had dispersed. Under cover of darkness, however, and at risk of punishment from the Germans, Sergeant Rose was secretly buried in the Spronck family plot at Soumagne Cemetery.

In 1948, Peter Rose's parents visited Soumagne where they were moved to receive the full story from M. Spronck. Soon afterwards, the IWGC intended to move Sergeant Rose to a communal war cemetery, but at this both the family and villagers protested. A compromise was reached when the authorities agreed that the pilot remain in the cemetery providing he was given his own grave marked by an official headstone. Today, every generation of Soumagne schoolchildren are told the story of 'their' pilot who died to make their freedom possible, and whenever the Rose family occasionally visits the grave, tributes of fresh flowers are always to be found.

*Corner of a foreign field: the crash site of X4495,1941 & 1988.*
*(Via M P Vierstraete)*

It is a fact, however, that little or no effort was made by the authorities to locate the whereabouts of Allied aircrew reported missing over the UK; had the reverse been a point of fact, it is unlikely that the need to write this book would ever have arisen.

Another relevant story concerns that of another 65 Squadron pilot, Pilot Officer Victor Lowson. On July 21st, 1942, 12 Spitfires 65 Squadron flew a Rhubarb to Zeebrugge. Various targets there were strafed, but shortly having crossed the coast Lowson's Spitfire was hit by machine-gun fire. He turned back out to sea and prepared to bale out by climbing to 1,500 feet and inverting the aircraft. At that point, the Spitfire plunged into the North Sea, taking its pilot to a watery grave. Although Warrant Officer Ron Stillwell orbited the spot, nothing more was ever seen of Lowson. The following day, 65 Squadron's CO, Squadron Leader DAP McMullen, wrote to Pilot Officer Lowson's parents:-

> It is with great regret that I have to write and tell you that your son, Pilot Officer Victor Lowson, is missing as a result of operations yesterday afternoon.

I am allowed to tell you in confidence that he was taking part in a low-flying attack against enemy troops and gun positions on the coast of Belgium near Zeebrugge. Whilst shooting up gun positions his Spitfire was hit and crashed in the sea about two miles off the Belgian coast. I am very much afraid that there is little chance of his having survived.

He was one of our best pilots, a section leader and potential flight commander. In fact during this flight he was leading a flight into the attack. He always showed exceptional promise as a pilot, officer and leader. It has come as a great blow to me personally that he is now missing.

Vicky was the best loved lad on our squadron, his quiet steadiness of purpose and gentle with having endeared him to us all during the long time he has been with us. He will always remain in the hearts of the rest of the squadron as one of the very best.

On August 8th, 1942, the Lowsons received a letter from Flight Lieutenant Hugh Tarrant, the 65 Squadron Intelligence Officer:-

*Plt Off Victor Lowson.*
*(Author via the late Mr J Lowson)*

I regret that we have received no further news of Victor. Should we hear anything at all in the future I will notify you immediately. I hope you will accept my personal sympathy. As an Intelligence officer I am naturally older and more experienced than the pilots in the squadron. I would like to assure you now that Victor was quite the finest boy that I have ever met in the Service. I am happy to think that he liked me and looked upon me as a friend. I miss his companionship in this squadron very deeply.

Even after receiving Tarrant's letter, the Lowsons had naturally prayed for a miracle, that some-how, against all the odds, Victor really had escaped the confines of his cockpit to be captured. On

November 24th, 1942, the Air Ministry wrote to Mr Lowson stating that in view of the time having elapsed since Pilot Officer Lowson had crashed into the sea, and no news having been received of him since, it had to be accepted that there was sadly little hope of him being alive. On February 27th, 1943, the Lowsons heard further from the Air Ministry, to the effect that as nothing had been heard of their eldest son since he was shot down, Victor must now be 'Presumed dead for official purposes'.

Of course in addition to the numerous Allied fighter pilots who went missing over the sea, so too did the crews of a great number of other aircraft. After the war, some thought had to be given regarding an appropriate means of commemorating all of these men. The Air Council Committee on War Memorials presented to the Air Council their recommendations regarding the commemoration of those members of the British Commonwealth and Empire who, while serving in or in association with the RAF, lost their lives and have no known grave. These proposals were approved in February 1948, and then referred to (what was then) the IWGC, so that appropriate memorials could be planned and built accordingly.

It was decided that in England there should be one memorial dedicated to men who lost their lives flying from bases in the UK, Iceland, the Faroe Islands, Northern Ireland and the Azores, and from bases on the Continent of Europe in France, Holland, Belgium, Germany, Denmark, Norway, Finland, Luxembourg, Czechoslovakia and Russia. These servicemen were from Fighter, Bomber, Coastal, Training and Maintenance Commands, and were from all parts of the British Commonwealth and Empire.

When considering a suitable site for the proposed memorial, the Commission wished to preserve a link with aircraft and favoured a position near Heathrow. Cooper's Hill was eventually chosen at Runnymede, scene of *Magna Carta*, near the Thames at Windsor. Sir Eugene and Lady Effie Millington-Drake donated six acres of land, and by the autumn of 1949 construction work, undertaken by Messrs. Holloway & Sons, had commenced.

The Runnymede Memorial was designed by Sir Edward Maufe and constructed in Portland Stone with Westmoreland green slate roofs. The memorial features a cloister, the names of the missing being recorded thereon, on the far side of which is a tower, akin to an airfield control tower, which contains a shrine as a place for quiet contemplation. At the southern end of the site are entrance gates to a central avenue leading to a triple-arched portico providing access to the cloisters which are located on the edge of a wooded hill, overlooking the Thames. Each cloister terminates in a look-out, one facing Windsor, the other Heathrow. The tower has a central arched opening above which are three figures representing Justice, Victory and Courage, the tower itself surmounted by a crown. The view from the top of the tower is quite stunning, with Windsor Castle to the west and Heathrow to the east. Indeed, aircraft approaching the busy airport are actually level with the viewing point high on Cooper's Hill. It could not have been better chosen and a visit is strongly recommended.

The names of over 20,000 missing aircrew, including Belgians and Czechoslovakians serving with the RAF but not Poles, are engraved at Runnymede. The official information plaque states that '...it is right for those with no known graves to be remembered here'. Walking around the cloisters in November 1997, it was moving to see poppy wreaths personally dedicated, by both relatives and squadrons, to various aircrew whose names sadly appear on the memorial. In the shrine's great engraved glass window, two angels hold a scroll with verses from Pslam 19:-

*If I climb up into*
*Heaven though art there*
*If I go down to Hell*
*Though art there also*
*If I take the wings of the*
*Morning & remain in the*
*Uttermost parts of the*
*Sea, even there also*
*Shall thy hand hold*
*Me and thy right*
*Hand shall hold me.*

HM Queen Elizabeth II inaugurated the Runnymede Memorial on October 17th, 1953, and thus did the British and Commonwealth establishment pay tribute to the missing.

*The impressive Runnymede Memorial to the Missing.*
*(Author)*

In 1943, Polish airmen stationed at Northolt considered erecting a stone tablet to commemorate their comrades killed during the Battle of Britain. Due to the continuance of the war and the increasing casualties, nothing further was done until after the cessation of hostilities. In the summer of 1945, a committee was established to consider how best to honour fallen Polish airmen. At the committee's request, MRAF Viscount Portal of Hungerford appealed to the British people via letters published in the *Daily Telegraph*. Contributions flowed in, and by the end of 1946, the Committee had at its disposal £8,172 7s 1d. It was decided that a memorial, designed by the well-known Polish sculptor, M. Lubeski, would be built close to RAF Northolt. On its reverse were to be the names of the 1,241 Polish aircrew killed on operational flights (the remaining 1,167 having lost their lives on non-operational sorties and not, therefore, individually recorded). Accompanying the names are the words 'I have fought a good fight. I have finished my course. I have kept the faith'. The Polish Air Force Memorial was unveiled, by Lord Tedder, on November 2nd, 1948, appropriately All Souls' Day in the Christian calendar.

As early as 1942, the Air Ministry decided to research and record the names of all aircrew killed in the Battle of Britain to facilitate a national memorial. Westminster Abbey was proposed as a site, and the easternmost of five small chapels therein was chosen. Appropriately, in September 1940, a piece of shrapnel from a German bomb had pierced the chapel's east wall, this being retained and protected by glass. The chapel's centrepiece is now the Memorial Window, designed and painted by Hugh Easton. On a lectern was displayed the Roll of Honour, printed on parchment and bound in blue leather. The Roll, however, includes the names of aircrew other than those

*Left: Polish Air Force Memorial at Northolt.*
*(Author)*
*Above: Battle of Britain Memorial Chapel,*
*Westminster Abbey.*
*(Via Lady Odette Dowding)*

relevant to Fighter Command, such as Bomber, Coastal, Training and Maintenance Commands, and the Fleet Air Arm. As the Battle of Britain was fought by Fighter Command, it is hard to understand the reason for including in this particular tribute the names of these other airmen. Nevertheless, this Battle of Britain memorial in Westminster Abbey was unveiled by HM King George VI on July 10th, 1947.

So far as the authorities are concerned, these acts of official commemoration should be the last word. The question we will later be asking is whether, in respect of certain cases, this is actually appropriate or indeed justified?

At the time, the fighting on September 15th, 1940, was considered significant, although the quantity of German aircraft claimed as destroyed has since been considerably reduced by post-war researchers able to cross-reference RAF and *Luftwaffe* records. Still recognised as a turning point in the battle, however, September 15th was dubbed *Battle of Britain Day* and celebrated annually. In the immediate post war period, although the armed forces demobilised, the RAF remained a significantly sized service, not least as a precaution against the perceived threat from the east. Many former 1940 fighter stations remained operational bases, such as Tangmere, Kenley and Duxford, and at such aerodromes the RAF annually hosted commemorative Battle of Britain air shows. The memory was overtly kept alive, and although wartime survivors tried desperately to 'get on with it', new generations became fascinated by the subject.

Naturally both the post war American and British film industries had a huge amount of material and ideas to commit to the silver screen. For at least 30 years after the war an apparently never-ending stream of war films were produced, covering many aspects of the conflict, such as *Dunkirk, Sink the Bismark, The One That Got Away, The Longest Day, Reach for the Sky* and the *Dambusters*. It must be appreciated that in those days home video entertainment was unavailable and, certainly during the 1950s, even television sets had yet to reach every household. The cinema, therefore, remained a vitally important focus of leisure and relaxation. Such films as *Reach for the Sky*, for example, really were the *Jurassic Park* and *Lost World* of their day. Also, in the wake of the Second World War, a plethora of literature was published, again covering all aspects, and authors such as Paul Brickhill, who not only wrote *Reach for the Sky* but also the *Dambusters* and the *Great Escape*, became wealthy men. Model kits also became popular, and both young and old built scale replicas of the aircraft, ships and armoured fighting vehicles which had fought in every theatre of war. An enthusiast cult had already begun.

The Battle of Britain itself commands all the elements of great dash and drama, so it is perhaps surprising that no-one, either in Britain or Hollywood, attempted to transfer the subject to the cinema screen until 1968. Films like *Reach for the Sky* and *Angels One Five* had included reference to the battle, but only as it affected a certain unit or individual; no attempt had been made to tell the story as a whole. In 1965, a former Polish Spitfire pilot, Ben Fisz, produced a story of Norwegian resistance fighters, *The Heroes of Telemark*, starring Kirk Douglas, but in September his next project, the story of General Ord Wingate, collapsed when the Wingates refused to sign the required consent agreement. Describing this as a 'punch in the solar plexus', Fisz was devastated and took to walking in Hyde Park to ease his distress. As he walked the green fields, Fisz heard a familiar sound - a Merlin engine - and saw a Spitfire overhead rehearsing for the Battle of Britain Day fly past over London just two days later. Immediately inspired, Fisz rushed back to his office and telephoned Freddy Thomas, head of the production division of the Rank Organisation. A positive reaction was given to Fisz's suggestion that he be commissioned to produce *The Battle of Britain*, although there was much work ahead before the film's premier in 1968.

During the making of *The Battle of Britain*, Group Captain Hamish Mahaddie, a former Path-finder of repute, was tasked with scouring appropriate period aircraft from wherever they could be found right across the globe. Spitfires and Hurricanes were located in various states, and restored to either flying or static condition. Incredibly, the Spanish Air Force remained equipped with Spanish built He 111s and Me 109s (albeit powered by Rolls-Royce Merlin engines!), and these airworthy machines were seconded to the film company. At Pinewood Studios a huge tented 'aircraft factory' was erected, producing replica Spitfires, Hurricanes, Me 109s and He 111s in both wood and fibre-glass. Some of the aerial filming was completed in the UK, despite somewhat variable weather, and so the skies of East Anglia and Southern England once more beheld a spectacle of yesteryear: cutting, thrusting fighters and blossoming parachutes. Many major stars of the 1960s were included in the cast, such as Sir Michael Redgrave, Robert Shaw, Christopher Plummer, and Michael Caine. The film's excelling marketing package suddenly made the Battle of Britain topical, and an international cinema going audience waited impatiently for the film's release. As a seven-year-old schoolboy I can personally remember accompanying my father to London on a business trip, and seeing the film's striking poster adorning every tube-station's walls. I still have a full set of *Battle of Britain Cards*, colour stills from the film available with (believe it or not!) *Battle of Britain Bubble Gum*, which we schoolboys enthusiastically chomped. Even before the epic's release, a new generation had been inspired.

*The Battle of Britain* was premiered in 1968, 28 years after the Battle of Britain proper was fought. Already the somewhat dramatic and never-to-be repeated conflict had passed into recent history, and the interest stimulated by the film inspired an increasing number of historically minded aviation enthusiasts to join those already undertaking their own research into the aerial combats of the past. A new interest with its own peculiar cult had been born: aviation archaeology; a significant milestone had been reached.

The very mention of the word 'archaeology' immediately conjures up an image of excavation, intrigue, the unknown, discovering the past in a time-travelling like experience. Again, I would refer to one of Mr Churchill's wartime speeches:-

> History, with its flickering lamp, stumbles across the trail of the past, trying to reconstruct its scenes, to revive its echoes, and kindle with pale gleams the passion of former days.

The essence of aviation related archaeology concerns the location and identification of an aircraft's crash site followed by the recovery of any remaining wreckage. Speaking from personal experience, so many years after the event this can often be a frustrating and sometimes impossible task, but sustaining indeed could be the discovery of an essential eye-witness account, a crucial snippet from official records, or ultimately the recovery of an important artefact - a control column top, for example, its gun button perhaps locked on 'Fire', the last person to touch it being the pilot concerned. Hours are spent pouring over contemporary records, interviewing witnesses and searching fields for visual clues: a shard of glinting perspex, a cartridge case or bullet, or perhaps a bright ingot of aluminium. Electronic metal detecting equipment is essential, to establish what lies beneath the ground. Ultimately there is often little finesse involved in a major recovery, wreckage being dug out using a mechanical wheeled or tracked shovel; these machines, with their long-reach extension arms and ramping techniques are capable of digging very many feet down with the minimum of time and effort, a far cry from the situation in 1940! Furthermore, who back then could have even imagined that the 'worthless' wreckage of 1940's air battles would so fascinate and motivate a generation then largely unborn?

Some may ask why such items have any importance; the answer is easy: it is quite simply, as Sir Alan Smith (Wing Commander Bader's No 2 during Tangmere Wing days) once described it, 'Memorabilia which this country can be proud of'. These twisted and battered remnants of wartime aircraft are poignant reminders of the sacrifice and violence of the Second World War. Today, we can enjoy the sight and sound of numerous airworthy Spitfires, but many of their parts are recently produced from original drawings or even patterns made from items recovered during 'digs'. Indeed, the Spitfire in which Charles Church was comparatively recently killed was dated as a 1988 production aircraft on its Certificate of Airworthiness, so many new parts did it have. During a recent interview by Central Television, filmed adjacent to a recovered Merlin engine now in the possession of the Malvern Spitfire Team, I said: 'Some may ask what importance could possibly be attached to such a bent and battered engine, but the point is that this is *real* Spitfire history, not a replica, a genuine Rolls-Royce Merlin which once powered a Spitfire into battle. There is quite a difference'.

Not surprisingly, in the interest's early days, Battle of Britain aircraft casualties were impatiently sought, artefacts being recovered by various groups and individuals, some of it eventually being displayed to the public, other items disappearing forever into private collections. Fierce rivalry existed, and, it has to be said, excavations by some of these aviation enthusiasts turned would-be amateur 'archaeologists' were often less than thorough. Research was frequently wanting and the end result questionable as, in some cases, engine after engine was stockpiled for no apparent purpose. Some groups lacked a stable base and, as members' interests diversified, they fragmented, these collections scattered to the winds and in some cases now lost forever. In other cases, however, the cause was genuine, the end result worthwhile; I can best refer the reader to the Kent Battle of Britain Museum (KBoBM), founded in 1969 by that rare and dedicated character Mike Llewellyn, now located at Hawkinge. There the remains of over 600 aircraft shot down during the Battle of Britain are intelligently displayed, an essential and tangible reminder of our 'Finest Hour'. Mike Llewellyn:-

> Due to the lack of specific information available in those days, my *modus operandi* was to get letters published in various Kentish newspapers appealing for crash eye-witnesses to contact us. In addition, a number of other interested parties came forward, and so our aircraft recovery group was formed. The other members would find the crash sites, with the help of eye-witnesses, and obtain the landowner's consent for an excavation. I then came in at that point with the money, transport and equipment necessary to undertake the task. Usually, therefore, I did not actually see a site until the recovery operation commenced. My reward was to obtain parts for display in (what was then) my proposed museum.

Considering the nature of an air crash, even one in which the pilot's body has been recovered, human remains were obviously going to be disturbed at some sites. Again Mike comments:-

> By nature of the work involved, I have no doubt that every recovery group encountered a certain quantity of human remains at certain sites. Once, back in the 1970s, I was exhibiting artefacts from our recoveries at the Biggin Hill air show where I was approached by (the now late) Group Captain Tom Gleave, one of the most respected of all Battle of Britain pilots. He asked me if I had found any human remains, and at the time I was able to honestly answer that we had not. He then said that, in his opinion, the best thing to do if ever we did was to 'quietly' re-bury them at the site. At the time there was no official precedent to follow, and so the movement, which was crying out for leadership and direction, was in a quandary.

Mike was soon to be faced with a personal 'quandary' which led to a veritable media storm.

CHAPTER THREE

# The Basic Right of Every Man?

At about mid-day on Sunday, August 18th, 1940, 11-year-old Michael Wigmore, of Link Cottage, Grove, watched the now familiar scene above him of vapour trails and blazing aircraft as yet another combat took place high over Kent:-

A Spitfire's engine was screaming as the plane came down, very close to me. It crashed with a loud thud and burst into flames immediately. It impacted at an angle of about 45 degrees. It was completely out of control, and the pilot, if he remained on board, made no attempt to pull out of the dive.

The fighter had crashed into the remote Grove Marshes at Wickhambreaux, near Canterbury; it was to remain there undisturbed for 31 years.

By 1971, Mike Llewellyn's KBoBM was most active in the area of aircraft recoveries. Eye-witnesses had pointed Mike in the direction of the crash site at Grove Marshes. It is of vital importance, however, for the reader to appreciate that at the time RAF and other wartime records remained secret and had yet to be released into the public domain (which was not to be until 1975, preserved thereafter at the PRO). Consequently these early explorers of the battlefield often faced a difficult task in identifying aircraft, both before and after a recovery.

Having no idea regarding the identity of the Grove Marsh aircraft, other than eye-witness evidence suggesting it to be a Spitfire, the KBoBM approached the landowner, the Nature Conservancy (which

protected the area as a bird sanctuary), for permission to dig. Permission was forth-coming but conditional: as no eye-witness evidence ex-isted to suggest a parachute, as a precautionary measure should human remains be disturbed, the police must be present. This was arranged, and on March 28th, 1971, Mike's team met on site with a superintendent, the Coro-ner's Officer (a constable), two sergeants and a police photographer in addition to a Range Warden.

*Mike Llewellyn (third right) surveys the recovered engine*
*together with various police officers and museum members.*
*(KBoBM)*

*The digger sloshes around Grove Marsh, giving a good impression of the water-logged conditions in 1971.*
*(KBoBM)*

Digging conditions were extremely difficult, the mechanical digger sloshing around in the marsh. At a depth of eight feet, the aircraft's powerplant was located, recovered and identified as a Merlin engine, confirming the aircraft to have been British. Another glutinous bucketful contained various items, including what was immediately identified as an unopened parachute pack together with what appeared to be human teeth and fabric.

In a single-seater fighter the pilot actually sits on his parachute, which is strapped tightly to him, and so the discovery of an unopened pack in such circumstances could only mean one thing, especially when coupled with the discovery of possible human remains (no matter how insignificant). According to Mike Llewellyn, this gruesome discovery was brought to the attention of the police officers present before the teeth were respectfully returned to the hole. As the presence of further human remains were suspected, Mike immediately discontinued the recovery. The KBoBM felt, quite rightly in my view, that it would be wrong for them, as an amateur civilian organisation, to continue with any further disturbance. As the police were both present and aware of the situation, Mike naturally assumed that the officers would notify the authorities who would in turn 'handle it'. For some unknown reason, however, the Grove Marsh Spitfire is not believed to have become the subject of a police report to either the RAF or MOD in 1971. Consequently the status quo and mystery regarding the missing pilot was maintained.

### Pilot Officer George James Drake: May 21st, 1972.

To travel in time back to the Battle of Britain itself, Monday, September 9th, 1940, was to claim more lives from both sides; No 607 'County of Durham' Squadron was particularly badly mauled. This was an Auxiliary Air Force (AAF) unit, the home station of which was at Usworth in Northumberland. 607 had participated in the Battle of France, and had been amongst those 12 & 13 Group squadrons intercepting the ill-fated *Luftwaffe* attacks against the north of England on August 15th. The great difference in operational conditions between the northern sectors and those in the south was that the range of the Me 109 prevented it operating any further north than the London area. There was naturally a very great difference in tempo between chasing lone, or small formations of, unescorted bombers, compared with mixing it with the *Jagdwaffe* over the *Kanal*. Squadron Leader Harry Welford was amongst 607 Squadron's pilots:-

After the Battle of France we received a number of replacement pilots, straight from OTU. Amongst them was a South African, Pilot Officer George Drake, who was only 19, with a boyish face, and always seemed to me to be far too young to be pitched into battle, but then, so were many others. He was very inquisitive as I recall, always interested in how we 'Brits'

*Last voyage: George Drake bids farewell to his sister & younger brother prior to embarking for England; they were never to meet again.*
*(David Buchanan)*

thought and lived. No bad thing that, though, as I daresay he expected to be amongst us for some time.

On September 8th, 1940, we moved south to Tangmere in 11 Group. We arrived at a completely blitzed aerodrome and were greeted by the pitiful remnants of 43 Squadron, some pilots on crutches, others with their arms in slings and yet another with his head swathed in bandages having had his face torn apart by an exploding canon shell. Though they had clearly suffered many casualties, it was amazing to see them walking about. Needless to say, however, they were delighted to see us, especially as they had just been up on the day's third sortie and were awaiting news of the latest casualties. We only had just enough time to refuel ourselves before we were scrambled for an evening patrol which transpired to be uneventful.

*Sqn Ldr Harry Welford in 1993, sadly he died in 1996.*
*(Dennis Williams)*

The following day, much to my great disappointment, I was not called upon to fly and inevitably the squadron later went off. As it happened I was the most fortunate, as in this, the squadron's first engagement since arriving in 11 Group, our Hurricanes were well and truly bounced by Me 109s: we lost six out of 12 aircraft; three NCOs were wounded and three officers were killed. Amongst the latter were my best friends, Stuart Parnall and Scotty Lenahan, and as no more was ever heard of young George Drake, his death was presumed. We were shocked, we just could not take it all in. No-one talked of it but we all hoped for news of the Missing from some pub or hospital. No news came so we just bit back our tears and sorrow; it was 'You heard about Stuart and Scotty, rotten luck wasn't it?', and someone would add 'And young George Drake, bloody good blokes all of them'. After that epitaph the matter would be apparently dismissed with the ordering of another round of drinks to avoid any further evidence of sentiment. The truth of it, though, is that it still hurts me to think of it even now.

Another aviation archaeology group active during the early period of aircraft recoveries was the Ashford & Tenterden Recovery Group (A&TRG), chaired by David Buchanan and founded in 1970. By 1972 the Group had recovered nine aircraft and possessed sufficient wreckage to justify a museum; that year the group was scheduled to open premises located at Brenzett, on Romney Marsh in Kent. Again, at this time wartime RAF records remained unavailable. Having received information concerning a 'Spitfire' which crashed near Goudhurst in Kent, Buchanan's team interviewed eye-witnesses in the area who described the pilot baling out, landing safely in a nearby hop field. The crash site was located and permission obtained to recover any aircraft remains at Bockingfold Farm on May 21st, 1972. David Buchanan:-

We nearly didn't find the wreck at all. We were searching a wood about half a mile away until a local woman said he thought we were in the wrong place. We checked the new site with metal detectors and there it was. Once we had located the spot we brought in the mechanical shovel. Each load that was dug out was piled next to the hole and later sifted through a metal screen for bits and pieces of wreckage. At the bottom of the hole we found the engine and bits of armour plate from behind the seat. The plane had crashed into the stream when it was shot down and we could not have got to it if the stream had not been diverted by the farmer four or five years ago. Even so, we were digging in mud and slurry and it was hard to find anything.

Amongst the wreckage discovered were certain items indicating that the fighter was actually a Hurricane and not a Spitfire as claimed by eye-witnesses; this was certainly not the first or last time that such eye-witness evidence, given and accepted in good faith, was found to be fundamentally flawed. On a piece of plywood airframe was found the serial P2728. When the mechanical digger exposed an opened parachute pack, its contents spilling out, the diggers faced a similar dilemma to that experienced by Mike Llewellyn at Grove Marshes the previous year. David Buchanan immediately halted the recovery and reported the matter to the local police. Whilst awaiting an officer's attendance, the 'spoil heap' was picked over, revealing personal effects of the pilot: a nail file and a silver coloured cigarette case.

Upon attendance the police officer was shown the unopened parachute pack and personal effects which indicated the presence of human remains. As such events were hardly a regular occurrence,

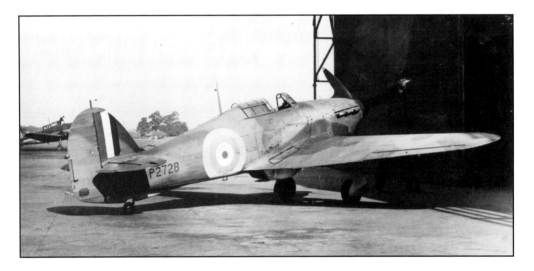

*Hurricane P2728: Missing in Action for 32 years.*
*(Via Norman Franks)*

the Constable not surprisingly sought advice, first from the Ashford Coroner, then from the CWGC. Consequently instructions were received for the recovery to proceed. Soon after work resumed, the pilot's remains were discovered in the smashed cockpit of his Hurricane (contrary to newspaper reports which described the cockpit as 'well preserved'). The total depth reached by the excavation was 4.5m.

In January 1998, David Buchanan, a softly spoken and modest man, told me:-

This was the first time we found human remains during an excavation. Normally if we heard of a wreck that may be that of a missing pilot then we did not dig. This time we did not know about the pilot, in fact we were searching for what we thought was a Spitfire, and went ahead. Having already notified the police, after the recovery the pilot's remains, which we treated with respect by all concerned, were handed over to them.

Having received the 'body', Chief Inspector Walter Smith issued a statement on behalf of Cranbrook Police:-

The MOD is virtually certain that they have identified the plane and pilot, but no names will be issued until they are absolutely sure and have had a chance to contact any relatives who may still be living.

From the aircraft serial number discovered at the site the MOD confirmed that the pilot found at Goudhurst was the South African Pilot Officer George James Drake (42398) of 607 Squadron.

The authorities soon successfully traced the pilot's family in Boksburg, near Johannesburg. Although his parents had both died, right up until the 1960s they had requested information from the MOD regarding their son's fate, receiving the usual response. The records of 49 MU confirm on September 10th, 1940, that a Hurricane came down at Goudhurst, Squadron Leader Goodman reporting that the aircraft was not salvaged. Nothing exists in the contemporary records to connect the Goudhurst Hurricane with Pilot Officer Drake. The pilot's oldest surviving brother, Arthur (56), was able to provide further information:-

Our family lived at Kroonstad, in the province of Pretoria, where our father was Stationmaster.

*Plt Off George Drake: First of the* Missing Few.
*(David Buchanan)*

George matriculated at the Paarl Boys' High School in 1938, and was a member of the Paarl branch of the St John Ambulance Association. He always wanted to fly but was rejected by our own Air Force due to being colour blind. Appreciating that in the event of war Great Britain would desperately require pilots, he then successfully applied for the RAF. To his younger brothers, Eric and myself, George was very much the hero; our father was

*Plt Off Drake's cigarette case and lighter.*
*(David Buchanan)*

secretly very proud but mother was naturally much concerned for her eldest son. George worked his way to England and realised his ambition to be a fighter pilot.

For the Drake family, the discovery also provided the opportunity to settle their parents' estate. Although the estate had been shared equally amongst their surviving children, the Drakes had included a proviso that if ever George should come home then his siblings must provide his share. As George's fate was now known, his restless shadow no longer fell over the Drake families affairs.

Naturally the case of Pilot Officer Drake had to be referred to Her Majesty's Coroner. The Coroner is a judicial office, quite independent of local and central government, who is required to act in accordance with certain laws. Any sudden or unexplained death must be reported to him, and it is the Coroner's duty to ascertain the cause of death and investigate any unusual circumstances. Sometimes the Coroner may be able to ascertain by simple enquiry whether the death was due to natural causes and that a Doctor is able to issue a death certificate. Such cases can then be registered, but in virtually all other instances the Coroner will require a post mortem examination. If that then indicates natural causes to be responsible, there would be no inquest. In other circumstances, however, such as those involving violence or a road traffic accident, the Coroner is obliged to hold an inquest. The purpose is to identify the deceased, ascertain when, where and how death occurred, and finally the cause of death. After the Inquest the Coroner can issue a certificate for burial or cremation

The Coroner's Inquest in respect of Pilot Officer Drake, held on November 7th, 1972, returned the verdict as 'Killed by an Act of War'. A Service funeral was arranged at the Brookwood Military Cemetery for 1430 hrs, November 22nd. The Drake family contributed to the cost of Eric's ticket, whilst Arthur's was kindly arranged by the *Johannesburg Star* in co-operation with South African Airways.

At the funeral, Pilot Officer Drake's coffin was lowered into his grave by servicemen from RAF Odiham, and a six-gun salute was fired by riflemen from the RAF Regiment. The pilot's two brothers and nephew were present, together with representatives of the South African armed forces, the Battle of Britain Fighter Association, the RAF Museum, MOD and A&TRG. The presiding RAF chaplain, the Rev. David Barnes, said:-

This young man came from a part of the Empire like so many others only to die fighting for the sacred cause of human freedom.

When he laid down his life pursuing what is the basic right of every man, he was a long way from his South African home and family.

When talking to the press afterwards, Arthur Drake added:-

Joining the RAF to fight for Britain was George's only ambition. He had to work his passage across here and then he went out to fight knowing that the odds were against him and his friends. He was very proud of what he was doing and we have always been proud of him down the years.

Before returning home, Eric and Arthur Drake received a guided tour of the new Brenzett Museum. Naturally they were moved to view parts of their brother's Hurricane, and they, grateful to the A&TRG, donated to the Museum the telegram reporting Pilot Officer Drake missing. The brothers were presented with the 'butterflies' from their brother's Hurricane's carburettors, these items being returned to South Africa for mounting with his medals as a memorial.

And so Pilot Officer George Drake made history in death as the first of Churchill's Few reported missing during the Battle of Britain to be recovered by an aircraft recovery group. The organisation concerned maintained a policy of non-interference of sites at which human remains may be encountered, and had undertaken this particular recovery in good faith, eyewitness evidence having suggested that the pilot of the aircraft concerned had baled out safely. When human remains were uncovered the discovery was both accidental and a great shock. What followed thereafter was entirely responsible: the police informed and further work only undertaken on the spot after authorisation from the CWGC. David Buchanan's actions were beyond reproach, and obviously much appreciated by the Drake family. At the funeral of Pilot Officer Drake, the Rev. David Barnes had referred to freedom as being 'the basic right of every man'; arguably a decent burial is another.

*Plt Off George Drake's last journey: Brookwood Military Cemetery.*
*(David Buchanan)*

### *Leutnant* **Werner Knittel: September 1973.**

The following year, the A&TRG hit the headlines again, this time following their recovery of the first German Battle of Britain casualty in similar circumstances to those in which they had already discovered Pilot Officer Drake.

In September 1973, at Burmarsh on Kent's Romney Marsh, David Buchanan's team discovered the remains of an Me 109 pilot buried with his fighter at a depth of 24 feet. Having notified the authorities, the body was removed to the mortuary at Folkestone's Royal Victoria Hospital. The South Kent Coroner, Mr John Clarke, told news reporters that 'We believe we can identify the pilot, but an Inquest is necessary so that the proper documents can be issued if, as we expect, the Germans wish to take him back home'. According to the *Daily Mail* report, 'Berlin has been asked for a formal declaration of the mission', and that the *Luftwaffe* had been requested to check its casualty records and confirm the pilot's identity'. The *Folkestone Herald* reported the words of an enthusiast involved in the recovery: 'Don't make us out to be grave-diggers. It was a shock to

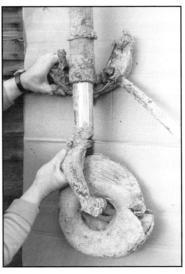

*Above: The recovery of* Lt *Werner Knittel,*
*1970s style.*
*Right: Tail wheel from Knittel's Me 109.*
*Below:* Lt *Werner Knittel.*
*(All: David Buchanan)*

us to find the pilot still in the plane'. Ultimately the Germans confirmed that the enthusiasts had found *Leutnant* Werner Knittel, a famous pre-war sport flier, Spanish Civil War veteran and *Gruppe* Adjutant of II/JG51. He had been officially *Vermisst* since failing to return from a *Freie Jagd* (free-ranging fighter sweep) over southern England on October 28th, 1940, and was the only outstanding German pilot from that particular day. The recovery stimulated great interest in Germany, not least due to Knittel's distinguished pre-war aviation past. In death, it seemed, Werner Knittel was also destined to become newsworthy as the first German airman to be recovered in such circumstances.

*Victors:* Lt *Werner Knittel (right)* & kameraden *survey bomb
damage in France, 1940.
(David Buchanan)*

By the day Werner Knittel lost his life, the Battle of Britain had degenerated into that inconclusive round of clashes between the opposing fighter forces which continued well into 1941. The fourth such enemy intrusion of British airspace that day occurred at 1642 hrs when three formations, comprising nearly 100 Me 109s, swept in at high altitude over the south coast between Beachy Head and Dungeness. Nine squadrons of Spitfires and Hurricanes responded, destroying two enemy fighters for no loss. One enemy aircraft crashed near Haywards Heath, West Sussex, the pilot of which was captured. The other was known by the British to have crashed at 1710 hrs on Fielding Land, Dymchurch; as we now know, however, probably due to the great depth involved and given the limitations of both equipment and resources available, its pilot was not recovered at the time.

When the story received international media coverage, it was reported that *Leutnant* Knittel may have been shot down by the CO of 257 'Burma' Squadron, the dashing 'ace' Squadron Leader Bob Stanford Tuck who, timed at 1645 - 1700 hrs, had claimed two Me 109 'probables' between Tonbridge Wells and Dungeness. Naturally Tuck himself readily accepted that this *could* have been the case, but now that RAF records are available, we know that there were claims by other RAF pilots:-

Sgt AS Darling, 603 Sqn:           One Me 109 probable, one damaged, Dungeness, 1655 hrs.
Sgt B Henson, 257 Sqn:             One Me 109 damaged, Dungeness, 1700 hrs
Fg Off DAP McMullen, 222 Sqn:   One Me 109 'shot down' near Dungeness, time n/k.

Although the time of the latter's claim is unknown, his sortie was between 1612-1745 hrs; any one of the foregoing pilots, therefore, in addition to Squadron Leader Tuck, could have shot down *Leutnant* Knittel. Despite the fact that the MOD's erstwhile Air Historical Branch (AHB) accepted Tuck to have been the victor, this exercise is a prime example of the difficulties in establishing exactly who-got-who in the spider's web of vapour trails, even on what was a relatively quiet day.

Just 48 hours after British newspapers carried the story that an Me 109 pilot had been recovered at Burmarsh, the German authorities successfully traced *Leutnant* Knittel's widow, Dr Inge Knittel, who was working in Paris; how Dr Knittel must have felt when given her husband's wedding ring, recovered from his body, can only be imagined. *Leutnant* Knittel had, in fact, been identified by his identity disc which provided his service number: B651782. After the Coroner's Inquest, the remains were not returned to Germany as Mr Clarke had anticipated, however, but interred with full military honours at the *Soldatenfriedhof*, Cannock Chase; his grave can be seen there today.

### *Gefrieter* Richard Riedel: November 1974.

Due to the sheer quantity of sites excavated, by 1974, the accidental discovery of long-lost fighter pilots was becoming an annual event for David Buchanan. In November of that year his group, now operating under the auspices of the Brenzett Aeronautical Museum (BAM), recovered the remains of another Me 109 pilot from Romney Marsh. The site had, in fact, been located and excavated to some extent by the London Air Museum (LAM, now defunct) only the previous month, but on that occasion there was apparently nothing discovered to suggest the presence of human remains.

*Recovery of* Gfr *Richard Reidel.*
*(David Buchanan)*

After some research, the West German Embassy in London named the *Jagdflieger* found by the BAM at Melon Farm, Ivychurch: *Gefrieter* Richard Riedel, of 2/JG3, reported *Vermisst* on November 17th, 1940. German records relate how the 109s were at a high altitude, around 30,000 feet, when the icing of windscreens and guns was experienced. When British fighters appeared some way off, the formation leader decreased altitude, but Riedel was seen to inexplicably peel off and crash. As enemy action was not therefore responsible, given the altitude concerned it is likely that his death was due to an oxygen system failure. Although Richard Riedel did not die within the official dates accorded the Battle of Britain by the British authorities, for our purposes this German casualty can be considered relevant. There was certainly no problem regarding Riedel's identification, as during the recovery his identity discs had been found together with a night pass and flying licence, all of which bore his name.

Unfortunately the Iron Curtain posed a problem with the tracing of Riedel's family, however, as his home at Muylenstrasse 11, Unteroblingen, was then in the Communist East German Democratic Republic. Nevertheless, the young former enemy pilot was also buried with all due military honours at Cannock Chase.

By November 1974, aviation archaeologists had presented a total of three pilots for burial: a South African Hurricane pilot and two German Me 109 pilots. At that time

*Richard Reidel's flying licence, bearing his signature.*
*(David Buchanan)*

the MOD was unaware of the disturbance of Flying Officer Gruszka in 1971, but nevertheless the authorities must have found alarming the rate at which missing pilots were being recovered. Many members of the general public, unfamiliar with the background circumstances as related by previous chapters of this book, were naturally astonished at the reported discoveries, and were unable to comprehend why these fallen warriors had not been either recovered at the time or at least recovered later by the authorities. It was the start of a public relations disaster for the MOD which unfortunately remains both ongoing and unresolved.

During the mid-1970s, many direct relatives of wartime casualties, of all nationalities, remained very much alive, and therefore the recovery of missing pilots at that time can only be considered as *extremely* sensitive. As media coverage of aviation archaeologists' activities increased, so too did the movement's growth, with numerous amateur museums and enthusiastic individuals all clamouring for, literally, a piece of the action. Many eyewitnesses remained alive and often readily offered help in locating wartime crashes, sometimes with unexpected and far-reaching consequences as with the case of Pilot Officer Drake.

On January 14th, 1975, the CWGC wrote to David Buchanan, after he expressed concern following an inaccurate article published in a local newspaper regarding the Commission's stance on aircraft recoveries; the letter clarified the policy:-

Notwithstanding the fact that the Commission has discharged its duty by commemorating on a Memorial the name of any casualty whose body could not be recovered for whatever reason at the time, it still has a duty to ensure the proper burial of the remains should they later be found. The Commission is also very conscious of the justified public disquiet caused by newspaper and other reports of present day interference with human remains in air and naval wrecks.

Despite this concern and the natural reluctance to disturb human remains after such a long period of time it must be accepted that the remains left in wrecked aircraft are not secure, nor are relatives or the Commission able to exercise any control over them. The Commission's policy therefore would tend to support the recovery of the remains and removal to a recognised cemetery provided it were done with care and reverence.

However, the Commission is not empowered to act in this matter since the Crown retains the ownership in and right to the possession of all crashed Crown aircraft and former German aircraft which are regarded as captured enemy property. It follows, therefore, that a preservation group wishing to investigate any such aircraft is required by law to apply to the Ministry of Defence (Air), which would ensure that any excavation was carried out in a responsible manner and that their conditions and Home Office regulations were observed.

It is only then at the final stage that the Commission, if required, takes over the remains from the Home Office (Police), or the appropriate Service Department, for reburial in a war cemetery or plot under its control. In the meantime all the Commission wishes to do is impress on each and every recovery group the need for the utmost care in its activities so as to avoid needless public concern.

This is certainly a well considered response from the CWGC, and certain points made are significant. Firstly, that the Commission's duty toward missing airmen had been discharged through the Runnymede Memorial (see Chapter Two). Secondly, the Commission rightly identified that, in view of the activities of recovery groups, long-forgotten remains left in aircraft wrecks were no longer 'secure'. Thirdly, it is worthy of note that despite Runnymede, the Commission supported, at this time, the idea of recovery to a recognised cemetery. It was incorrect, however, to state that any law, as such, applied to the activities of recovery groups at this time.

For the MOD, the rate at which missing Battle of Britain airmen appeared to being recovered must have been alarming, not least due to the 'justified public disquiet' such discoveries caused. At that time, of course, the number of missing airmen still buried with their aircraft was unknown. Consequently the MOD issued a set of guidelines in March 1975, to which aviation archaeologists were expected to adhere; these regulations included reference to the fact that if accidentally discovered then human remains should be treated with respect, work ceased immediately and the authorities informed. Also, the MOD demanded that in such an event, under no circumstances should the suspected name of the pilot concerned be released to the media until the establishment had traced and notified NOK accordingly. A previous, and most experienced, author on the subject once wrote that these guidelines were 'well conceived' but of limited value as they 'carried no great legislative weight'; the fact is that they relied entirely upon good will and carried *no* 'legislative weight' whatsoever. Any contravention, therefore, carried no fine or other punishment, only a cessation of co-operation from the MOD. This fundamental problem was to be the major stumbling block for over 10 years to come, and incredibly even beyond, as we shall see.

### Flying Officer Franciszek Gruszka: April 15th, 1974.

After the Grove Marsh excavation in March 1971, the KBoBM felt that it had absolved any responsibilities it may have regarding this site as the police had been present; it was assumed that the Kent Constabulary would, therefore, deal with matters as appropriate. The wreckage recovered was therefore cleaned and displayed at the KBoBM's premises at Chilham Castle, where the pilot's the parachute was displayed. Further research had indicated that the most likely owner was Flying Officer Gruszka, the artefacts being captioned accordingly. This was ultimately to have far reaching consequences.

*Fg Off Franciszek Gruszka.*
*(Author via Mrs B Sykes)*

In England, like Franek Surma, Flying Officer Gruszka and his comrades had been trained to fly modern RAF fighters. On August 5th, 1940, Pilot Officer Szulkowski arrived at Hornchurch in Essex to fly Spitfires with 65 Squadron's 'A' Flight; Flying Officer Gruszka joined him just two days later. A British pilot with 65 was 19-year-old Pilot Officer David Glaser who befriended the Poles:-

They were both older than me and had obviously been experienced and respected pilots in their own air force before the war. They were having a hard time coming to terms with the language and so on, and I used to try and teach them English during the time we spent together on Readiness. I looked up to them, no question about it.

*Plt Off David Glaser (;eft), friend of Gruszka and later instrumental in organising his recovery. (Author via Chalmers)*

'A' Flight was commanded by an Australian, Flight Lieutenant Gordon Olive, under whose command was a remarkable civilian, Supermarine's Chief Test Pilot, Jeffrey Quill. A former service pilot, Quill had requested the opportunity to serve under operational conditions to assist with the Spitfire's evaluation. In addition to his own observations, he wanted to listen and learn from other fighter pilots. In 1995, he told me:-

When I arrived at Hornchurch I assumed that I would be operational immediately, but the CO, Squadron Leader Sam Saunders, asked me to lead a section of three recently joined pilots for an air firing exercise at Sutton Bridge. These men were Pilot Officer David Glaser, a mere youth at the time, and two Poles, Pilot Officer Szulkowski and Flying Officer Gruszka. In the Mess at Sutton Bridge I had tried to talk to the Poles about their escape, but their English was limited. They had certainly endured a most traumatic time and my heart went out to them, although I was worried about how they would understand orders over the R/T. To be fair, they spent hours studying an English dictionary with David's help.

Indeed, amongst other English terms, Franek Gruszka wrote in his diary the Polish translation of the following essential flying terms: trimming, brakes, throttle, rudder bar, undercarriage, aileron, flaps and fuselage; the Spitfire's Air Ministry Pilot's Notes must have made daunting reading for Gruszka and his comrades.

On Sunday, August 18th, 1940, various of Fighter Command's vital Sector Stations were subjected to sustained attack. By the end of that day, both sides had suffered more aircraft destroyed or damaged than on any other day throughout the entire Battle of Britain: 69 German machines were destroyed, as were 73 of Fighter Command.

Jeffrey Quill:-

In 65 Squadron we did not fly the useless formation comprising vics of three, but instead flew our four sections of three in line astern. This could be rapidly opened out sideways and, like the German line abreast *Schwarm* formation, required minimum concentration when flying (unlike the vics, which is what was so dangerous about them). Everyone was therefore able to search the sky for the enemy and I am sure that this increased our chances of survival. Nevertheless, we suffered certain casualties, of course. August 18th was a hectic day, and once combat was joined, our two Poles were inclined to go chasing off on their own, so determined were they to get at the enemy. Gruszka sadly failed to return from our lunchtime engagement over Kent, and as we received no reports of any Spitfires having crashed inland, assumed that he must have crashed into the sea. Back at base, Szulkowski was terribly upset but could shed no light on his friend's fate.

If not for aviation archaeology, the story would probably have ended there. Word eventually reached David Glaser, who was retired from the RAF but working as a test pilot for BAC at Weybridge and Hurn, that the parachute of his friend Gruszka was openly displayed at Chilham despite the fact that officially the pilot's fate remained unresolved. Appreciating the possible implications, Squadron Leader Glaser was naturally incensed. He contacted Squadron Leader Boleslaw 'Gandy' Drobinski, who had escaped from Poland with Franek Gruszka (but had not been posted to 65 Squadron himself until after his friend was killed); Drobinski was equally angered, and the pair complained to the MOD, insisting that the RAF should mount an official excavation to recover their friend's body for a decent Christian burial.

Accordingly, on April 15th, 1974, an RAF team recovered the remainder of Spitfire R6713 together with the mortal remains of 30-year-old Flying Officer Franciszek Gruszka. The pilot was identified from an inscription on his gold-coloured propelling pencil, a gift from a PAF comrade before the war. The post mortem was conducted by Dr AC Ogilvie, a consultant pathologist at the Kent & Canterbury Hospital. The skull was found to have suffered multiple fractures, consistent with the violent impact of an air crash, but no indication was found of the pilot having been shot or hit by shrapnel.

On May 1st, 1975, the Coroner's Inquest took place at the Canterbury Coroner's Court regarding the death of Flying Officer Gruszka. The MOD's official, a Mr Kenneth Wall, provided evidence from contemporary records which stated that the Spitfire concerned 'was last seen chasing enemy aircraft between Canterbury and Manston at about 1450 hrs on August 18th, 1940'. The eyewitness Mr Wigmore also gave his evidence. During these proceedings the Coroner, Mr Wilfred Mowll suggested that the Museum had been more concerned with the recovery of Gruszka's Spitfire than the pilot himself. Incomplete, the case was adjourned to be continued the following week. When the case so far was reported in the *Kent Herald*, articles suggested that the enthusiasts concerned had reflected a lack of respect for the dead pilot. A representative of the Museum wrote to the editor insisting that the published reporting represented a 'gross distortion' of the truth. It was only the beginning.

When the inquest resumed, Mike Llewellyn told the Coroner that on March 28th, 1971, he informed the Coroner's Officer, who was on site, immediately he suspected that a body might be present. This, however, both Superintendent 'X' and PC 'Y' denied. As Mike said during the inquest, 'We felt morally obliged not to continue. I reported it at the time to the Coroner's Officer'. Mr Mowll then asked why he had then discontinued the excavation, to which Mike's response was 'Because we were then acting in the dark, and legally, morally and religiously, we were not sure of our position in carrying on'.

As we have seen, at the time of the first Grove Marsh excavation in 1971, there were no laws or regulations directly concerning the recovery of crashed aircraft, nor precedents to follow when Flying Officer Gruszka's remains were first disturbed. It is not therefore surprising that the enthusiasts were confused regarding their position and unsure of what to do next. Personally I would entirely support Mike Llewellyn's decision to suspend operations on legal, moral and religious grounds. To accord due respect to the likes of Flying Officer Gruzska, to whom we all owe so very much, surely, if one has time to take stock and plan ahead, *only* the RAF should undertake the recovery of human remains in, as one would expect, a thoroughly professional and dignified manner? Mr Llewellyn also told the Court that his actions in 1971 actually reflected the spirit of the guidelines for aircraft recoveries laid down by the MOD in 1975.

The two police officers remained unmoved, however, adamant that they had no knowledge of the teeth; Superintendent 'X' stated that during the dig he was shown a rudder pedal, 'and expressed surprise that if the body was there, human remains had not been found. During my presence no part of the uniform, clothing or part of the body were pointed out to me.' Mr Mowll asked whether he had seen the teeth, but the Superintendent replied that he had not, and continued: 'There was some discussion about continuing the dig, but Mr Llewellyn did not want any more parts of the plane. It was agreed that the dig should cease'. When Mr Mowll inquired whether the teeth had been returned to the marsh with his knowledge, the senior policeman stated: 'They were not. Had they been brought to my notice I would not have let them be buried.' When questioned by Mike Llewellyn's solicitor, Mr Frederick Tickner, the Superintendent agreed, however, that Mr Llewellyn could not be criticised for anything he had done in 1971. The inquest had clearly become a witch-hunt by this stage, as Mr Tickner pointed out: 'I am beginning to wonder if this inquest is to find the cause of death or if people are trying to avoid the blame.' When PC 'Y' also denied having seen any human remains in 1971, Mr Tickner pointed out that as Mr Llewellyn had informed the police of the dig, why should he not then show the officers any human remains subsequently discovered?

From my own experience in dealing with 'sudden deaths', having been an operational police officer between 1983, I would suggest that in the event of being shown what were possibly teeth, the police should have, in the first instance, seized those grisly items, together with the unopened parachute pack and recovered aircraft wreckage. The Coroner should then have been informed together with the MOD. Both officers maintained throughout the 1975 proceedings that they had never seen the teeth to which Mike Llewellyn had referred. From a policing viewpoint given such circumstances, I would also tender that the teeth alone are *not* the crux of *any* argument; more so, and constant in both accounts, is the unopened parachute discovered at what was the crash site of a single-seater fighter. The police were certainly aware of this item, indeed photographic evidence exists to confirm this fact. It is fair to ask, therefore, why the officers did not, on the basis of the unopened parachute alone, seize that evidence and inform the Coroner and MOD for their information and guidance? For some reason, however, this basic matter was not raised during the Inquest.

Mr Mowll explained that he could not understand why no effort had been made by the KBoBM to recover the pilot in 1971 for a decent burial; Mike Llewellyn:-

> The decision was mine and there were women and children turning up. Even now I don't think it was right for us to continue. I told the officers present that there was every chance the pilot was present and discontinued the excavation. I thought that the police would then report the matter to the appropriate authorities for them to recover the chap.

The Coroner then accused the KBoBM of 'not having been interested in the body'; Mike Llewellyn responded:-

> You could not be more wrong. Nothing could be more wrong than to suggest that we had no respect for the body. I left the matter firmly with the authorities, the onus lies with them, not with us.

Also present in Court had been both Squadron Leaders Glaser and Drobinski. They were understandably incensed that although their comrade's parachute had been displayed and captioned, the KBoBM had made no effort to notify the MOD that, even so long after the recovery, it had positively identified the aircraft concerned as belonging to a missing pilot. When this was put to him, Mike Llewellyn responded that he 'did not really know (why the MOD was not informed), we were more concerned with acquiring aircraft'. To put that statement into context, having been formed in 1969, by 1971 the KBoBM had already excavated the sites of at least 50 aircraft. By 1975 there were many more to add to what was a rapidly growing list of important artefacts. Also, so far as the Museum was concerned, the authorities were already aware of the situation but had made no move, prior to the involvement of Squadron Leaders Glaser and Drobinski, to take any action. One could argue that in those circumstances there was no need for the KBoBM to notify the MOD, although equally it would certainly have been prudent to do so. In my view, this is the only area where any criticism could be perhaps be levelled at the Museum, given all the circumstances, throughout the entire affair. Mike Llewellyn responds:-

Hindsight is, of course, a wonderful thing. In those days we trusted the authorities, and having informed those present at the dig of the circumstances, we assumed that they would take over - that is, of course, why they were there! We wondered what was going to happen, and local rumour suggested that the location would be turned into a war grave. Another rumour was that due to the Cold War the *status quo* had been maintained. Whatever, so far as we are concerned the authorities were already aware and there was no requirement for us to later notify them of the aircraft's serial number - they already knew.

Ultimately, Mr Mowll's Inquest returned a verdict that Flying Officer Gruszka had died from injuries sustained during war service; he said:-

It rings with gallantry. A man of 30 of the Polish Air Force not content with fighting in Poland, came to this country to fight gallantly with our Air Force as a member of the famous 65 Squadron. On August 18th, 1940, for reasons not accounted for, he dived into the marshes. It is a moving story, and one must do honour to this man. I hope I have done so.

Arising out of it has been the perhaps unfortunate recovery of the engine, but not the body in 1971. Mr Llewellyn's evidence regarding the interring of the teeth has been challenged by the police, who were present with the express purpose of reporting anything found. I must adhere to the line I took that in fact no part of the body was found - unless Mr Llewellyn did find the teeth which makes the story even more unpleasant..... I am satisfied that he (Flying Officer Gruszka) died through injuries during war service and as it happened during the war years I do not have to return any more than that. I should add that this group (KBoBM) is carrying out an onerous task which has undoubtedly established quite a lot of data of value. My only comment is that if there is a body suspected the Coroner should be given pre-eminent place.

In the wake of the inquest, further reports appeared in the newspapers, headlines as ever attempting to create a sensation in a distasteful and inaccurate manner: *'Plane Hunters Lack Respect for the Dead' says Coroner*. Needless to say, such articles provoked further correspondence from the KBoBM, copies of which were sent to both the Home Secretary and Lord Chancellor. As Mike Llewellyn says today, 'If we had done anything wrong, why then did the RAF present us with the wreckage of R7913 after they had recovered the body? We had nothing to do with the 1975 recovery directly but co-operated in every other way possible to ensure that Flying Officer Gruszka was ultimately recovered by the authorities, which is as it should be, and given a fitting Christian burial'. The remains of the Gruszka Spitfire, in fact, are displayed at the KBoBM's current premises and are a typically moving reminder of yet another sad casualty.

In 1998, Mike Llewellyn reflected on the incident:-

I feel strongly that certain of the Coroner's comments were outrageous and made without listening carefully to the true facts of the case. There seemed to be a very definite attempt by the authorities to shift any blame on to us. The Coroner asked why it had taken us so long to exhibit the engine, suggesting that we had something to hide, and his remark that I 'did not want any more aircraft parts' was completely out of context. My response is that, at the time, space was a problem at the museum, and the Gruszka engine was not that historically important and nor was it in particularly good condition. Secondly, I discontinued the operation because I suspected that substantial human remains were present, *not* because we had recovered sufficient aircraft parts to satisfy our interest. Regarding the suspected teeth, I have to say that they were only fragments and, in the eyes of the law, I am unqualified to identify them anyway. As a matter of interest, the RAF invited me to attend the second recovery, which I did, but left when other members of the group were denied access.

It may surprise many current enthusiasts to know that, despite having been recovering aircraft for several years prior to the Gruszka case, the Inquest was our first contact with the MOD. in fact, a civil servant said to me at the time that so far as he was concerned we had done nothing wrong and so he couldn't see what all the fuss was about. The KBoBM was represented at the funeral by members Major John Hollis and Tony Webb; they were thanked on behalf of the Polish people present.

*The last journey of Fg Off Gruszka: Northwood Cemetery.*
*(Mrs B Sykes)*

Recent contact with the Gruszka family has enabled the story of this Polish freedom fighter to be recorded:-

For official purposes, Flying Officer Gruszka was 'presumed dead' on October 3rd, 1941. Earlier that year, his comrade Wladyslaw Szulkowski managed to get a letter through to his friend's parents, telling them that he had last seen their son at a height of 3,000', in no apparent difficulty, and was still, therefore, 'waiting for him to come back'. In 1975, following the recovery and identification of Flying Officer Gruszka, attempts by the British authorities, via the Polish Embassy, to locate the Gruszkas failed due to Poland also being behind the Iron Curtain. Consequently no relatives were present when Flying Officer Gruszka was buried at Northwood Military Cemetery at a Service funeral organised by RAF Uxbridge. Participating were the Queen's Colour Squadron and the Central Band of the RAF. Jeffrey Quill remembered:-

> As I understand it, after the second dig, Gruszka's remains were eventually handed over to the Polish Air Force Association (PAFA) in London. Dave Glaser, Gandy Drobinski and myself all attended from 65 Squadron, in addition to about two coach loads of Poles from their London community. I had previously no idea that there were so many Poles over here. The service was conducted by a Church of England parson and a Polish priest (Greek Orthodox).

*Proud relatives: the sister and niece of*
*Fg Off Gruszka at his graveside.*
*(Mrs B Sykes)*

Despite the difficulties in tracing the Gruszka family, there were actually relatives resident in the UK. They learned of the funeral from the newspapers, and consequently passed on the information to the NOK in Poland. Piotr Gruszka, Franciszek's younger and closest brother, actually heard the news himself on the BBC World Service. In 1976, Miss Barbara Sekowska, a neice of Flying Officer Gruszka, defected to the UK and, via Anglo-Polish friends, made contact with the PAFA in London which handed over her uncle's personal effects, recovered with his body the previous year. It was a moving moment when Barbara stood at the grave of the uncle she had never known, but of whom had heard so much. The grave was later visited by her mother, the pilot's sister. Barbara also contacted Squadron Leader Glaser who paid tribute to her late uncle over dinner. Many years later, in May 1995, and by sheer coincidence, Barbara passed by the launch of my fifth book, *A Few of the Many*, at the Guildhall, Worcester; there she was moved to see the Malvern Spitfire Team's display concerning Flying Officer Surma. We have been good friends ever since, and I can now, therefore, fill in many gaps regarding Franciszek Gruszka's life and times. Piotr Gruszka:-

My dear brother was born on January 21st, 1910, in a village near the Polish city of Lwow, an important cultural centre. Being just one year younger than 'Franek', we were very close.

The first four years of Franek's primary education were spent at the local school before we attended together a preparatory school in the city. After passing the required entrance exams, we then went to grammar school, science being Franek's leading subject. As we progressed through the school, our lessons changed, which at one point were of a neo-classical and Latin emphasis. This was in the hope that at least one, if not both, of us would become a Roman Catholic priest. Franek matriculated on May 5th, 1931, there automatically following one year's service in the army; as I was a year behind him, we feared that there would be a parting of our ways forever. After his time at the Military College for Infantry Cadets at Rawa Ruska, between November 15th, 1931 - August 15th, 1932, he gained air experience on observation balloons at Torun. There he decided that he wanted to pursue a career in the Air Force and become a pilot. He then succeeded in passing entrance exams to the Officer Cadets' Flying School at Deblin. By August 11th, 1934, he had successfully completed the course and was a fully qualified pilot with the rank of 2nd Lieutenant. His flying, however, was so precise that instead of joining a fighter squadron, as he wished, my brother was posted to be an instructor at the Flying Training School (FTS) at Lwow. By then I was studying at the Humanitarian Faculty of the University of King Jan Kazimierz, in Lwow, so we were able to share lodgings.

One day when we lived together in Lwow, Franek suggested that I should take a pleasure flight with him. It was a September morning in 1934, and I arrived at the aerodrome early, as we had arranged. Having checked on the weather, Franek said that we were to fly at 100-200m, below the clouds. I was both excited and curious regarding what was to be my first flight. By 0700 hrs the plane, a Polish monoplane, was ready. First in climbed Franek, then me, both of us wearing flying suits and helmets. After no time at all were up to 100m. I could see that the airport was getting further and further away, the buildings and trees getting smaller and smaller. Soon we were under the first cloud layer; one second the plane was flying in a horizontal attitude, then, without warning, diving. I felt my stomach coming up into my throat and was just about to shout out in fear when my brother calmly explained that we had hit a vacuum, an air pocket, and had dropped like a stone. Unfortunately on that flight there were many vacuums and each time I thought that we would crash! We then approached a church steeple at about the same height, swerving to avoid it at the last moment. Then off to Zimna Wodka for Franek to wave to his fiancee, Eugenia. I wondered why we needed to climb so high; suddenly the engine stopped and the plane plunged almost vertically towards some houses. Out of one of them ran some people, one of whom I recognised as 'Gena'. My brother's skilled hand then changed our direction and we adopted a normal attitude just above some trees. After waggling his wings in greeting to those on the ground, we returned to the airport. My first flight was one I will never forget!

My brother had many friends and was very popular. Even before his military days he was known for his great courage and generosity. He liked music and was a splendid mandolinist, I accompanying him on the guitar. He had no match in wrestling and aviation was his passion. I know that he trained his cadets in a most professional manner for which he was commended.

When war broke out on September 1st, 1939, I was called up and sent to defend Warsaw. On September 17th, Franek received orders to escape across the Roumanian border. Having done so, he obtained a Polish passport via the Polish Consulate in Bucharest, and then, via the former Yugoslavia and Italy, arrived in France on October 7th. The following day registered at the alien assembly point in Paris, but he and other Polish pilots, namely Wladyslaw Szulkowski, Boleslaw Drobinski and Joseph Szlagowski decided that the British were more likely to resist the Germans than the French. Consequently they were the first Polish pilots to arrive in the UK, in February 1940. My brother was immediately commissioned in the RAFVR as a Flying Officer, No 76785. The rest you know.

Although Flying Officer Gruszka's remains were the first to be disturbed by aviation archaeologists, this pilot was actually the fourth such casualty to be recovered in the space of three years: three by David Buchanan's teams, Franek Gruszka himself eventually by the authorities. Although the *Daily Mail's* headline reporting the discovery of *Leutnant* Werner Knittel in 1973 had proclaimed him to be *The Last of the Many*, time was to prove that the pilots covered in this chapter, Drake, Knittel, Riedel and Gruszka, were actually the *First* of the Many.

*The coins, purse, diary, damaged Madonna & child pendant and propelling pencil recovered with Fg Off Gruszka. The coins include several Victorian pennies, and currency from Poland, Roumania, Italy and France. An inscription on the pencil positively identified this pilot. The author arranged issue of Fg Off Gruszka's medals to the family, and these represent a typical Battle of Britain group: The 1939-45 Star, Aircrew Europe Star with Battle of Britain Clasp, and the 1939-45 War Medal.*
*(Author)*

CHAPTER FOUR

# Roll Call of the Lost: and Found?

After the March 1975 Guidelines were issued, the activities of recovery groups continued unabated. There was fierce rivalry between them, and the race was on to excavate as many sites as possible. Considering that it was not uncommon for a group to dig *several* sites in *one* day, the available evidence suggests that the appended research was often less than thorough, and, due to the activities of some, the interest attracted an unprofessional image. As a *serious* and worthwhile historical exercise the activity was undoubtedly questionable. In view of the increasing interest in aviation archaeology however, when offset against the number of aircraft crash sites available and therefore recoveries to be undertaken, it was just a matter of time before the next missing airman was recovered. This chapter catalogues the relevant recoveries between 1976 and 1986.

### *Oberfeldwebel* Karl Herzog & *Obergefrieter* Herbert Schilling: August 1976

On October 7th, 1940, Me 110s of ZG26 escorted the Ju 88s of II/KG51 to attack the Westland aircraft factory at Yeovil, in Somerset. The RAF's response was swift, and bitter fighting again took place over the West Country. At about 1600 hrs, 10 miles NW of Portland, Squadron Leader ML Robinson of 609 Squadron found a defensive circle of Me 110s, consequently attacking one of their number, '... from dead astern and it dived vertically into the ground about five miles north of the coast (Little Bredy)'.

*The tattered uniform of Me 110 gunner* Obgefr *Herbert Schilling,* Vermisst *1940, recovered 1976. (Andy Saunders)*

The enemy aircraft, of 6/ZG26, crashed near Kingston Russell House, Long Bredy, near Poole in Dorset. What remains of the crew could be found were originally buried at the crash site as 'unknown'. The graves were then marked by two wooden crosses made by British soldiers; each recorded simply: 'A German Soldier'. After the war these airmen were removed to Cannock Chase.

In August 1976, the site became the subject of a major recovery by the Wealdon Aviation Archaeological Group (WAAG), during which a substantial amount of both crewmen, together with many personal effects including cards bearing the names of Herzog and Schilling, were discovered. Surprisingly, however, the Central Dorset Coroner, Mr Morris Bailey, refused to accept the evidence before him as conclusive proof that the two airmen concerned were indeed *Oberfeldwebel* Herzog and *Obergefrieter* Schilling. A Destruction Order was then placed on the human remains, but as the WAAG was totally dissatisfied with the Coroner's decision, members petitioned the German War Graves Commission. Eventually the *Volksbund* accepted the WAAG's evidence and the remains were then interred at Cannock Chase, the headstone being named accordingly. In fact, Herzog and Schilling were to join Werner Knittel in Grave 162, Block 8, Row 7.

### Sergeant Edward James Egan: September 11th, 1976.

Referring back to Chapter One, we have heard how, on September 17th, 1940, Sergeant Tony Pickering watched powerless whilst his friend, Sergeant Eddie Egan, was shot down over Ashford. Upon his own safe return, Tony reported the crash location, in a wood, only to receive a visit several months later by Air Ministry staff requesting that he pinpoint the exact position on their map. This he did but heard no more about it until Eddie Egan hit the headlines when his remains were recovered by the LAM in Daniels Wood, Tuesnoad, near Bethersden, on September 11th, 1976. John Tickner was present on this occasion and comments:-

In these early days, we just used to drive to a village, seek out elderly residents and ask whether they could recall any aircraft crashes in the vicinity. We would then locate these with a view to a recovery, but frequently until that went ahead we were actually unaware of even what type of aircraft was involved, much less its identity. This was so in the case of Sergeant Egan's aircraft, prior to the excavation we genuinely had no idea that a missing airman was concerned. It is difficult to understand, however, why the authorities were unable to locate the wreck in 1940 as it was, in fact, easily accessible.

*Sgt E J Egan shortly before his death in action. (Author via Mrs J Somerville)*

At the Inquest on February 25th, 1977, the Croydon Coroner was satisfied that the human remains recovered were those of Sergeant Egan. As no serial numbers had been found on the wreckage, however, or anything with the pilot to confirm his ID, the MOD refused to accept this identification, despite the fact that Sergeant Egan was the *only* outstanding pilot from the day in question. I am at a loss to understand the MOD's inflexibility. My detective experience suggests that burglars do not leave behind them signed confessions, and so other forms of evidence have to be found in order to prove the case beyond *reasonable* doubt. In the absence of any identification at the crash site, surely the process of elimination regarding casualties proved identity beyond all *reasonable* doubt? Due to the MOD's stance, however, the CWGC was obliged to bury the pilot as unknown in the Brookwood Military Cemetery. Relatives of Sergeant Egan attended the funeral, including his sister, Mrs Jane Somerville, who had accepted that her brother had been found.

In November 1978, a number of recovery groups co-operated to re-excavate the Daniels Wood crash site with a view to confirming the aircraft's identity beyond any dispute. Fortunately the manufacturer's plate was found bearing the serial number P3820: Sergeant Egan's Hurricane. The MOD thereafter accepted, on the basis of this crucial evidence, that the pilot was indeed Sergeant Egan and a named headstone at Brookwood was immediately authorised.

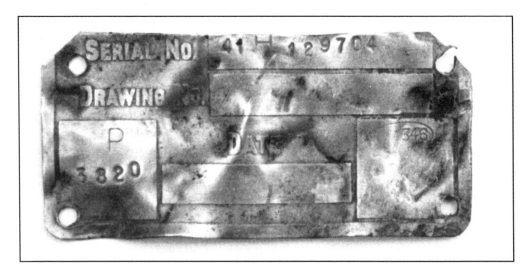

*The plate conclusively identifying the Daniel's Wood Hurricane as P3820,*
*last flown by Sgt Egan.*
*(Steve Vizard)*

### *Oberleutnant* Ekkehard Schelcher: October 1st, 1977.

Oblt *Ekkehard Schelcher,* Stab *III/JG54*
Grunherz.
*(KBoBM)*

At about noon on Monday, September 2nd, 1940, a formation of some 250 German fighters and bombers crossed the south coast, bound for various Fighter Command airfields. The raiders were intercepted by around 70 Spitfires and Hurricanes as a huge melee developed over Kent. Amongst those enemy units embroiled were the Me 109s of JG54. That day, the *Grunherz Geschwader* lost two pilots killed in a collision over Calais shortly after take-off, another captured and *Oberleutnant* Schelcher, the III *Gruppe* Staff Officer, was *Vermisst.*

Many years later, both the landowner and MOD refused permission for recovery groups to excavate the crash site of an Me 109 located behind mountain Street, Chilham, Kent. Although a previous publication claimed that the site was, in fact, recognised by the Germans and registered as a war grave, I have been unable to substantiate this. Locals can recall a white cross being in existence many years ago, some 50 yards from the actual site, and perhaps a fence around it. Such arrangements, however, were of a purely private nature. Permission was eventually given to a local Territorial Army formation, No 590 Explosive Ordnance Disposal Unit, to excavate the site as an 'exercise advantageous to squadron training'. This subsequently took place on October 1st, 1977, and much of the aircraft, together with the remains of *Oberleutnant* Schelcher were recovered. The *Jagdflieger* was later buried with full military honours at the *Soldatenfriedhof* with both his brother and sister-in-law present.

Mike Llewellyn, of the KBoBM and who had previously been involved in the Gruszka case, adds:-

> In this case, I was called in by the EOD unit concerned to identify the aircraft as Schelcher's Me 109E. This I did and at the Inquest was praised by the Coroner, in direct contrast to the Gruszka fiasco; you just cannot win!

**Note of Guidance to Recovery Groups, July 1979.**

These further recoveries of long missing airmen and the ever increasing momentum of aviation archaeology provoked a revision of the Note of Guidance issued by the MOD in 1975. Four years on, the new note read in its entirety:-

MINISTRY OF DEFENCE
AIR FORCE BOARD SECRETARIAT
CRASHED MILITARY AIRCRAFT OF HISTORICAL INTEREST
NOTE OF GUIDANCE TO RECOVERY GROUPS

1.    One result of the growing public interest in the history of aviation and the Second World War in particular, is that a number of groups have been formed to recover, preserve and exhibit some of the military aircraft which crashed during the war and have never been recovered. The level of activity is such that it is considered necessary to issue this Note of Guidance on matters which are of particular concern to the Ministry of Defence.

Ownership of aircraft and equipment and retention of recovered items.

2.    Crashed British military aircraft and their equipment remain the property of the Ministry of Defence until such time as the Crown decide to dispose of them (see para 4 below). Crashed enemy aircraft and their equipment lying within the United Kingdom are regarded as captured enemy property which has been surrendered to the Crown. For all practical purposes the Ministry of Defence can exercise possession of both categories and deal with any question arising on them. Should the Royal Air Force undertake any of the recovery work in connection with human remains (see para 10), any additional non-prohibited items thereby recovered will be offered to the group concerned.

Permission to recover.

3.    Any recovery group wishing to recover the wreckage of military aircraft should first approach the Ministry of Defence to obtain their consent as owner. Consent will normally be given, subject to the various requirements contained in this Note and to the condition that the

work will be carried out in a responsible manner. Consent may be withheld, however, in cases where the Ministry of Defence wishes to make its own arrangements for the recovery and/or preservation of an aircraft. Consent must be obtained with respect to each and every recovery operation, and groups should note that the Ministry of Defence is not prepared to grant sole rights or recovery to any one group for any one site.

4.    The Ministry of Defence requires to know what items have been recovered by groups who have been granted permission to recover crashed military aircraft. A report is to be rendered on the proforma attached at Annex and returned to the Ministry of Defence at the address shown in para 16 below when the project is completed. Recovery groups will then receive, in due course, formal written notification from the Ministry of Defence that the items listed on the proforma may be regarded as their own property. Until such time as they have been notified, however, recovery groups are reminded that the items remain the property of the Crown and are not to be considered their own.

5.    Any failure to follow the guidance in this Note will result in a recovery becoming an unlawful interference with Crown property and could lead to civil or criminal proceedings. In this respect particular attention is drawn to para 9 concerning firearms, ammunition and explosives, and a para 10 concerning human remains.

Entry on to land

6.    In all cases the permission of landowners and occupiers should be obtained before any recovery project is undertaken. Once permission is granted, full liaison should be maintained with the landowner or occupier in order to ensure the minimum of inconvenience and damage to property.

Wreckage lying in coastal waters

7.    Groups wishing to recover aircraft lying in coastal waters are advised that, in addition to approaching the Ministry of Defence, as laid down by this Note, they must also contact the local receiver of Wrecks, who is ultimately responsible for determining ownership of any such aircraft.

Safety Precautions

8.    Recovery operations should not commence until adequate safety precautions, commensurate with the dangers likely to be encountered, have been taken. For example, if an aircraft lies on a former bombing or gunnery range, or if the presence of any firearms, ammunition or explosives is suspected, expert advice should be sought from the police or any Service Unit. (See also paragraph 9).

Firearms, ammunition and explosives

9.    The possession of firearms, ammunition and explosives is subject to strict control under the Firearms Act 1968 and the Explosives Act 1875, and any person having unauthorised possession of them would commit an offence. The finding of firearms, ammunition and explosives should be notified immediately to the police. This applies in all cases irrespective of the condition of the items found, and recovery work is to cease until the items have been removed by

properly authorised persons and the site declared safe. The Ministry of Defence specifically reserves its rights of ownership in respect of prohibited weapons and ammunition (whatever the condition) detailed under Section 5 of the Firearms Act 1968, that is, any firearm designed or adapted to contain any such noxious thing. The retention of any firearm or ammunition under Section 1 of the Firearms Act 1968 is, of course, subject to the possession of a Firearms Certificate.

## Human remains

10.   In many cases crews will have escaped from aircraft before they crashed, but there is still a possibility of human remains being found. These must not be touched and they should be treated with due respect. Their discovery must be reported immediately to the police and the Ministry of Defence, AR9 (RAF), Adastral House, Theobolds Road, London WC1X 8RU, Tel 01-430-7577. Recovery activities must be suspended and nothing should be taken from the site until both the Royal Air Force and the police have made their investigations and the human remains have been removed. The feelings of relatives of deceased aircrew cannot be emphasised too strongly. Irreverent handling of human remains would be particularly distressing to them and it is most important that no information about the discovery of human remains should be given to presumed relatives or the news media, or indeed to anyone outside the police or the Ministry of Defence, until the facts have been properly confirmed. A coroner's inquest may have to be held. The Ministry of defence will take all necessary steps to notify the next-of-kin or other relatives, and in no circumstances is a recovery group to act in this respect.

## Personal property

11.   Items might be found in wreckage which were the personal property of crew members. These must be handed over to the police or any Service Unit.

## Books, documents and papers

12.   All books, documents and papers found during excavation, whether official or personal crew property, must be reported to the Ministry of Defence, who will then decide which items, if any, may be retained by the group in question.

## Legal responsibilities

13.   It must be clearly understood that the Ministry of Defence will not under any circumstances accept any responsibility whatsoever for any consequences arising from the activities of recovery groups, for example compensation for injury to any persons or damage to any property. This Note is not therefore to be construed as an authority from the Ministry of Defence to recover aircraft, but rather as a guide to the circumstances under which the Ministry of Defence may consent to an application for recovery. Groups are urged to consider their position before embarking upon a project.

## Adverse publicity

14.   The Ministry of Defence is concerned that the Services should not become involved in any adverse publicity as the result of any recovery activities. Groups are requested to take all possible steps to prevent this.

US military aircraft

15.  Any enquiries concerning the investigation or recovery of US military aircraft of historical interest are to be directed to the Ministry of Defence, who will act on behalf of the US authorities.

Reports, applications and enquiries

16.  Reports of items recovered (see para 4 above) and any applications or enquiries regarding recovery operations covered by this note should be addressed to:

Ministry of Defence,
Air Force Board Secretariat,
Room 8239,
Main Building,
Whitehall SW1

The Air Force Board Secretariat rapidly distributed the newly revised Note of Guidance to Recovery Groups. The new Note differed from previous editions in that the MOD required a report to be rendered detailing items recovered during every excavation. The letter accompanying the Notes drew particular attention to the paragraphs concerning human remains, firearms, ammunition and explosives. Groups were 'requested to follow these instructions closely'.

Again, however, the Notes had no supporting legislation, and so the activities of those involved in the recovery of missing pilots remained arguably unaffected by this latest paper chase.

**Sergeant Alexander Logan McNay: September 1979.**

Alexander McNay, a Glaswegian, joined No 73 Squadron at Church Fenton, the northern most Sector Station of 12 Group, on July 21st, 1940. On August 15th, 73 Squadron's Hurricanes were amongst those RAF fighters intercepting the *Luftwaffe* raids directed against targets in northern England. During the ensuing combat, known to the RAF as the '*Junkers* Party', Sergeant McNay claimed two Ju 88s destroyed. On September 5th, 73 Squadron was sent south, to Castle Camps in the Debden Sector of 11 Group, north of the Thames Estuary. Having previously operated against unescorted bombers, 73 Squadron was to be roughly handled in its first traumatic encounter with Me 109s: five Hurricanes were shot down (whilst a further aircraft returned to base in a damaged state), one pilot being wounded and another posted missing: Sergeant McNay.

Essex County Council records indicate that at 1530 hrs on September 5th, 1940, the Eastern Report Centre noted that 'one Hurricane crashed and burnt out at rear of Post Office, North Fambridge. No trace of pilot'. The Billericay Region Air Raid Precaution (ARP) Warden's Log Book provides more significant evidence:-

At 1530 hrs North Fambridge near Post Office. Machine burnt out. British markings. Occupants - no trace. Plane buried 10 to 15 feet in ground. Pilot believed to be in wreckage.

Mr Jack Friedlein provides important eye-witness evidence:-

I was working near my cattle sheds at Whitehouse Farm, North Fambridge. My wife, Winnie, my parents and two other works were in the shelter. Personally I rarely went to the shelter during air raids as they were becoming so commonplace the disruption was too frequent to be practical. As so often in the past, I could see a formation of twin-engined bombers making their way up the river towards London. Suddenly I heard a mighty explosion, and looked up to see a huge ball of flame next to my chicken sheds. The flames quickly spread to the adjacent pig sheds. The sow was severely burned and I assume she must have been smothered in aviation fuel. She died, as did her piglets with no mother to suckle. The aircraft must have gone in at an extremely shallow angle from the east for me not to have seen it. It clipped the tops of some trees and piled in. An RAF salvage team arrived later and over a period of about a week various items of wreckage were recovered. The crater was guarded by Scottish soldiers who told me that the pilot had been shot on his way down but had not burned. No race of him was ever recovered so I presumed that he had been blown to pieces. For years afterwards Winnie used a section of the Hurricane's self-sealing rubber fuel tank as the children's' bath mat.

In September 1979, the LAM and WAAG excavated the North Fambridge crash site. The shattered Merlin engine of the Hurricane concerned was recovered together with various cockpit items, including the pilot's head armour, pieces of the pilot's Sutton harness and even a map on which the name 'McNay' was recorded; beyond doubt the enthusiasts had found P3224 flown by Sergeant Alexander McNay. No 'tangible' human remains were discovered, however, and so this

*Corner of an English field: the crash site of Sgt McNay's Hurricane 1940 and 1979. (Above: Philip Harvey, Below: Steve Vizard)*

pilot remains missing to this day. John Tickner, present at the dig, recalls that only 'a few pieces of lifejacket were discovered, nothing else connected with the pilot' (as a matter of interest, during the course of my research, the staff of a local crematorium confirmed that to incinerate human remains a minimum temperature of 820 degrees centigrade is required). This is actually a great pity, given that identification was found amongst the wreckage, not withstanding the fact that Sergeant McNay remains the only Hurricane pilot reported missing on September 5th, 1940.

### Flight Lieutenant Hugh Richard Aden Beresford: September 29th, 1979.

Amongst those RAF squadrons scrambled in defence of the capital when the big raid came in on the afternoon of September 7th, 1940, was No 257 Squadron. After what was the squadron's fourth sortie of the day, however, the unit's clerk had to record that following this intense combat over the Thames Estuary, both flight commanders were missing: Flight Lieutenant Beresford and Flying Officer Mitchell.

*Flt Lt H R A Beresford, subject of BBC 2's 40 Minute documentary.*
*(Andy Saunders)*

On October 4th, 49 MU received information that a Hurricane had crashed on the Isle of Sheppey, East Kent, and suggested that a Bren Gun Carrier from RAF Eastchurch might be best suited to dragging the wreckage across the marsh. For some unknown reason, however, the RAF actually failed to undertake any work at this site.

In 1971, the KBoBM had partially excavated the site concerned, located at Elmley, Spithead Point, Sheppey, during which time the serial number P3049 was confirmed. When RAF records became available, this was found to be Beresford's Hurricane. In 1979, however, the BBC decided to make a *40 Minute* documentary relating to aviation archaeology, the provisional title being *Missing - no known grave*. The assistance of the WAAG was obtained, and the Spithead Point crash site chosen as the subject. It is fair, I think, to suggest that all involved knew full well that this was the crash site of a missing pilot and that there was every liklihood of Flight Lieutenant Beresford's remains being recovered in front of the cameras. No attempt whatsoever was made to seek the view of the deceased airman's NOK prior to the recovery going ahead.

The recovery took place on Sunday, 29th September 1979, and it will come as no surprise to the reader to learn that Flight Lieutenant Beresford was indeed found. The police at Sheppey were informed and took away the pilot's remains. The MOD were then presented with the unenviable task of tracing and informing the Beresford family. It was discovered that the Flight Lieutenant's widow had remarried but died prematurely in 1966. His sole surviving relative was found to be his 62-year-old sister, Pamela, who later admitted that she had always clung to some remote belief that her brother may still be alive.

The Inquest was held at Sittingbourne on October 19th, 1979. HM Coroner, Mr Lionel Skingley, heard from the Pathologist, Dr John Dales, that Hugh Beresford had died instantly. When summing up, Mr Skingley quite rightly described the 24-year-old Flight Lieutenant as 'one of our national heroes'.

*The recovery of Hugh Beresford,*
*Spithead Point 1979.*
*(Andy Saunders)*

On November 16th, 1979, Flight Lieutenant Hugh Beresford was finally laid to rest at the Brookwood Military Cemetery. By co-incidence, between that date and the recovery of Beresford's remains, the unrelated funeral took place in Austria of the *Jagdflieger* who may have shot down this particular Hurricane pilot: former Major Josef Fozo (at the time *Staffelkapitaen* of 4/ JG51).

Nearly 20 years later, Andy Saunders of the WAAG and a prime mover in the operation, remarks:-

Looking back, what we did was wrong, and I admit that. We should not have recovered the pilot without first seeking the views of his family. I would not operate in such a way now.

### Sergeant Hubert Hastings Adair: October 6th, 1979.

Like *Gefrieter* Richard Riedel (see Chapter Three), Sergeant Adair was killed just outside the officially accepted end of the Battle of Britain (October 31st, 1940), but his story is also relevant.

On November 6th, 1940, the main engagement of the day took place when Me 109s of JG2 *Richthofen* clashed with Hurricanes and Spitfires over Portsmouth. Amongst the responding RAF fighters were the Hurricanes of Tangmere's 213 Squadron. Flight Lieutenant Geoffrey Stevens (see Chapter One) remembers:-

Having joined 151 Squadron in early August 1940, I became very friendly with a fellow NCO pilot called Paddy Adair who was posted to us in early September. He had been with a Fairey Battle squadron attacking bridges in the Low Countries and France and was lucky to have survived. When I volunteered to go to a squadron in the south, Paddy, who by then was my best friend, somehow managed to follow me to 213 Squadron. We were therefore able to continue our friendship. He was a volatile redhead who could fly off the handle only to return to earth just as quickly. We had many violent arguments but these never made the slightest difference to our close friendship.

On November 6th, 1940, I did not have a serviceable aircraft and was therefore left on the ground. I watched the battle in the air, over the Portsmouth area, from the tarmac and saw a lone fighter plunge in an almost vertical dive from about 15-20,000'. I remember thinking 'Poor devil, whoever you are'; of course I had no idea whether it was one of ours or theirs. I had even less idea that it was Paddy, who was sadly killed.

As his best friend, I was sent by transport to identify Paddy Adair, but there wasn't very much to see. It was most unpleasant and very depressing.

Sergeant Adair's Hurricane, V7602 (AK-D), was shot down by none other than the famous *experten* and *Kommodore* of JG2, Major Helmut Wick. The 23-year-old British pilot was officially posted missing and later commemorated on the Runnymede Memorial.

By August 1979, the crash site at Pigeon House Farm, Cosham, had become of interest to the WAAG. Via the MOD, the group confirmed that in the action concerned, two pilots were killed: Sergeant Adair and 238 Squadron's Flying Officer James Tillett, the latter being buried at Gosport. With all other RAF fighters accounted for on November 6th, the Pigeon House Farm Hurricane had to be that of the missing Sergeant Adair. Consequently the MOD forwarded a letter from the WAAG to the NOK's last known address, but no reply was ever received.

*Sgt H H Adair.*
*(Andy Saunders)*

It can only be thought surprising, considering both policy and the content of the then current Note of Guidance (providing that the MOD was made aware of *all* the circumstances relating to this particular aircraft), that permission was given to the WAAG to recover the Pigeon House Farm Hurricane.

The Hurricane recovery took place on October 6th, 1979. Shortly after 1000 hrs the first parts of the fighter were discovered at a depth of three feet below the ground. Present at the excavation was the tenant farmer, Mr Robert Ware, himself an eyewitness, and the aviation historian and author Alexander McKee who had also seen the Hurricane crash. Mr Ware remembered that after the crash, 'air force people came to the scene and stood guard for several days. After that, a long trailer came and removed the part of the plane above ground. To my knowledge there was no attempt made to remove the body of the pilot'.

As the excavation went on, all eight Mk II Browning machine-guns were discovered in addition to the remains of a body which consists of a quantity of bones and part of a flying boot. As in the case of Sergeant Egan, no sign of identification could be found. The police were duly notified, the guns being seized and conveyed to Cosham Police Station, whilst the human remains were removed by the Coroner's Officer.

*The recovery of Sgt Adair.*
*Note the chalky ground and all*
*eight Browning machine-guns.*
*(Steve Vizard)*

On October 22nd, 1979, the Coroner's Officer reported:-

Since the discovery of the aircraft I have had several discussions with both Mr 'X' of the Ministry of Defence, Whitehall, and Mr 'Y' of the Ministry of Defence, Adastral House. Mr 'Y' assumed responsibility for enquiries in that department. As a result of a discussion with him the Browning machine-guns were collected from Cosham Police Station on 11.10.79 by Sergeant Rutter of the RAF Bomb Disposal Unit. On 22.10.79, I received a telephone call from Mr 'Y' to the effect that he was unable to trace any next-of-kin in this case and that in any event cannot positively identify the plane or pilot. His attitude and that of his superior, Mr 'Z', is that this matter is best dealt with by NOT holding an Inquest. By calling the pilot an unknown aviator and by disposing of the remains locally. He further stated that of course it was your decision to make and that if you elected to hold an Inquest then he would be pleased to attend and offer as much assistance as he could. He is sending a letter confirming this.

On October 24th, the MOD wrote to the Coroner's Officer:-

I would like to state at this point that the established policy of the Ministry of Defence in connection with the identification of deceased aviators is that identification must always be positive.

During our investigations we have examined the records related to the loss of the particular Hurricane which have been suggested by the recovery group, and all other Hurricane crashes around the approximate date of the crash. Unfortunately we have been unable to positively identify the aircraft or the pilot.

So far as the wreckage is concerned, it has been established that it was a Hurricane fighter, which as you probably know, was used extensively by the Royal Air Force in WWII. The location of the human remains indicate that they are those of a pilot. In view of this limited evidence, positive identification has not been possible.

There was no inquest. Although such a decision was that of the Coroner, would such a course of action been taken, I wonder, if not for the MOD's suggestion? Another question that must be asked is what happened to the remains recovered at the time and viewed by Pilot Officer Stevens? There is no record of any 'unknown' burial which could relate to this case.

Although in 1979 nothing was found in the wreckage to confirm that the aircraft concerned was V6702, statements made to the police by both Mr Ware and Mr McKee confirm the crash to have occurred on November 6th, 1940, on which date Sergeant Adair, known to have been lost in the Portsmouth area, remained Fighter Command's only outstanding pilot. As we have seen, the MOD's inflexible insistence that 'positive identification' had to come from either the aircraft or body has often been found to be impractical in certain circumstances. When considering the facts of this case, however, the reader must remember that this recovery took place just a week after that of Hugh Beresford, which was continuing to receive the media's attention. A similar situation, especially so soon, must have been the last thing the MOD needed, but when Mr 'Y' suggests that 'the matter is best dealt with by NOT holding an Inquest', what does he mean, 'best' for whom? Certainly not for poor Sergeant Adair, whose mortal remains were not even buried as unknown at Brookwood but cremated at Portchester and scattered in the Garden of Remembrance there on October 29th, 1979. Again curiously, although the Coroner's file is titled 'Unidentified remains', the letter by the Superintendent and Registrar, Mr EC Appleton, confirming disposal of the remains in question refers to them belonging to 'the late Hubert Adair'.

I would suggest that the evidence available does *confirm* that the pilot concerned was Sergeant 580088 Hubert Hastings Adair (alphabetically the first of the Few). One last point would I make: on this occasion as there was not even an 'unknown' burial at Brookwood, as in the case of Sergeant Egan, even if the Department did now accept that the airman concerned was Sergeant Adair, there would be no headstone to name. As he remains officially missing, Adair is still remembered on Runnymede; as his remains were 'disposed of', would any other commemoration now be either possible or appropriate? The fact of the matter is, that regardless of whether identity is accepted as Sergeant Adair, the MOD's treatment of this case is unacceptable.

Steve Vizard, present at this recovery, comments:-

Whilst it was again wrong of us to present the family, which was traced by the MOD some time *after* the recovery, with such a *fait accompli*, given the evidence how can the MOD justify both not accepting the pilot's identity and destroying his remains?

How indeed?

### Pilot Officer John Benzie (Canadian): 1980.

September 7th, 1940, saw not only the change in emphasis of *Luftwaffe* targets, but also the first sortie of the controversial 12 Group Wing, based at Duxford and lead by Acting Squadron Leader Douglas Bader. At a height disadvantage, however, the Duxford Wing's first foray was not a resounding success; although the formation's Spitfire squadron, No 19, suffered no loss, the two Hurricane units did: 310 (Czech) lost one Hurricane destroyed and another damaged; two 242 Squadron Hurricanes were damaged (including Bader's), and Pilot Officer Benzie was reported missing from the combat over the Thames Estuary. It was naturally assumed that he had crashed into the water.

*Plt Off John Benzie: is he the Theydon Bois airman? (Andy Saunders)*

Following a protracted search, the LAM located a crash site at Blackacre, Theydon Bois, Essex, which was excavated in 1980. A Hurricane was discovered together with the pilot's remains. However, as no identification of either the machine or pilot could be found, the Inquest at Epping was inconclusive; the pilot was buried as an unknown airman at Brookwood. Three Hurricane pilots were reported missing on September 7th: Flight Lieutenant Beresford and Flying Officer Mitchell of 257 Squadron, and Pilot Officer Benzie of 242. By the time of the Theydon Bois excavation, Beresford had been recovered, so in fairness, still with two outstanding pilots, the MOD cannot be criticised on this occasion for not accepting the enthusiasts' view that Pilot Officer Benzie had been found. Again, those concerned with this recovery have to accept critiscm for going ahead with such an operation prior to seeking the family's views (as indeed they now accept).

### Sergeant John Joseph Brimble: September 14th, 1980.

Amongst 73 Squadron's more experienced pilots was Sergeant John Brimble who had fought with the unit during the Battle of France. By September 14th, 1940, he had survived nine days of fighting in the 11 Group area, but on that day his luck ran out. In combat shortly after 1600 hrs, three 73 Squadron Hurricanes were lost, a further four damaged (one the victim of a 'Friendly Fire' attack by a Spitfire); again, just one pilot was to remain missing: Sergeant Brimble.

In May 1980, Steve Vizard's organisation, the Tonbridge Aircraft Museum (TAM) applied to the MOD to recover Hurricane L2118, safely abandoned by 73 Squadron's Sergeant Griffin on September 14th, 1940. The excavation, which took place on September 14th, 1980, was at Parkhouse Farm, Chart Sutton; the aircraft discovered was P2542, together with its pilot: Sergeant Brimble. To say that this recovery was untimely was an understatement: the *Missing* documentary, concerning Hugh Beresford, having been premiered the previous week.

A veritable media storm brewed over the recovery of John Brimble, one headline reading *Death Plane Dig Runs into Flak*. The RAF claimed that it was 'upset and angry' because the application made, and permission given, concerned another aircraft. Steve Vizard maintained that his actions were justified in view of the fact that Sergeant Brimble would now get a decent burial: the basic right of every man?

*The recovery of Sgt Brimble. Note propeller reduction gear in right foreground.*
*(Steve Vizard)*

On October 16th, 1980, Sergeant John Brimble at least received a fitting burial, as was the TAM's intention, when he too was buried at Brookwood with full military honours. Again, Steve Vizard comments:-

> This is another case regarding which I would now act differently. It was another *fait accompli*, the pilot's brother, Bill, again being found by the authorities *after* the recovery. Fortunately he was supportive, although those of us responsible for the recovery were physically prevented by the authorities from speaking to the family at the funeral.

The MOD was indeed clearly unimpressed and revoked existing permission for *all* aircraft recoveries. The major UK groups were then called to a meeting in London on January 7th, 1981; the subsequent MOD (RAF) press release was dated the following day:-

> Senior RAF officers and officials in the MOD met representatives of organisations and individuals interested in the recovery of crashed wartime aircraft, at their request, to discuss the Ministry's current policy towards their activities, especially the problems that arise when human remains are thought to be in the wreckage.

> Air Commodore Henry Probert RAF (Ret'd), Head of the Air Historical Branch, took the chair, and others present included representatives of the Commonwealth War Graves Commission, Royal British Legion, SSAFA, War Widows Association of GB, Royal Air Forces Association, RAF Benevolent Fund, Imperial War Museum, RAF Museum, National Farmers' Union, British Aircraft Preservation Council, British Aviation Archaeological Council, and a number of independent aviation archaeologists.

> Representatives of the MOD said that some recent digs involving the discovery of human remains had led to controversy, and the purpose of the meeting was to enable all those with an

interest in the subject to put their views forward. The Ministry's current policy was to permit the excavation of wrecks where there was no liklihood of human remains being found and no risk from explosives. Otherwise permission was normally withheld.

Views on the policy were then expressed by representatives of the BAPC and BAAC and by several independent archaeologists. The majority expressed general support, while suggesting a number of practical improvements in the way the policy was implemented, including protection of landowners' interests. Some of the independents, however, felt strongly that all wrecks containing human remains should be excavated with the consent of next-of-kin and the bodies recovered for burial in consecrated grounds.

Representatives of the ex-Servicemen's' Associations and the war widows stated that most of their members agreed with the present policy and strongly opposed the digging up of wreckage thought to contain human remains; this was very upsetting for next-of-kin, many of whom are now of advanced age.

Summing up the Chairman said there were no easy answers. They had to face a wide range of strongly held views. There were those who very sincerely felt that recovery of human remains should be undertaken. A lot of others felt equally strongly that aircraft wrecks should be a last resting place. The meeting had heard as many expressions of view opposed to recovery as those for it, and the associations present represented very many people. He therefore asked all aviation archaeologists to have respect for the Ministry's policy based on the very sincerely held views of a great many people.

On the question of ownership of parts of aircraft recovered by groups the Ministry made it clear that since 1974, all such parts were Crown property until ownership was formally transferred to the finders. While the Ministry would not in general seek to recover past unauthorised finds, it would be in everyone's interests for the Ministry to be informed in general terms of what had been found if groups wished to retain their discoveries.

The meeting agreed there could be advantages in developing a system of Ministry accreditation of archaeologists through a limited number of groups. The Ministry would then hold further meetings with such groups to monitor developments.

Although in certain respects the meeting was a valuable public relations exercise, enthusiasts attending felt that the MOD had presented its own *fait accompli* in that although their views were listened to, there was never any chance of policy being influenced. Personally, I feel strongly that human remains should not be deliberately disturbed without the prior permission of the NOK (excepting in exceptional circumstances, see Chapter Six, case of Sergeant Caldwell refers); it is noteworthy that the suggested way forward expressed by enthusiasts present was exactly that, all present accepting that without such prior knowledge and consent such discoveries could be greatly upsetting. On the contrary it could equally be argued, I would suggest, that families would be relieved to know at last, to have a tangible full stop; the evidence equally supports this reaction. Nevertheless, at this point I think all were agreed (even those personally involved) that the previous *fait accomplis*, such as the cases of Beresford and Brimble, were unacceptable.

We must remember that at this time the quantity of wrecks containing human remains was unknown. Had the MOD agreed with the enthusiasts' view, the flood gates could have been opened for a host of families clamouring for recoveries and service funerals, a budget for such a major operation being unavailable. Although *our* foremost interest is in the Battle of Britain, the Few being held in especially high regard, the MOD has to consider the *overall* subject of casualties, from *all* services in *all* theatres of war and in *all* conflicts: in this context we are talking about millions of men, thousands of which remain missing. If an exception was made in respect of one casualty, a precedent would have been set, after which the debate could have opened on a huge scale. Although our hearts may not agree with the MOD, practicality and reality have to be appreciated, and so we can at least understand the policy of 'letting sleeping dogs lie'.

David Buchanan:-

I was at the meeting and a particular enthusiast stated his view that he considered it improper for tractors and so on to be active, for example, on the crash site of a missing pilot who crashed on agricultural land. He did not feel that the site should be so disturbed and argued that recoveries should take place so that those casualties concerned could be reburied in cemeteries where they could rest in peace. A clergyman present, however, confirmed the religious view that as the spirit left the body, it did not matter. It was an interesting point.

Mike Llewellyn:-

I attended both the first, and a second meeting (the latter involving but a select few). I pushed hard at both to have either the RAF recover the outstanding missing pilots or the sites marked appropriately. An RAF chaplain present at the second told me that there could be no better burial than at a crash site as it would be impossible to recover every fragment for burial; so much for the 'basic right of every man'. In my opinion, the real change in attitudes took place after those with a commercial interest were permitted to recover gold from HMS Edinburgh, a recognised war grave.

### Pilot Officer Colin Dunstone Francis: August 23rd, 1981.

As my general research progresses, time and time again it emerges that squadrons new to the rapid and lethal tempo of battle in the 11 Group area were hammered on their first combats. On August 29th, 1940, the Hurricanes of 253 Squadron arrived at Kenley, fresh from resting at Prestwick in Scotland after the Battle of France. During the morning of August 30th, 253 met the *Luftwaffe* with disastrous results: four Hurricanes were damaged, four more destroyed; one pilot was wounded but two were killed (one of which, Pilot Officer DNO Jenkins, was machine-gunned during his parachute descent by enemy fighters). A third, Pilot Officer Colin Francis, was posted missing.

Having located a crash site in a field north of Wrotham, Kent, the TAM applied to the MOD to recover Spitfire X4248, in which Flying Officer Jack Bell of 616 Squadron had been shot down and killed in combat over West Malling on August 30th, 1940; Bell was not missing, however, as his body was recovered at the time and buried at Eastgate, Lincoln. Permission for the excavation was therefore given by the MOD, but the aircraft actually discovered at Wrotham was Hurricane L1965. From records available the enthusiasts knew that the aircraft concerned belonged to a missing pilot: 19-year-old Pilot Officer Colin Francis. This, together with the discovery of shreds of uniform fabric, led to the site being closed down and protected overnight by the placing of an iron grid over the hole. A telephone call was made to the MOD the following morning (Monday).

*Plt Off C D Francis.*
*(Andy Saunders)*

It was decided that the recovery could continue the following Wednesday under the supervision of RAF personnel from Biggin Hill. This was duly done, and the RAF consequently removed the pilot's remains to the local police station. The MOD then traced the NOK of Pilot Officer Francis, a cousin, before the Inquest was held at Tonbridge on September 8th, 1981. The verdict was 'Death whilst on active service'. On September 29th, 1981, Pilot Officer Francis received a Service funeral at Brookwood.

Allowing the TAM to continue with the excavation in the presence of RAF personnel was a first, but if anyone felt that policy had been influenced and was changing, they were wrong.

*The battered plate identifying L1965 flown by Plt Off Francis.*
*(Steve Vizard)*

*Restless spirit? The recovery of Plt Off Ramsay and his Hurricane.*
*(Steve Vizard)*

### Pilot Officer John Basil Ramsay: August 11th, 1983.

*Plt Off J B Ramsay.*
*(Andy Saunders)*

Like Flying Officer Gruszka, Pilot Officer Ramsay was reported missing on August 18th, 1940. His squadron, No 151 based at North Weald, attacked the He 111s of KG53 over the Essex coast. The bombers' fighter escort was provided by the Me 110 *Zestorers* of ZG26 which lost no time in making a counter-attack, as a result of which Squadron Leader Gordon baled out wounded, Wing Commander Beamish forced-landed at Martlesham Heath, and 21-year-old Pilot Officer Ramsay - an experienced pilot - was reported missing. Again, there the matter may have rested if not for Steve Vizard:-

We were searching for a Spitfire at Holliwell Point, near Burnham-on-Crouch in Essex, but found the modification plate confirming the aircraft to be a Hurricane. Further research indicated that the aircraft concerned was that flown by Pilot Officer Ramsay. By coincidence, around the same time, his mother's death notice appeared in the *Daily Telegraph*, placed by his cousin, Miss Joan Worth. Andy Saunders contacted this lovely lady, who actually worked for the MOD and had grown up with Pilot Officer Ramsay. The facts were put to Miss Worth who concluded that her cousin *must* be recovered as her aunt had always agonised over her son's fate.

It is noteworthy that in this instance instead of going straight out and recovering the Holliwell Hurricane themselves, the enthusiasts pursued the matter through Miss Worth, who personally presented the case to the MOD. This raises a most important issue, however. The MOD will not accept any evidence to identity an aircraft other than a serial number from the wreckage itself, as indeed we have already seen in the cases of both Sergeants Egan and Adair. Such evidence, of course, can only be discovered if the site is excavated. As policy dictated that no permission will be given in the case of missing pilots, it was therefore impossible for such conclusive evidence to be found prior to a full recovery. Such an operation, of course, the MOD would neither task the RAF to undertake or authorise the enthusiasts to go ahead. The MOD still argues that without such conclusive proof it will not excavate any site as the aircraft may transpire to be that of another pilot, the last resting place of which his family may not wish disturbed. Miss Worth's request for an official inquiry and recovery was therefore refused. The reason given was that another pilot had been reported missing during the same action: Squadron Leader RHA 'Dickie' Lee of 85 Squadron, although contemporary accounts confirm that he was lost 30 miles out to sea.

This was the first known case where co-operation between relatives and enthusiasts had led to such an approach by a family; the MOD's response was not encouraging.

Naturally Miss Worth was disappointed, but a personal visit to Holliwell Point confirmed the lady's resolve to see her cousin provided a decent burial, come what may. Consequently, at Miss Worth's request, the enthusiasts undertook a major recovery at the site on August 11th, 1983. The mortal remains of Pilot Officer Ramsay were duly recovered and reported to the local police. After the subsequent Coroner's Inquest, Pilot Officer Ramsay was buried with full military honours at Brookwood. Steve Vizard:-

> This time we had the backing of a relative, but the MOD still refused to co-operate. Our unauthorised recovery was only undertaken as a last resort, therefore. At the funeral the MOD again tried to prevent us from communicating with the relatives, but Miss Worth kindly took us back to her hotel where a buffet tea had been arranged for us. That, I think, indicates the level of support she gave us and reflects the family's appreciation.

Clearly not even the direct and personal intervention of relatives could be counted upon to affect the MOD's decision regarding such matters. Some may, with some justification, consider the Department to have acted both insensitively and unreasonably in this case.

### Flying Officer Michael Duke Doulton: April 27th, 1984.

On August 13th, 1978, the Essex Aircraft Historical Society (EAHS) excavated the crash site of a Hurricane south of Wennington Church, near Romford, Essex. No confirmation of identity was discovered in the wreckage. The enthusiasts' research indicated that the Hurricane had crashed on August 31st, 1940, and they believed the most likely candidate to be P3159; the pilot of that aircraft, 26-year-old Pilot Officer Jaroslav Sterbacek remained missing. Human remains were not reported by the EAHS, however, so it is hard to understand why, as at least one other Hurricane remained outstanding but whose pilot was safe, such a firm conclusion was reached that a missing pilot was involved.

Pilot Officer Sterbacek was amongst the original Czech pilots of Squadron Leader Sacha Hess's 310 Squadron, formed at Duxford on July 10th, 1940 (see *Bader's Duxford Fighters*, also by this author). Like the Poles, however, the language created some difficulties, and so the Station Commander and 'Boss Controller', Wing Commander AB 'Woody' Woodhall had the BBC produce a recording which provided a translation of flying commands and terminology. Also, a policy of 'double-banking' was operated so that the Czech officers had British counter-parts. For example, although Hess was the Czech CO, overall the squadron was commanded by Squadron Leader Douglas Blackwood, whose British flight commanders were Flight Lieutenant's Sinclair and Jefferies. On August 31st, the Czechs met the enemy for the first time.

Situated at Duxford, 12 Group's southern most Sector Station, the fighter squadrons there were required to protect their own area in addition to providing reinforcement to Air Vice-Marshal Park's No 11 Group. At lunchtime on August 31st, such assistance was requested. Squadron Leader Bader led his 242 Squadron on a patrol of London, but landed with nothing to report. 310 Squadron was vectored to Hornchurch where, with 11 Group units, the Czechs attacked a formation of 'Do 215s' escorted by Me 110s and Me 109s. Four bombers and one Me 109 were subsequently claimed destroyed. Two Hurricanes were lost: Pilot Officer Kredba baled out safely, but Pilot Officer Sterbacek was missing. The 310 Squadron Operations Record Book states that:-

Pilot Officer Sterbacek's aircraft was seen to go down very steeply. Presumed that he went into the Thames. Pilot Officer Sterbacek has the proud distinction of being the first Czech fighter pilot to give his life for England.

Some years later, the Medway Aviation Research Group (MARG) questioned the belief of the EAHS that Pilot Officer Sterbacek's Hurricane had been found. More likely, the MARG believed, the aircraft was that of Pilot Officer Kredba, and on that basis the MOD gave permission for a recovery. The MARG were aware, however, that the Sterbacek family were 'very keen that Jaroslav should be found and buried', as member David Smith recalls; he continues:-

*The MARG recovery underway at Wennington.*
*(David Smith)*

On Friday, 27th April, 1984, a group of enthusiasts gathered at the Purfleet Rifle Range's offices in Essex. At 0845 hrs a low-loader arrived with a tracked excavator. The day was bright and sunny and April had turned into a very dry month, unlike the preceding March which had been wet in the extreme. John Burton who lived in Wennington at the time of the crash, clearly remembered the aircraft coming down from out of a dogfight. He thought it might have been hit by AA and saw a parachute come down. The RAF came to the site out on the marsh, about two days later. They cleared the surface wreckage and told local people that the pilot had escaped. John also remembered another aircraft coming down in the Purfleet Sandpits.

On the day of our recovery, the range was quiet as it was a maintenance day, and the ground conditions were good. A factor hampering the previous recovery attempt was the very wet conditions prevailing at that time. The site had to be reached by crossing three drainage dykes and lay just south of the main Southend to Fenchurch Street railway line. Fortunately all of those involved in our effort had considerable experience in aircraft recovery having been involved in the hobby for some 10 - 15 years. Nevertheless we knew it would not be easy as the wreckage was likely to be buried very deep due to the nature of the crash and the marshy ground conditions.

Dave Bernhardt, the digger driver, got the machine to the crash site without any major problems. All that was visible on the surface was a minor indentation in the ground and small surface parts of the aircraft scattered around. The first task was to ramp the digger in and the first item to see the light of day was a railway sleeper left behind from the 1978 recovery attempt.

Having reached a depth of 15 feet, we had to rescue the digger from its ramp when its tracks became stuck in the clay. By that time very little of the aircraft had been found. Also time was moving quickly on and it was getting on towards mid-afternoon. At a depth of about 20 feet the digger lifted out a tail wheel assembly, complete with its rubber tyre still inflated. The digger then dug down a further five feet and lifted out something that shed a totally different light on the operation: a complete and unopened parachute pack! We knew then that the aircraft could not be Kredba's. Nobody was now in the Range Offices and a decision had to be taken regarding the next move. The ground conditions would not allow any new attempt at a recovery if the digging was stopped. The pilot was obviously still in the wreckage, and as the knew that the aircraft had definitely crashed on August 31st, 1940, casualty records indicated that Fighter Command had two missing pilots that day: Pilot Officer Sterbacek and Flying Officer Michael Duke Doulton of 601 Squadron; which had we found?

Due to circumstances as previously explained, we decided to carry on. Of course although we all feel inspired by the Battle of Britain and are moved by the sacrifices of those involved, our experience is not personal; this, coupled with our belief that if it was a relative of any of those present we would unanimously wish to see the remains recovered for a decent burial, influenced our thinking. It was not a decision we reached lightly, however, especially realising that someone, somewhere, was going to have their life turned on end by the result. In addition to recovering the pilot, it was of vital importance to identify the aircraft so that the MOD could officially identify the pilot.

As the excavation continued with renewed vigour and purpose, Dave Bernhardt ramped the digger in even deeper. At a depth of well over 25 feet the remaining wreckage and pilot were recovered. A panel from the aircraft's tail was found bearing the number R4215, and then the main ID label was found confirming the Hurricane as R4215. Thus the pilot was identified as Flying Officer (90235) Michael Duke Doulton of 601 Squadron, Royal Auxiliary Air Force. The local police were called and Michael Doulton was eventually identified by the South Essex Coroner. He was buried at Salehurst, Sussex in what was a private funeral, surrounded by his family and friends in an intimate ceremony as I am sure this quiet man would have wished.

For those concerned with his recovery, Michael Doulton will always be a person remembered, not so much as a man we knew but as a very tangible reminder of the debt we owe for the freedom that today can be so taken for granted. For his family the discovery came as a great shock, but as the years go by hopefully, that shock decreases as they are at least aware of the circumstances surrounding his disappearance. He now has a marked grave and younger members of the family know more of this very brave man. The ancient Egyptians believed that if a person's name is remembered and spoken they never die, that will certainly be true of Michael Doulton.

For the record, Michael Doulton himself, a professional engineer and member of the famous Doulton China family, at 31-years was an old man by fighter pilot standards. At six feet and eight inches he was also rather tall to be a pilot but was nevertheless an experienced one having been a member of an Auxiliary squadron, No 604, between 1931 and 1936. He then became a reservist, but was called to full time service with 604 when the country mobilised for war in August 1939.

*The control column of R4215, gun button locked on 'Fire', and the last pilot to touch it: Michael Doulton pictured in far happier times.*
*(Via David Smith)*

Doulton then flew Blenheims from various bases, and his experiences included operational sorties during the Dunkirk evacuation. In June 1940, however, many Hurricane-equipped squadrons required replacement pilots to make good losses suffered during the fall of France and Belgium; knowing certain members of 601 (another AAF unit), Doulton therefore requested a transfer to that squadron. When the Battle of Britain commenced, 601 was operating from Tangmere, moving to Debden on August 19th. Before his own death in action, Doulton had shared in the destruction of two enemy aircraft and personally destroyed two more. David Smith tells us more:-

On the Saturday he died, Michael Doulton should not have been at Debden but actually *en route* to enjoy leave with his wife at their rented cottage in Sussex. They had been married 18 months and their first child was expected. An unexpected 'hitch' had kept him on duty, however, and whilst Flying Officer Doulton sat at Readiness he read a book borrowed from Tangmere's Station Library.

On August 31st, No 601 Squadron was scrambled at 1300 hrs with orders to patrol Colchester at Angels 15. Meanwhile, the Do 17s of KG3 proceeded to their target - Hornchurch - escorted by the Me 109s of JG26 and a number of Me 110s. Battle was joined over the Thames Estuary, 310 Squadron intercepting the same raiders. David Smith relates the balance sheet:-

> Hornchurch was badly hit, but the interception of both 310 and 610 Squadron must have made a difference; it could have been worse. Hornchurch Sector Station remained operational, in fact, this being crucial to Fighter Command at this time. The day was that of Fighter Command's highest casualties throughout the whole battle: 39 RAF fighters lost against 41 *Luftwaffe* aircraft. Five Allied pilots were killed. In the lunchtime engagement over Essex, 601 Squadron claimed four enemy aircraft destroyed, three probables and two damaged. This was offset against four Hurricanes lost, one pilot (as we now know) having been killed. The library book borrowed by that pilot was returned to Tangmere 44 years late, but no-one asked for the overdue fine which had already been paid - in full.

There is no doubt that the Battle of the Airfields represented a crucial phase during the Battle of Britain (again see *Bader's Duxford Fighters*), and the sacrifice of both Flying Officer Doulton and Pilot Officer Sterbacek really did occur during our Darkest Hour. Tragically, the only thing Michael Doulton's son (born in April 1941) was ever able to do for the father he never met was arrange his funeral.

In Czechoslovakia, the Sterbacek family, already aware of the 1978 excavation, was excited to hear of the 1984 recovery. The Czech pilot's brother travelled to England hoping for confirmation that Jaroslav had been found. Sadly the MOD had to tell Mr Sterbacek that the remains were actually those of Flying Officer Doulton, and that in fact his brother's crash site had *never* been found. The family was, quite naturally, devastated; David Smith:-

> For the Sterbacek family the anguish still goes on. It is easy to be critical with the benefit of hindsight, although Michael Doulton's recovery did raise many issues; hopefully the decisions taken at the time proved to be the right ones for his family.

As we have seen, a long-standing argument presented by the MOD is that without positive proof before an excavation, in the event the wrong aircraft could actually be found leading to both disappointment and distress for hopeful relatives. Likewise distress could also be suffered by relatives if presented with such shocking news 'out of the blue'. Again, the recovery team had acted in good faith, however, upon eye-witness evidence received of a parachute (also see Chapter Three, case of Pilot Officer Drake refers), which provides another example of just how unreliable such accounts can be. Although the recovery of Michael Doulton was, therefore, a genuine accident it nonetheless provided the MOD with an example to vindicate its policy.

The question of the *Missing Few*, however, was now reaching a head.

### *Unteroffizier* **Fritz Buchner: September 22nd, 1984.**

Fritz Buchner was the first *Luftwaffe* airman to be recovered since Ekkehard Schlecher in 1977.

In 1975, the BAM excavated a site at Shuart Farm, St Nicholas-at-Wade, on the Isle of Thanet, but the operation was abandoned due to the limitations of mechanical equipment available and given the great depth at which wreckage lay. The ground around the open hole crumbled and caved in, the digger then experiencing difficulties. During this preliminary excavation, however, the aircraft's *Werke Nummer* was discovered: 3874, confirming it to be an Me 109E-1 of 6/JG3 shot down by 56 Squadron's Flying Officer Ken Marston on August 26th, 1940; the pilot, *Unteroffizier* Fritz Buchner remained missing.

*The first dig for the St Nicholas-at-Wade Me109 in 1975.*
*(David Buchanan)*

On September 21st, 1984, a team led by Andy Saunders and Steve Vizard commenced work at the site. The engine and cockpit section were recovered at a depth of some 40 feet, together with the remains of the pilot, with which were found *Unteroffizier* rank badges and a handkerchief embroidered 'FB'. As the BAM had previously confirmed the aircraft's identity in 1975, all concerned were left in no doubt that they had found Fritz Buchner. Other finds, such as the aircraft's unit and individual designation markings, together with further personal possessions, seemed to confirm this.

For some reason, however, the Germans were unwilling to accept that the pilot found was Fritz Buchner, and on March 20th, 1985, indicated that the remains were to be buried at Cannock Chase as unknown. The authorities seem to have put little effort into locating the NOK, and ultimately this was left to the enthusiasts to arrange for themselves. Consequently 80-year-old *Frau* Emma Heumos was traced living in Augsburg and told that her brother had been discovered.

Incredibly, however, the Inquest at Broadstairs was not held until July 1st, 1986, nearly two years after the discovery of the German airman concerned. Proceedings lasted some three hours, during which a letter from the pilot's nephew, expressing gratitude to the enthusiasts involved, was read to the Court. In conclusion, the Coroner, Rebecca Cobb, agreed that Fritz Buchner had indeed been found, and furthermore confirmed that he had been shot down by Flying Officer Marston.

Uffz *Fritz Buchner.*
*(Andy Saunders)*

*Unteroffizier* Fritz Buchner was laid to rest under a named headstone at Cannock Chase. In view of the fact that in 1975 the BAM had confirmed the Shuart Farm site to be that of a missing pilot, the question which has to be asked is whether, not being in contact with any relatives and being aware of the MOD's stance, was it right for the 1984 excavation to go ahead? Whatever your view, it will no doubt be appreciated why those personally concerned consider this case to be a triumph over the apparent apathy, insensitivity and inflexibility of authority which, on occasions, appears equally indefensible.

## The Protection of Military Remains.

Between 1972 and 1984, the MOD had been presented with the remains of 16 Battle of Britain and related airmen: a South African, a Pole, a suspected Canadian, seven British and six German. In an area where feelings often ran high, as we have seen in certain cases the MOD's regulations were openly and blatantly contravened. The MOD, however, was unable to take any significant action against those concerned for, as previously indicated, the regulations were not legally binding and therefore offered no deterrent in the event of contravention. The general public weighed its opinion down heavily against the establishment, unable to comprehend why more had not been done at the time to recover the airmen concerned. On at least one occasion, public opinion was cemented by the enthusiasts having the support of the family involved. The MOD remained unmoved, however, and had matters in hand to provide legislation in support of their policy.

The MOD's cause received support from a Conservative Member of Parliament who was himself a former army officer: Michael Mates MP. On January 30th, 1986, his Private Members Bill, the Protection of Military Remains, received its second and third reading in the House of Commons. The process then dictated that it had to be passed by the House of Lords prior to receiving Royal Assent and becoming enforceable legislation.

The Bill was not just directed at aviation archaeology, but did seek to formalise the existing regulations then in force concerning aircraft recoveries. In addition, it sought to introduce a system whereby enthusiasts would actually be issued with a formal Licence by the Secretary of State, rather than just written permission from the MOD. Most importantly, the last resting places of missing airmen would become prohibited sites, contravention carrying a punishment. Naturally the enthusiast movement as a whole was concerned, but the object was not to curtail the activities of those many organisations going about their interest both within the law and giving due regard to the Notes for Guidance, but specifically those who felt so strongly about the question of the *Missing Few* that they were prepared to contravene the MOD's guidelines and policy.

**Pilot Officer Charles Barber, September 1st, 1986.**

News of the impending Protection of Military Remains Act (PMA, see Chapter Five) had been filtering through to the enthusiast culture for some time, the subject being frequently reported in *Fly Past* magazine, arguably the UK's premier and most read aviation enthusiast periodical. It was widely known that the PMA would become legally binding on September 9th, 1986. On September 1st, Andy Saunders led a team which recovered the remains of Pilot Officer Charles Barber, whose 140 (PR) Squadron Spitfire crashed into a marsh adjacent to the River Brede at Udimore, near Winchelsea, on April 24th, 1942. Although not a Battle of Britain casualty, again this story is significant.

On the day of his death, Pilot Officer Barber, 22, based at RAF Benson, was tasked with photographing the French coast between Calais and Boulogne. It is likely that, again, anoxia caused by oxygen system failure was the cause of his fatal crash. Just 55 minutes after the impact, Inspector Amos of Rye Police completed his 'Crashed Aircraft Report' confirming the fact that the Spitfire X4784's unfortunate pilot remained 'buried in wreckage'. Upon attendance, however, personnel from 49 MU decreed recovery to be beyond their means, due to the depth involved and nature of the marsh. The men collected surface wreckage which included an F.8 camera, sufficient to connect the crash with Pilot Officer Barber. For some reason, however, it took the Air Ministry five months to confirm, in writing to the pilot's father, that although Spitfire X4784 had been found, recovery of the pilot's body was impossible. Six months later, Pilot Officer Barber's death was officially presumed.

Mr Barber could not accept that the recovery of his son's body was impossible, and took up the case with his MP, who wrote to (the then) Parliamentary Under-Secretary of State for Air, Captain Harold Balfour. On November 26th, 1942, Balfour responded to the effect that a recovery was 'impracticable ...... salvage work would mean the damming of the river, and there are other difficulties to be considered'. Given the limitations of equipment then available, recovery was, in fairness, unrealistic in 1942. The Barber family could not accept this, however, as not even an attempt had been made. As a result of Mr Barber's persistent correspondence, in 1943 the Air Ministry sent him a map, indicating the location of his son's crash site so that he could make his own assessment. Following a moving pilgrimage, Mr Barber made no further requests for salvage. When the Runnymede Memorial was dedicated in 1953, however, the Barber family did not attend, but instead held its own service on the Udimore crash site.

In 1970, the BAM approached the landowner with a view to recovering X4784, but he, quite rightly, refused on the basis that the family's wishes had not been sought. In 1985, during the course of his research with Pat Burgess regarding the air war over Sussex, the crash had become of interest to Andy Saunders who felt that a memorial would be an appropriate marker. Andy traced the pilot's brother, Raymond, who not only enthusiastically supported his plans but also related details of the whole saga dating back to 1942. As recently as 1968, Mr Raymond Barber had taken the case up with the authorities. The (then) Minister for Defence, Merlyn Rees, merely re-stated the 1942 view. This has to be questionable, given the advancements of technology, but again we have to consider the MOD's position regarding casualties as previously reported. According to Raymond Barber, this letter 'destroyed the last remaining flicker of hope that we as a family had to lay our Bertie to rest, properly, back home'. Both of the pilot's parents died soon afterwards.

On February 6th, 1986, Raymond Barber visited the crash site at the invitation of Andy Saunders. Like Miss Joan Worth in the case of Pilot Officer Ramsay, Mr Barber's visit confirmed his resolve to recover his brother. Under the auspices of the TMAM, a letter was sent stating the case to the Minister for Defence that as both the landowner and family required a recovery, a licence should be issued for the work to go ahead. The MOD's response was that such licences were never 'unreasonably refused'. At the MOD's request in April 1986, Mr Barber quickly confirmed in writing his desire that the recovery should go ahead, and provided proof of his relationship with Pilot Officer Charles Barber. It took three months, however, for the MOD to respond, stating that a firm decision was expected in 'the not too distant future'. How can such a delay be justified? Further letters from both Mr Barber and the TMAM urged the MOD that a swift decision would be appreciated given both the farmer's calendar and impending Protection of Military Remains Act (which would become law on September 9th). By August 28th, a decision had still not been reached.

With the foregoing circumstances as a backdrop, the TMAM decided to go ahead with an unauthorised recovery over the period August 29th - 31st, 1986, inclusive. The TMAM stated that this decision was regrettable, but that the recovery team felt 'morally obliged to do so, for if they had waited until after September 9th, and the MOD had then refused a licence, the wishes of the family would never have been carried out unless in direct contravention of the law'. Was the MOD against setting a precedent for an *authorised* but *private* recovery? The date of September 9th is *not* actually that relevant as the Secretary of State can authorise whoever he chooses to undertake such work (see Chapter Five); arguably he could have issued a licence to the TMAM, although this can only be considered doubtful. Was the MOD, however, awaiting September 9th's events so that the Secretary of State could dictate that the RAF alone be tasked with the recovery? The enthusiasts, of course, argue that such a course of action would have been inappropriate as the family wished for their involvement, but others would argue that the issue was Pilot Officer Barber's recovery, not who was involved. On the other hand, there was no guarantee that the MOD's decision would ultimately have been positive. Unfortunately we can only speculate at the MOD's intentions as I am told that such things are 'not a matter of public record'.

*The TMAM's digger encountering problems during the ambitious and successful recovery of Plt Off Barber.*
*(Andy Saunders)*

Whatever readers' personal views are, the recovery operation was a true epic which even saw the River Brede's volume and flow controlled. By the end of the operation, which had seen the added complication of the Poclain digger becoming stuck fast in the glutinous mud, the pilot's remains had been recovered. Identification was not an issue in this case, but discovery of the pilot's identity discs proved beyond doubt that Pilot Officer Barber was no longer missing. In this instance, the NOK, Mr Raymond Barber, received swift notification of the recovery via his local police and expressed his gratitude to the recovery team.

Surprisingly an inquest was not held, and on September 3rd, 1986, the remains of Pilot Officer Barber were released by the Home Office to RAF Halton. On October 15th, 1986, at the family's request, Charles Barber was finally laid to rest in the churchyard of St Oswald's, near their Yorkshire home. It is appropriate to allow Raymond Barber the last word: 'To me I can never think of how Bertie might be today; to me he will forever be just 22'.

### *Leutnant* Helmut Strobl: September 5th, 1986.

September 5th, 1940, was another day of intensive aerial activity over southern England. Sergeant CAL Hurry of 43 Squadron was engaged that day, and recently recalled the drama:-

> I cannot recall what I was doing before the engagement with this 109, but I do remember what led up to it. I was returning to Tangmere on my own, flying at about 10,000 feet on a southwesterly course, when I saw a *Staffel* of 11 E/A (Me 109s), in close 'V' formation, flying West. I was up sun so rolled the Hurricane over to starboard and dived on their rear - hoping that they had not seen me. I was just about to open fire when the outer 109 spotted me, and he half-rolled and dived away under the formation. Immediately I did the same thing and followed him nearly to the coast near Rye. I was naturally expecting a hornets' nest of 109s, but we were going pretty fast in the dive or perhaps they did not see me against the ground. The singleton 109 was flying straight and level when I caught up with him over Appledore and I gave him a short burst from 200 yards. He immediately burst into flames and dived into the ground. The pilot did not bale out.

*Sgt Charles Hurry.*
*(KBoBM)*

Lt *Helmut*
*Strobl.*
*(Andy*
*Saunders)*

Sergeant Hurry's victim crashed close to Appledore Railway Station. Amongst the *Vermisst Jagdflieger* that day was *Leutnant* Helmut Strobl of 5/JG27; he had been killed on his 25th birthday.

Again, this site was excavated by the A&TRG (later the BAM) in 1971. Some highly prized items were recovered, including many cockpit items such as the *Revi* reflector gunsight, the pilot's parachute harness release buckle and Iron Cross. The excavation also confirmed the aircraft concerned as being WN 3627, Strobl's Me 109E-1. In 1978 the site was re-excavated by another enthusiast who apparently recovered further plates and the aircraft's oxygen apparatus. As no human remains were reported on either occasion, we must assume that none were discovered; to be realistic, the aircraft parts found does suggest otherwise.

On the 46th anniversary of the Appledore Station crash, September 5th, 1986, just four days before the PMA came into force, a third excavation was undertaken there, organised by an individual enthusiast but attended by many of those actively involved in the recovery of Battle of Britain aircraft. Perhaps inevitably the mortal remains of Helmut Strobl were recovered together with various items confirming his identity, including the all conclusive identity disc. The disturbing fact, however, is that Helmut Strobl's remains were discovered contained in a *plastic carrier bag*; there are clearly some 'enthusiasts' who should be absolutely *ashamed* of themselves.

The identity of the Appledore *Jagdflieger* was officially established at the Coroner's Inquest held in March 1987. At the request of his family, *Leutnant* Strobl's remains were interred at the family grave at Kolbnitz, near Badgastein, Germany. Some years later, the pilot's sister wrote to the man who shot him down; Charles Hurry:-

> The letter caused me to do some heart-searching. It was a courteous letter, and I responded accordingly. I was glad that she didn't ask how her brother had died; I was shot down, in fact, 13 days later and I would not wish the experience on anyone.

As from September 9th, 1986, the PMA became a part of the law of this land. By rights, therefore, Charles Barber and Helmut Strobl should have been the last unauthorised recoveries.

CHAPTER FIVE

# The Protection of Military Remains Act, 1986

Firstly let us all be aware that an Act of Parliament is:-

Enacted by the Queen's most Excellent Majesty, by and with the advice and consent of the Lords Spiritual and Temporal, and the Commons, in this present Parliament assembled, and by the authority of the same.

According to the Protection of Military Remains Act's Preamble, it is:-

An Act to secure the protection from unauthorised interference of the remains of military aircraft and vessels that have crashed, sunk or been stranded and of associated human remains; and for connected purposes.

In short, regardless of any personal feelings regarding the MOD's policy concerning the *Missing Few*, from September 9th, 1986, onwards, the PMA has been a part of the law of this land. The Act 'applies to any aircraft which has crashed (whether before or after the passing of this Act) while in military service'. Much of the Act concerns vessels sunk at sea, so references here will be those specifically relating, or applicable, to aircraft.

Before we examine the Act in detail, it is necessary for us to be conversant with the definition, in this context, of certain words and phrases used therein:-

'Aircraft' includes a hovercraft, glider or balloon.

'Controlled site' means any area designated as such a site under section 1 (see below).

'Remains', in relation to, or to part of an aircraft or vessel which has crashed, sunk or been stranded, includes any cargo, munitions, apparel or personal effects which were on board the aircraft or vessel during its final flight or voyage (including in the case of a vessel, any aircraft which were on board) and any human remains associated with the aircraft or vessel.

The Secretary of State may 'designate as a controlled site any area (whether in the United Kingdom, in United Kingdom waters or in international waters) which appears to him to contain a place comprising the remains of, or of a substantial part of, an aircraft to which this Act applies or a vessel which has to be sunk or stranded'.

With regard to the size of a controlled site:-

An area designated as a controlled site shall not extend further around any place appearing to the Secretary of State to comprise remains of an aircraft or vessel which has crashed, sunk or been stranded while in military service than appears to him to be appropriate for the purpose of protecting or preserving those remains or on account of the difficulty of identifying that place ...

For the purposes of this Act, a 'place' is a 'protected place' if:-

It comprises the remains of, or of a substantial part of, an aircraft, or vessel to which this Act applies; and
it is on or in the sea bed or is the place, or in the immediate vicinity of the place, where the remains were left by the crash, sinking or stranding of that aircraft or vessel.

The 'power to designate any land as, or as part of, a controlled site shall be exercisable in relation to Crown land as it is exercisable in relation to other land'.

The Section 2, subsection 1 of the Act is quite specific regarding 'Offences in relation to remains and prohibited operations'. It tells us that 'a person shall be guilty of an offence':-

(a)  If he contravenes subsection (2) below in relation to any remains of an aircraft or vessel which are comprised in a place which is part of a controlled site;

(b)  If, believing or having reasonable grounds for suspecting that any place comprises any remains of an aircraft or vessel which has crashed, sunk or been stranded while in military service, he contravenes that subsection in relation to any remains by virtue of which that place is a protected place;

(c)  If he knowingly takes part in, or causes or permits any other person to take part in, the carrying out of any excavation or diving or salvage operation which is prohibited by subsection (3) below; or

(d)  If he knowingly uses, or causes or permits any other person to use, any equipment in connection with the carrying out of any such excavation or operation.

Subsection 2 continues:-

A person contravenes this subsection in relation to any remains:-

(a)  If he tampers with, damages, moves, removes or unearths the remains;

(b)  If he enters any hatch or other opening in any of the remains which enclose any part of the interior of an aircraft or vessel; or

(c)  If he causes or permits any other person to do anything falling within paragraph (a) or (b) above.

Subsection 3 clearly defines when a diving or salvage operation is prohibited:-

(a)  If it is carried out at a controlled site for the purposes of investigating or recording details of any remains of an aircraft or vessel which are comprised in a place which is part of that site; or

(b)  If it is carried out for the purpose of doing something that constitutes, or is likely to involve, a contravention of subsection (2) above in relation to any remains of an aircraft and vessel which are comprised in a protected place or in a place which is part of such a site; or

(c)   In the case of an excavation, if it is carried out for the purpose of discovering whether any place in the United Kingdom or United Kingdom waters comprises any remains of an aircraft or vessel which has crashed, sunk or been stranded while in military service.

Subsections 4, 5 and 6 provide statutory defences; in plain English these are:-

1.      If the defendant can prove that what he did, or caused or permitted, was under and in accordance with a licence.

2.      That reasonable grounds existed for the person concerned not to believe that the area disturbed was a controlled site.

3.      That whatever was done was undertaken in the urgent 'interests of safety or health or to prevent or avoid serious damage to property'.

Subsection 7 states that a person who is guilty of an offence under this section shall be liable:-

(a)   On summary conviction, to a fine not exceeding the statutory maximum;

(b)   On conviction on indictment, to a fine.

In my view, 'summary conviction', i.e. at a Magistrates Court, is most likely given the circumstances with which we are most concerned; the current 'statutory maximum' fine in such circumstances is now £5,000. This means that a fine can be imposed, appropriate to the circumstances of the case in question and means of the defendant, up to, but not above, that figure.

In England and Wales, proceedings under the PMA can only be brought with the consent of the Director of Public Prosecutions (DPP), and in Northern Ireland by the DPP for that country. Curiously, Scotland is not mentioned in the Act, which is strange considering the quantity of vessels sunk around its coast - HMS Royal Oak at Scapa Flow being just one example.

Section 4 of the PMA provides the Secretary of State with the power to grant licenses authorising work at controlled sites in those circumstances where such work would not lead to an offence being committed under subsection 2. Such Licences can be granted to a particular person, 'persons of a particular description' or to 'persons generally'. The Secretary of State is also at liberty to impose any conditions in respect of any licence, 'for any purpose connected with protecting or preserving any remains to which the licence relates'. During the course of the licence, the Secretary of State can make any amendments necessary until such time as the Licence is either revoked or expires (whichever is soonest). Any amendments or revocation has to be notified to the licensee, either personally or published in such a manner as appropriate for bringing the matter to the attention of those concerned.

As a precaution against some of the situations which developed during the 1980s, subsection 5 creates further offences in respect of licensing if a person (whether for himself or another or for persons of any description):-

(a)   Makes a statement, or furnishes a document or information, which he knows to be false in a material particular; or

(b)   Recklessly makes a statement or representation, or furnishes a document or information, which is false in a material particular.

The liabilities in respect of the foregoing are:-

(a)   On summary conviction, to a fine not exceeding the statutory maximum;

(b)   On conviction on indictment, to a fine.

At last the MOD had a deterrent against anyone contravening its policy. In September 1986, the MOD's S10s(Air) department issued a small blue booklet to recovery groups which contained a further Note of Guidance. In this new Note, the effects of the PMA concerning aircraft recoveries was laid down clearly. It states that:-

The remains of all aircraft which have crashed in military service (whether on land or at sea) are protected by the Protection of Military Remains Act 1986. It is an offence under that Act to tamper with, damage, move or unearth the remains unless the Secretary of State has issued a Licence authorising those things to be done and they are done in accordance with the conditions of the licence.

Regarding 'Application and issue of a Licence', the Note continues:-

Any group wishing to recover the wreckage of a military aircraft must first approach the Ministry of Defence, S10s(Air), Room 607, Adastral House, Theobolds Road, London WC1X 8RU (Tel: 01-430 7020/7569) to obtain a licence. Licences will be granted to a named individual but will enable other people to assist him at his request. A licence will normally be issued *for one year only* and will authorise activity within a defined area. It should also be noted that the Ministry of Defence is not prepared to grant sole rights of recovery to any one group for any one site.

The paragraph concerning 'Preliminary explorations' is also of importance:-

The Ministry of Defence is not prepared to issue a licence for preliminary explorations in order to establish the identity of an aircraft when wreckage is situated on land.

The effect of this rule is that it remained impossible to legally establish the identity of an aircraft from wreckage at the crash site prior to a recovery taking place. This question of identity raises an important issue: if the MOD will not accept the identity of an aircraft unless its serial number can be provided from wreckage at the crash site, how, in the absence of such evidence, can the Secretary of State refuse to issue a licence? For the answer we must refer to Section 1, subsection 1:b, which states that the Secretary of State can designate as a controlled site any area which 'appears to him to contain a place comprising the remains of, or of a substantial part of, and aircraft to which this Act applies'. 'Appears' is the all-important word in that sentence, and of course no licence would be issued to an amateur civilian group in respect of a 'controlled site'.

This is confirmed by the 1986 Notes for Guidance:-

### Human Remains

In many cases crews will have escaped from aircraft before they crashed but there is still a possibility of human remains being found. On receipt of an application to recover a crashed aircraft the Ministry of Defence will try to determine if there is a possibility of human remains being found in the wreckage. If it is known or suspected that there might be then a licence will not normally be issued.

'Not normally be issued' is an interesting phrase, as to the best of my knowledge a licence has *never* been issued in such circumstances. The Note continues:-

If, however, despite these precautions human remains are discovered by chance the licence is *automatically suspended and the discovery must be reported immediately to the Ministry of Defence* or to the police. Recovery activities must be suspended until an officer of the Ministry of Defence says it can continue. This is normally a condition of the licence. On no account are the remains to be touched and they should be treated with due respect at all times. Recovery activities will normally be allowed to recommence when either the police or members of the RAF have made their investigations and the human remains have been removed. The feelings of relatives of the deceased aircrew cannot be emphasised too strongly. Groups are reminded that the presumed identity of the aircrew should not be divulged in advance of an inquest to anyone except the police, coroner or Ministry of Defence. The Ministry of Defence will take all the necessary steps to trace and notify the next-of-kin or other relatives, *and in no circumstances is a recovery group to act in this respect.* Any breach of these conditions will normally lead to withdrawal of the licence.

The final italics of the foregoing paragraph are of interest. Although the intention is quite clearly for recovery groups not to seek relatives *after* the discovery of a missing airman, no provision is made to counter the long-standing *modus operandi* of them seeking to establish such contact *before* any recovery takes place.

Regarding 'Personal Property', the Note states:-

Any items which are personal property of the pilot/crew members (e.g. rings, watches) found amongst the wreckage must be handed at once to the local police or forwarded to the Ministry of defence (S10(Air)). The Ministry of Defence cannot transfer title to personal property.

Regarding 'Adverse Publicity':-

The Ministry of Defence is concerned that neither the Services or the Department should become involved in any adverse publicity as the result of any recovery activities. Groups are requested to take all possible steps to prevent such an occurrence.

In the event of human remains being recovered and you are approached by the press for information concerning the identity of aircrew, you should ask the press to contact the Ministry of Defence .... *On no account should groups divulge the possible identity of the aircrew.*

Finally, the Note points out:-

**Reminder**

Failure to follow the guidance given in these Notes could result in a recovery becoming an unlawful interference with Crown property and could lead to civil or criminal proceedings. Particular attention is drawn to paragraph 2 concerning the Protection of Military Remains Act; paragraphs 9 and 10 regarding risks and safety precautions and legal responsibility; paragraphs 11 and 12 concerning human remains; and paragraphs 13 and 14 concerning firearms, ammunition and explosives.

Quite clearly the MOD intended to uphold the provisions of the PMA and would only tolerate both enthusiasts and recoveries which observed the law.

The reader may be wondering what powers a coroner has in the circumstances covered by the PMA. Mr RAH Davies, HM Coroner for the County of Hereford & Worcester:-

Apart from the Protection of Military Remains Act, in law I can find no other reference to this subject.

My observations are that firstly, it is clear from Section 4 that a Licence has to be granted by the Secretary of State to any person, or body of persons, wishing to carry out an excavation of military aircraft remains. This must mean that no-one, not even a member of a family of the deceased, nor a Coroner on his own initiative, can authorise an excavation.

Once an excavation has begun (Licensed or otherwise) and a body is found, then the Coroner has to be informed. The law is that whenever a body is found, the Coroner, in whose jurisdiction the body has been discovered, has to be informed. It is then, at this stage, that a Coroner has to decide what action to take. Exhumation hardly applies, because the body has already come to light by the excavation itself.

In any event, the Coroner would have no power, in the first place, to order an excavation under the guise of it being an exhumation. The Coroner can only order an exhumation in certain circumstances, and regarding those I would refer you to the book *Jervis on Coroners* which states:-

*A coroner may by a warrant signed by him order the exhumation of the body of a person buried 'within the area within which he has jurisdiction', when either of two conditions is satisfied. These conditions are, first, where it appears to the coroner that it is necessary for the body to be examined for the purpose of holding an inquest into the death or of carrying out any other coronial function in relation to the body or the death, and, secondly, where it appears to the coroner to be necessary for the body to be examined for the purposes of any criminal proceedings either instituted or contemplated in respect of the death in question, or any other death which has taken place in circumstances connected with the death in question.*

Clearly a coroner's power does not apply to sites protected by the PMA *prior* to the discovery of a body. In a nutshell, a coroner has *no* power to act independently of either the Secretary of State or PMA, and cannot authorise a recovery at a site suspected to contain the remains of a missing airman. Of equal importance is the fact that relatives of the deceased likewise have no power to authorise any recovery, which brings us back full circle to the Secretary of State and the provisions of the PMA. Technically the Secretary of State is not obliged to task the RAF with the recovery of a missing airman, so could licence a private individual; despite this legislation, therefore, the old debate continued unabated.

CHAPTER SIX

# Restless Spirits?

Two days after the Protection of Military remains Act came into force, a
certain event took place on Romney Marsh which was quite the opposite: the dedication of a
memorial to a missing RAF pilot.

**Pilot Officer Arthur William Clarke: Memorial dedicated September 11th, 1986.**

Situated on the south-west Kentish coast, in 1940 the residents of Romney Marsh were daily eye-
witnesses to aerial combat, as indicated by the diary of one local resident, Miss Homewood of
Wills Farm:-

August 24th        Planes came over in the evening, met by fighters, turned and dropped bombs
at Ruckinge, Newchurch and Dymchurch. Bomb at Newchurch was in our field. Later walked
over and saw crater. No other damage done.

August 31st.        Dornier made a crash-landing in the evening across the Bilsington Road.
We laid in dyke and plane came right over us, very low. watched RAMC go out to the plane
from Newchurch with ambulance. Walked over and saw the plane later.

September 1st.      Me 110 came over us as we laid in a dyke and came down by Bilsington.
Plane was later sent to America.

September 2nd.      Me 109 came down in flames at Bilsington this afternoon.

September 7th.      Heavy raid on London this evening, wave after wave of bombers came over
us. A Hurricane came down by Newchurch, pilot safe.

September 11th.     He 111 made a crash-landing at Burmarsh, crew set fire to plane. Hurricane
crashed at Newchurch burying itself deep in the ground.

September 15th.     Me 109 came down at Ruckinge, at lunchtime, killing a mother and baby.
The plane was a yellow-nosed fighter. Went over and saw it in the evening. Saw four parachutes
in the sky this evening.

On September 11th, the *Luftwaffe* had continued its intensive attacks against London - codenamed
*Loge* after the Nordic God of fire, and various Thames-side factories and warehouses. In addition
damage was caused to a number of buildings in Central London, including Buckingham Palace;
clearly the Royal family was now 'in it' just as much as the Eastenders. Amongst the squadrons in
11 Group on that date was No 504 'City of Nottingham', of the AAF; at the time, Mike Bush was
a Sergeant Pilot:-

We flew south from Catterick and arrived at Hendon on September 5th. I recall that when we
were at Readiness, awaiting the call to scramble, our favourite number was appropriately Vera
Lynn singing 'In Room Five-hundred-and-four'! The following day we intercepted the big raid

on London, during which a cannon shell passed through my instrument panel and into the reserve petrol tank beyond. I was damned lucky not to catch fire as petrol splashed all over me. I forced-landed my Hurricane at Eastchurch but, due to repairs being carried out, did not return to Hendon with my aircraft until September 9th. I was given the next week off to recover, and did not fly again until September 17th.

*Plt Off A W Clarke.*
*(Allan White)*

On September 11th, the rest of 504 Squadron, flying in three vics, each of three aircraft, engaged a formation of 30 bombers escorted by fighters about 10 miles west of Folkestone. After the combat, 20-year-old Pilot Officer Arthur William Clarke was missing; Sergeant Ray Holmes: 'I don't think anyone knew what had happened to him, I certainly didn't. Pilot Officer Clarke simply disappeared'.

At about 1500 hrs on the day in question, the He 111s of I & II/KG26 had left their French bases bound for England. After rendezvousing with their 200 strong fighter escort, the bombers headed up the Thames Estuary for London. From 1530 hrs onwards, Fighter Command squadrons attacked the enemy formation but were unable to reach the bombers until after bombs started exploding in the docklands below. The Me 110 escorts withdrew to the south, where they formed up in defensive circles over Croydon to cover the bombers' homeward journey - back over the shortest route, re-crossing the English coast between Dungeness and Dover. Inaccurate routing on the approach, however, led to the Me 109s expending too much fuel, and they were forced to break off prematurely. These units included JG2, JG26, JG51, JG53, JG54 and LG2, a substantial protecting force indeed. Over London, therefore, the Heinkels were left without protection. Not surprisingly they suffered heavy losses: 10 were shot down and 12 more were damaged. In terms of aircrew casualties this equated to 50 killed or missing, and at least a further 12 wounded. In response to this particular raid, Fighter Command lost some 23 aircraft destroyed, eight of their pilots being killed or missing, including Pilot Officer Clarke.

As 504 Squadron's combat had taken place near the coast, when no report was received indicating that the wreckage of Clarke's fighter had been found, it was assumed that he had crashed into the sea. On September 19th, the CO, Squadron Leader John Sample, wrote to the missing pilot's parents describing the circumstances in which their son was lost. He confirmed that after the action there was no sign of Pilot Officer Clarke's aircraft and no-one had seen what had happened. Sample suggested that he could have baled out over the sea only to be 'rescued' by an enemy vessel, but concluded that this was, in fact, unlikely.

Pilot Officer AW Clarke was later remembered on the Runnymede Memorial.

In 1971, the KBoBM discovered and excavated a crash site on Romney Marsh. The aircraft was the Hurricane to which Miss Homewood had referred in her diary entry on September 11th. The actual site lay 300 yards south of 'Starve Acre Bridge', where the St Mary-in-the-Marsh to Newchurch Road crosses the Sheaty Sewer (all land drainage dykes on Romney Marsh are called sewers or gutters), Rookelands Farm being located some 400 yards to the north. Digging conditions were again difficult in the soft, water-logged ground which is a mere two-three feet above sea level (2,000 years ago, Romney Marsh was actually a part of the seabed). The excavation was eventually abandoned, but not before many items had been recovered, including the shattered Rolls-Royce Merlin engine and other relics of a more personal nature: a map storage box containing a complete set of air maps, a pair of pilot's silk inner gloves, and, most poignantly of all, a handkerchief inscribed 'CLARKE'. No human remains were discovered, however, and nor were they reported following excavations by the several other groups which have visited this site over the years.

On September 11th, 1940, several Hurricane pilots were reported missing, but only one named Clarke; the only Clarke killed in the Battle of Britain was, in fact, Pilot Officer AW Clarke of 504 Squadron. Without any doubt, it was his aircraft discovered at Rookelands. By the 1980s, the site had become of interest to the TMAM, and Andy Saunders spent three years attempting to trace the Clarke family. Although ultimately successful, in a letter dated July 30th, 1986, the pilot's sister, Mrs KL Freeman, confirmed that the family 'proposed to leave Bill's remains where they lie and hold a memorial service close to the spot'. This family's reaction, and indeed that of the enthusiasts, is of great importance.

As we have seen, the MOD's policy is one of non-disturbance. The Department argues that without conclusive proof of identity, it would be wrong to go ahead with a recovery which may actually lead to a different aircraft being discovered, the relatives of which pilot perhaps preferring non-disturbance and therefore being caused unnecessary distress by an accidental discovery. To their great credit (contrary to popular and unfounded rumour), the enthusiasts entirely respected Mrs Freeman's wishes; indeed it was Andy Saunders himself who subsequently organised the memorial on the family's behalf.

*The privately arranged*
*memorial to Plt Off*
*Clarke: well worth a visit.*
*(Andrew Long)*

This modest monument commemorating Pilot Officer Clarke was erected at the roadside, the nearest practicable spot to the crash site located in the field behind. At mid-day on September 11th, 1986 - 46th anniversary of the crash - the Rev. Walker conducted a memorial service in the church at Newchurch, before dedicating the privately funded memorial. As the stone reads, it is an appropriate marker to 'One of the Few'. Like the grave of Sergeant Peter Rose in far-off Soumagne (see Chapter Two), it is heart-warming to always find fresh flowers at Pilot Officer Clarke's memorial, together with an appropriate verse:-

> *Think of me as you pass by*
> *Reflect on why I had to die*
> *So many young lives*
> *Such senseless wars*
> *We surrendered our future*
> *So you could have yours.*

**Sergeant Ernest Scott: December 15th, 1990.**

*Fighter pilot: Sgt Ernest Scott pictured at Hornchurch*
*with the Spitfire of 222's CO, Sqn Ldr John Hill.*
*(Via Mark Kirby)*

The next instalment regarding the *Missing Few* was not to occur until December 15th, 1990 - appropriately the Battle of Britain's 50th anniversary year - when the mortal remains of a missing Spitfire pilot, Sergeant Ernest Scott, were recovered; significantly this work was undertaken by the RAF Aircraft Salvage & Transportation Flight (AS&TF) based at Abingdon.

Ernest Scott was born one of a family of six at Doncaster, Yorkshire, on December 30th, 1916. In 1935, he left St John's College, York, briefly becoming a foundry engineer before joining the RAF as a regular airman on October 9th. By March 31st, 1940, he was a fully fledged service pilot and joined 222 Squadron at Duxford, which had only recently converted from Blenheims to

Spitfires. Having been declared fully operational in the day fighter role on April 17th, 222 Squadron participated in air operations covering the Dunkirk evacuation in late May and early June, flying from Hornchurch in Essex. Afterwards the squadron moved north, to Kirton-in-Lindsey. On August 29th, Squadron Leader John Hill led his pilots south to Hornchurch, 222 having been posted there to relieve 65 Squadron. From then on, Sergeant Scott and his comrades were to frequently find themselves in action against the *Luftwaffe*.

Sergeant Scott's combat claims were impressive: two He 111s shared destroyed on September 1st, a Do 17 damaged on September 2nd, a Do 17 and an Me 109 destroyed on September 3rd, an Me 110 on September 7th, two Me 109s damaged on September 9th, and an Me 109 destroyed on the morning of September 27th. On the latter date, 222 Squadron was scrambled again at 1510 hrs, but, as they desperately clawed for height, Hill's Spitfires were perfectly bounced by Me 109s. So sudden and swift was the attack, that none of the Spitfire pilots were able to respond. The *Kommodore* of JG51, Major Werner Moelders subsequently claimed his 41st victory, a Spitfire: only Sergeant Scott failed to return.

Consequently, personnel from No 49 MU inspected the crash site of a British fighter in a cherry orchard at Greenway Court, near Hollingbourne in Kent. They found an item bearing the serial number 'P9364' - Scott's Spitfire; in the unit's records, therefore, the whereabouts of this Spitfire are stated as being in the 'Hollingbourne district'. Sergeant Scott remained officially missing, however, and was also amongst those gallant airmen remembered on Runnymede. His father had previously written to Mr Churchill himself, imploring that all possible efforts be made to find airmen reported missing in the Battle of Britain; he was assured that this would indeed be the case.

In 1977, Steve Vizard located the crash site:-

I was only 19 then and just could not organise a dig in the two days I was given by the farmer's schedule. We had not contacted the family at that time, so with the benefit of hindsight I now think it for the best that we did not go ahead and recover Sergeant Scott at that time.

Some years later, aviation archaeology enthusiast Mark Kirby was to play a part in such a saga for the first time:-

In 1990, I visited a local enthusiast friend from whom I learned that he had Sergeant Scott's brother coming down. Because I had a car, this friend of mine asked me to do the driving on the day. It was a foggy day, one of those when the inside of the car mists up. I will never forget the brother, Albert Kent, sitting in the back of my car and wiping away enough condensation to peer out across the fields at the crash site. He was crying. It moved me almost beyond belief and from that day, what was previously a hobby changed into a deeply serious quest. Albert himself got out of the car and went over to the farm. He spoke to the landowner and showed him a photograph of Sergeant Scott, saying 'This is my brother, please let me take him home'. The farmer responded that he could not possibly stand in his way, and Albert returned absolutely animated, so happy that at last his brother would be brought home to rest. Unfortunately the landowner almost immediately had a change of heart, and no amount of pleading by the family had any effect on this.

Both the family and enthusiasts now faced a dilemma. The PMA prevented the enthusiasts from undertaking a recovery without the Secretary of State's permission, but they had no confidence in obtaining this. Nor was there any confidence in the MOD being persuaded to act, and of course the landowner's refusal to co-operate was of crucial importance. Consequently the pilot's sister, Mrs Irene Hukin, wrote to the Prince of Wales, His Royal Highness consequently providing an encouraging response on November 30th, 1990, by asking the MOD to look into the matter.

On December 13th, 1990, the RAF Personnel Management Centre wrote to Mr Albert Kent:-

We have now gathered together sufficient information from official wartime records to tell us something about Ernest's fine Service career and the period leading up to his last tragic mission. Regrettably our research also confirms that a breakdown in the lines of communication probably occurred immediately following the crash and vital information about the possible crash site was not passed on to the Air Ministry's Central Casualty Office in London for evaluation. At this late stage I can only hazard a guess that this lack of information was due to constantly changing and sometimes confused conditions at the time which led the Casualty Office to conclude that Ernest's aircraft had crashed into the sea. Hence the explanation which was given to your mother in the Air Ministry's letter dated February 28th, 1941.

However, the strongest evidence to emerge during our research to suggest that Ernest's aircraft had crashed at Greenway Court Farm comes from the records of 49 Maintenance Unit Faygate; at the time this Unit was tasked with the salvage of all crashed aircraft in the Kent area. The records show 'Spitfire P9364' as being in the 'Hollingbourne' district, but there is no confirmation that any wreckage was recovered.

Frankly I am saddened to discover that the clues as to the aircraft's whereabouts were not investigated at the time of the crash or followed up at a later stage. I understand that RAF Support Command has now been assigned the task of examining the field on Greenway Court Farm and I can assure you that if Ernest's remains are found we will certainly ensure that they are treated in a befitting manner and that you will be kept fully informed.

Although in Chapter One we have examined the volume of work faced by the authorities in 1940, it is perhaps worth quantifying this through the records of 49 MU: between September 1st and November 29th, 1940, the Unit dealt with 618 RAF aircraft alone! Against the entry regarding Sergeant Scott's Spitfire is the remark 'In hand'; sadly it was not, in fact.

In December 1990, over 50 years since he crashed, Sergeant Scott was recovered by the RAF's 'Crash & Smash', the authorities having persuaded the landowner that this was the appropriate course of action. Fortunately, various paperwork was found to confirm the pilot's identity. According to the newspapers, Mrs Hukin's response was that 'It now seems that they (the authorities) knew, very early on, where Ernest's plane could be located. It is sad it has taken all this time but we are indebted to Prince Charles'.

Following a post mortem conducted by Dr Michael Heath, the Inquest into the death of Sergeant Scott was held at Maidstone on January 29th, 1991. HM Coroner for the Mid Kent and Shepway District, Mr Roger Sykes, recorded that 'the cause of death was unascertainable' but concluded that 'Sergeant Scott was killed in action'. A funeral service was held at RAF Manston on February 1st, 1991, after which Sergeant Scott was laid to rest in the station cemetery.

Mark Kirby:-

> This case influenced me more than anything else, seeing the relatives so upset but then so happy after a successful recovery. It made up my mind that if families required an excavation, then this should be done, regardless of the MOD. To me the likes of Albert Kent were the only people whose opinion and wishes mattered. I had experienced the relatives' reaction first hand, and this left a lasting impression vivid to this day.

### Sergeant Eldon Howard Caldwell: Inconclusive (official) recovery, spring 1993.

In early 1993, I was to have some experience myself of an operation within the same spirit as the case of Sergeant Scott.

*Sgt E H Caldwell.*
*(Allan White)*

Living in the Midlands, there is obviously a considerable distance between my friends and I and the geographical area of England over which the Battle of Britain was fought. Nevertheless, in 1986 we formed the MST to further original research, publish our findings, erect memorials and raise money for charity, recover aircraft for conservation and display. I would defy anyone to deny that we achieved this with distinction. It was also of crucial importance for us to provide as professional an image as possible and stringently operate within the law. Being formed at roughly the same time as the PMA came into force, arguably this could be described as a 'new wave' and standard of aviation archaeology and research.

The emphasis of our work always concerned RAF fighters, although almost exclusively the crashes in our area were of a training nature rather than combat casualties. Many of these aircraft, however, had previously participated in the Battle of Britain before perishing in flying accidents, and as one looked back into their history, some fascinating stories were to emerge (virtually all of which have been both published and/or exhibited). By early 1993, an opportunity arose for us to make a contribution to the question of the missing pilots; although this did not concern a Battle of Britain casualty the story is of significance for several important reasons.

The River Severn rises at its source high in the Welsh hills, rushing along its upper reaches into Shropshire, until sedately meandering through southern Worcestershire; downstream, at Gloucester, the river becomes tidal, soon joining the River Wye and discharging into the Bristol Channel. The Severn Estuary is amongst the most dangerous in the world, and is respected and feared by both fishermen and sailors alike. During the Second World War, its tidal reaches were to claim the bodies of a number of Allied airmen.

To the east of the Estuary is Aston Down, during WW2 a busy RAF station and home of a Spitfire OTU. The rate of attrition from training flights was high, and Spitfires from this unit crashed, in various circumstances, all over the area throughout the OTU's existence. One such incident occurred on Tuesday, 26th January, 1943. At 1030 hrs that morning, Spitfires from 52 OTU fired at a drogue during a gunnery exercise over the Severn Estuary. Purple Section was ordered to attack the target, and Sergeant Clarke, in Spitfire P8027, swung round over the eastern bank of the Estuary to close in. As he did so, Sergeant Caldwell, in P8208, executed a similar manoeuvre from the west side, according to eye-witnesses roaring over the sea wall at about 500 feet. On a head-on course, over the water the two Spitfires collided. Clarke's Spitfire belched black smoke, although he maintained control of the aircraft and made a safe forced-landing on the beach at Magor. P8208, however, span straight in, and crashed into the water some half-a-mile out from the Redwick sea wall. Although the tide was in, when an RAF team arrived shortly afterwards, locals recount how they told the airmen that if they waited just a short while the wreck would be accessible on foot. Eye-witness testimony suggests, however, that little or no attempt was made to reach the Spitfire. Sergeant Caldwell, a 22-year-old from Alberta, Canada, was simply reported missing.

Group Captain FG Argyle-Robinson, RAF Aston Down's Station Commander, wrote to Sergeant Caldwell's parents:-

It is with deep regret that I have to write you of the accident in which your son, Sergeant Pilot Eldon Caldwell, was involved whilst serving in this unit.

The aircraft in which Sgt Caldwell was flying on January 26th, 1943, was seen to dive into the River Severn after it had collided in mid-air with another Spitfire. Although every effort was immediately made to recover the pilot, this could not be done and so your son has been officially posted as missing. But I am afraid there is no doubt that he has in fact been killed, and I wish to express to you the very sincere sympathy felt by myself and the officers and airmen serving on this station with your and your family in this grievous loss.

The accident has been thoroughly investigated but no satisfactory reason for the mid-air collision has been found. The accident was witnessed both from the air and from the shore, and no attempt to bale out was observed. The Severn is a tidal river and attempts to recover the machine have so far proved unsuccessful, though it has been located. Following Air Ministry procedure, Sergeant Caldwell has been posted as missing. There will be some delay in presuming death unless his body is recovered.

Sergeant Caldwell was first posted to this unit for target towing duties, but, at his own request, was transferred to operational training. He was a most likeable boy, very popular with his instructors and with other pupils on this station and there is no doubt that he would have made an admirable fighter pilot. By his untimely death both the Royal Air Force and Royal Canadian Air Force have been deprived of the services of one of the finer type of lads who are the backbone of the force.

Sergeant Caldwell's death was eventually 'presumed' on August 19th, 1943. His was later to become yet another name recorded on the Runnymede Memorial, and yet again, if not for aviation archaeology, doubtless there the matter would have rested.

In the Severn Estuary it is worth mentioning that the sands are constantly shifting, revealing, and then just as quickly hiding, various relics of the past that came to grief in these murky waters. Amongst the other aircraft known to remain on the seabed is a Blenheim, but the aircraft has long since been swallowed by the ever shifting sand; if ever it is uncovered and quickly found, before the salt water can overly attack the airframe, the Blenheim, a rare Mk IF, is likely to remain in reasonable condition. By 1984, the story of P8208 had been brought to the attention of the Severnside Aviation Society (SAS), who searched from the seawall for sight of the wreckage. As the tide went out the Spitfire was located, and the members present, without a doubt, put their lives at risk by walking out across the treacherous mud and sand. All of P8208's major components was found to be in situ, but instead of considering how to lift these out in their entirety, the wreck was picked over and those items which could be man-handled were recovered to the shore. These relics included many cockpit components together with the complete tailwheel assembly. Later, oil drums were attached to the Merlin, which still had both the reduction gear and complete propeller attached, with a view to a lift, on the incoming tide, which would ultimately resulted in the engine bobbing ashore 12 months later. Unfortunately, however, due to a lack of knowledge regarding conservation, the Merlin no longer exists.

Conversely, the MST was fortunate to have access to the expert assistance of Dr Dennis Williams, a metallurgist, who has, over the years, painstakingly conserved many Spitfire parts recovered by the Team. These have become exhibits of the highest possible standard and reflect completely the spirit in which the Team was both founded and operated. In 1992, Dennis and I obtained many of the P8208 recovered by the SAS, and my friend then set about his long process of conservation. During the late 1980s I had actually researched the 'life' of this Spitfire, confirming, for example, that it had been built at the Castle Bromwich Aircraft Factory before being test flown by Alex Henshaw himself. P8208 had then flown on operations over France with 303 'Kosciuszko' Squadron, a part of No 1 Polish Fighter Wing at Northolt, before arriving at Aston Down.

Dennis and I found that the tip of one of the duralumin propeller blades had been nearly cut through with a hacksaw in an unsuccessful attempt to obtain a souvenir from the wreck before it was recovered. We were later provided accurate information suggesting that on one particular visit to the site, what was believed to be a human femur had been found. Naturally we found quite abhorrent the fact that the last resting place of a missing pilot was being frequently picked over by souvenir hunters. As the wreck was so easily accessible at low tide, we felt that it was not within the spirit of the PMA to leave it there as such a focus for souvenir hunters. Consequently I contacted Mr Martin Hill, the head of the MOD's S10 department which, at that time, dealt with all such cases. I explained the situation and suggested that a joint operation be mounted between the MST and MOD with a view to clearing the site, the RAF then having the opportunity to search for Sergeant Caldwell in the process. This, I felt, would thus prevent any further unauthorised interference. Furthermore, it was made clear to Mr Hill that although, via a Ramrod Publications customer, Mike Parry in Ontario, we had traced Sergeant Caldwell's brother, we would be making no attempt to make contact at that time; if any human remains were found, we felt strongly that the approach should not come from us, but from the Department, as indeed policy dictates. Also, we had secured the professional assistance and advice of Chris Carne, an old friend and former police officer but then the National Rivers Authority's bailiff in the area concerned. Having Chris's expert help was of vital importance to the safety of the operation, and there is no way that I would have suggested that we entered the Severn Estuary without having such a professional involved. There had already been at least one occasion whereby aviation archaeologists had to be rescued by helicopter from a similar site, and the MST was not in the business of such irresponsible behaviour. Given the circumstances, Mr Hill agreed immediately to my request, and the RAF AS&TF based at St Athan, near Cardiff, was authorised to assist.

On February 8th, 1993, the MST and RAF AS&TF met at Redwick's village inn. We immediately set about convincing the service unit's CO, Flight Lieutenant 'Tex' Dallas, of the depth of our interest and quality of work undertaken to date. I have to say that there was an awkward atmosphere at first, which is hardly surprising given aviation archaeology's unfortunate, but in some cases quite deserved, often poor reputation. It did not take long, however, for the airmen to warm to our enthusiasm and approach, and in a very short time we found ourselves working as one team, rather than two groups of people thrown together by circumstances but not necessarily choice.

By 1330 hrs, on what was a very dull and generally depressing sort of day, our party had gathered together on the sea wall. Upon Chris Carne's advice we had very carefully chosen the date due to it being that of the first low spring tide. By utilising MST honorary member Peter Earp's Robinson helicopter, our plan was for Dennis and Peter to fly down the Estuary to Redwick, undertaking a survey en route of any other wrecks which may have become visible, before locating the remaining P8208 wreckage from the air. As the tide went out, exposing an almost lunar like seascape, the little Robinson appeared from the North-East. Our party, guided by Chris, had already started carefully making our way on foot to the crash site. Progress was slow and, if you remained in one place for too long, frightening as the sand beneath shifted. The best technique was found to walk as quickly as possible, sloshing through the mud, until the bed of hard shale was reached on which the wreckage lay. Hovering over the water, Dennis excitedly reported an undercarriage leg - still gleaming chrome - sticking up through the water; to us its appearance was like Excalibur! Peter landed his machine on the shale, adjacent to the wreck, which had now become virtually completely exposed.

We immediately set about searching the area and discovered many items still lying on the surface: both undercarriage legs, still attached to the mainspar, all sections of armour plate, the radiator, the fuel tank. Of course the salt water's action had destroyed all skinning, and the remains of fishermens' nets on the wreckage suggested that such fouling had helped break up the Spitfire over the years. Much of the aircraft, however, had sunk down into the shale and required digging out, having the appearance of barnacle encrusted lumps of rock. As we all dug furiously in the cockpit area, in what was a race against time, a rudder pedal and the reflector gunsight were soon found. Soon, two bones were discovered, but no further trace of any remains; it was impossible to distinguish whether these were human or animal and so Tex retained them for examination by the St Athan Medical Officer (MO).

All of the wreckage discovered was placed in one pile, but we were unable to consider, with safety being the principle concern, recovering the items to the shore ourselves. The small helicopter was only able to carry a selection of smaller items, so we left our finds and retreated to the sea wall, allowing good time for the tide to come in. As Chris explained, the water also rises up through the sand and so it is very easy to unwittingly get trapped.

This is, I think, typical of the manner in which relatives are treated by the majority of researchers.

Throughout 'Operation Estuary', the MST had clearly acted in both a professional and responsible manner, proving just what level of co-operation could be achieved from the MOD given the right approach. We had also earned the respect of the RAF AS&TF, and the whole scenario gave me personally some confidence that given a continued projection of such professionalism, it may eventually be possible to influence the MOD's policy with regard to the *Missing Few*. I remain convinced that operating in such a manner, i.e. within the law and in support of the MOD, is the only approach likely to have any positive effect on the decision making process. The exercise also convinced me that service professionals *must* be involved in any such recovery, and I have yet to be persuaded otherwise. As these airmen lost their lives in the service, indeed the defence, of this country, surely the onus of any recovery should rest with the authorities? However, as illustrated by the story of Sergeant Caldwell, there also exists a case for enthusiasts and the MOD sharing resources and knowledge in respect of such an operation.

*Dilip Sarkar (centre) with members of the MST, RAF AS&TF & Bristows Helicopters staff, Redwick, March 1993. A large quantity of Spitfire P8208 can be seen, including the main spar, undercarriage legs and all armour plating.*
*(Mark Postlethwaite)*

### Sergeant John Hugh Mortimer Ellis: September 1993.

In late 1993, the *Missing Few* were back in the news, the events of September 1st, 1940, coming under close scrutiny. On that day, the *Luftwaffe* continued attacking Fighter Command airfields in southern England, in addition to London's docklands in retaliation for Bomber Command's nocturnal raids on Berlin. Amongst Air Vice-Marshal Park's battle weary squadrons was No 85, based at Croydon. In four days the squadron had been in action seven times, losing nine Hurricanes; even its CO, Squadron Leader Peter Townsend DFC, was wounded and in hospital having been shot down only the previous day. During the morning of September 1st, Flight Lieutenant Geoffrey 'Sammy' Allard led 85 Squadron against nine Me 109s which were attacking the Dover balloon barrage. Allard himself pursued a 109 across the Channel and shot it down 10 miles off Cap Gris Nez - a very dangerous place indeed for a lone Hurricane.

At lunchtime, Major Adolf Galland's entire JG26 prepared to escort the Do 17s of KG76 on a raid against Kenley airfield. No 85 Squadron was soon scrambled, as the Operations Record Book relates:-

Squadron again airborne at 1350 hrs to intercept enemy formation approaching Tunbridge Wells/ Kenley area. At about 1355 hrs about 150-200 aircraft (Do 17, Me 109 and Me 110) were sighted near Biggin Hill at 15,000 feet. When sighted the Squadron was still about 5,000 feet lower, and while climbing were attacked continuously by the 109s and 110s. Allard attacked a straggling Do 17 whose rear gunner baled out and whose pilot attempted a forced-landing near the railway line at Lydd. Allard's oil pressure dropped so he switched off and landed at Lympne, but while the aircraft was being serviced the airfield was bombed and his aircraft was hit (one groundcrewman killed and another seriously wounded). Pilot Officer English carried out carried out two quarter attacks on a Do 17, stopping its starboard engine; the enemy aircraft landed between Ham Street and Hythe, and two crewmen were seen to emerge. Evans attacked and destroyed an Me 109 with a seven-second burst, and another with a five-second burst but was unable to identify the location of the crashes. Howes attacked and shot down a Do 17 just south of Tunbridge Wells, two crew members baling out; he also damaged an Me 109. Gowers was hit by a cannon shell and baled out with severe burns on hands and face; his Hurricane crashed at Oxted. Booth's aircraft was hit by cannon shells; he baled out near Purley, and his aircraft crashed at Sanderstead. His parachute did not open properly and he suffered a broken back, leg and arm. Patrick Woods-Scawen was posted Missing and his body was found near Kenley on 6th September - his parachute unopened. Sergeant Ellis was also killed in this fight. Six Hurricanes - all that remained of the squadron - landed at Croydon between 1430 and 1500 hrs, and Lewis had to land wheels up.

No 85 Squadron had clashed with Galland's 109s, and were joined in the fray by the Hurricanes

of 79 (Biggin Hill) and 253 (Kenley) Squadrons. Three of the former squadron's Hurricanes were hit: Flight Lieutenant Haysom forced-landed back at base, Pilot Officer Bryant-Fenn baled out, wounded, as did Pilot Officer Noble; his Hurricane, L2062, crashed at 1445 hrs in Court Road Orchard, near 'Highways', Chelsfield, Kent. Unfortunately, 253 Squadron's only casualty was a fatality: Pilot Officer Clifton, whose Hurricane crashed at Clapper Lane, Staplehurst. For 85 Squadron, the Battle of Britain had reached its climax. It was particularly tragic that Flying Officer Patrick Woods-Scawen had been lost, as within 24 hours his brother, Pilot Officer Tony Woods-Scawen of 43 Squadron, was also killed in action (their father later received his tragic sons' posthumous DFCs from the King). Of 85 Squadron's Sergeant Ellis, however, there was no news: he was consequently reported Missing. After this engagement, the squadron's pilot strength had been so depleted that on September 3rd, 85 was relieved by 111 Squadron.

*Sgt J H M Ellis.*
*(Mark Kirby)*

Fellow aviation historian and publisher Peter Osborne takes up the story:-

The question of a missing pilot is not simply that of the body of a missing airman remaining buried in the wreckage of an aircraft which is located at an identified site. It can be much more complex than that as illustrated by the case of Sergeant John Hugh Mortimer Ellis. He had always joked with his colleagues that he would be lost at sea because Mortimer was similar to the French *mort à Mer* (loosely translated as: 'die at sea'); for years this was presumed to have been his fate.

In 1986, some friends of mine were negotiating for a bungalow at The Highway, in Chelsfield, one of the three roads which boarder the area where a Hawker Hurricane was thought to have crashed. They asked me to look at a few aspects of their prospective home and I was delighted to oblige, but whilst there I remembered that Colin Lee and Colin Brown, two aviation archaeologists, had once suggested that a fighter had crashed in that area during the Battle of Britain. When hearing that the vendor had occupied the bungalow since its pre-war construction date, I just had to ask if she remembered an aircraft crashing nearby. I was quite unprepared for the most affirmative answer and, further, that a chap still living opposite was an eye-witness. This *had* to be pursued. The eye-witness told me that he had been with the Army at an anti-aircraft site nearby when he'd seen the aeroplane falling, trailing smoke. There had been an impact which could be felt through the ground and then all was quiet. He had, with his NCO's permission, jumped on a bike and peddled furiously towards where he thought the aircraft had come down. There he found a crater on the edge of an apple orchard, surrounded by pieces of wreckage, in particular a complete undercarriage leg. Little did he know, however, that buried with the rest of the aircraft were the remains of the pilot.

Further research indicated that this aircraft had been incorrectly identified in 1940. Exactly why is unclear, but one local story is that a pilot came to the field on a fire engine and said, *"That's my bloody kite!"*. The aircraft concerned was identified as Hurricane L2062 (Noble's machine) and not as L2673 (Ellis's aircraft). In any event there was apparently no rush to excavate the site after the RAF arrived from Uxbridge later that day, removing the surface wreckage but leaving the engine and other deeply buried wreckage until later. Some two weeks on, a recovery team arrived in Chelsfield, the substance of their report being as follows:-

REPORT TO SQUADRON LEADER GOODMAN

R.A.F. DEPOT  22-9-40

HURRICANE L 2062.  Chelsfield, N.N.W Sevenoaks.

I located the site where the above aircraft crashed as under; Court Road Orchard (At the junction of four cross roads adjoining a road called Highways, Chelsfield).
        I interviewed the Officer commanding 472 Battery R.A.s on duty at a Listening Post in Highways, Chelsfield. He informed me that his men had been guarding the crashed aircraft by day but there was no guard at night. He also informed me that the fuselage of this machine had been cleared by an R.A.F. Squad which he believed came from Uxbridge approximately two weeks ago; they informed him that they were returning for the engine later. Upon inspection I found that this machine had gone five to six feet into the ground, a propeller blade was visible

embedded in the bottom of the crater made by the machine; the engine was still in the ground; one or two pieces of broken fuselage remained.

I have instructed the gang to clear the remainder of the wreckage, i.e. the engine etc:, to-day the 23rd September.

(Signed) A V Nicholls

But all was not to be so simple, a further report followed hot on the heels of the first.

SUPPLEMENT TO REPORT DATED 22-9-40

REPORT TO SQUADRON LEADER GOODMAN

R.A.F. DEPOT  22-9-40

HURRICANE L 2062.   Chelsfield, N.N.W Sevenoaks.

My gang arrived on site of crash at Court Road Orchard, Chelsfield in the forenoon September 23rd. Commenced digging operations to remove the embedded engine etc.: They came across a "Flying" boot containing a foot; digging further they came across an unopened parachute, pulling on the parachute exposed pilot's body. Police were called  to the site by gang supervisor, digging operations continued under surveillance of the Police, came across money (2/11 1/2 d), opened Pilot's pocket, found cigarette case also small wallet containing photograph of two ladies. All the above articles handed over to police.
The Officers of the Police present were the local constable stationed at Chelsfield and two Mobile Police Officers from Orpington. The Police took charge of the Pilot's remains. We cleared all remaining fuselage, one propeller blade and engine parts; filled in the crater and left tidy.

(Signed) AV Nicholls

What happened then is a matter of conjecture as no further written records have been discovered. *Presumably* the police would have informed the coroner who would have had have held an inquest at which, presumably, he would have asked the R.A.F. for some positive proof of identity of the remains. The reports refers to the Pilot's 'body' and they were able to search at least one pocket so the remains must have consisted a substantial amount of the unfortunate pilot's body. However why the remains were not identified is not know, but it is almost certain that they were buried in plot number 128 at Star Lane Cemetery, St. Mary Cray, near Orpington. The reasons for making this supposition are that Orpington did not have a mortuary, but some temporary ones were established in the area, one at Tugmutton Green, Starts Hill (near Farnborough, Kent - about three miles by road from the crash site) and there was one at RAF Biggin Hill (about five miles by road). The Ordnance Survey map of 1937 shows one at Star Lane Cemetery (also about three miles by road from Chelsfield), although it is not certain it was in use in 1940, but it seems likely that any remains held there would be eventually buried in the cemetery. In addition, the Orpington Urban District Council minutes for UDC Fire Brigade, Parks, Cemeteries and Allotments Committee November 9th, 1940, (page 400) indicates that

Grave No. 128 was purchased by 'The Directorate of War Graves, War Office'. The headstone is inscribed: 'An Airman of The 1939-45 War, Royal Air Force, October 12th, 1940'. Considering that the 'remains' concerned were found on September 23rd, and the date on the headstone shows October 12th, (the date of burial rather than the date of death - there are no pilots unaccounted for on October 12th, 1940) it seems about the right timing, just over two weeks, for investigations to take place and for the Coroner to decide the remains could not be positively identified and order the burial.

After this the site was then left undisturbed until the late seventies/early eighties when Ken Anscomb, one of the new *Aviation Archaeologists*, relocated the site and sought the owner's permission to dig. According to a witness they were on a tight time constraint because the field was being ploughed as they worked and they had only time to remove some easily accessible parts before they had to back-fill the hole. They had always meant to go back, but in the event they didn't and the exact location was lost. None-the-less what had been recovered included the main maker's label from the engine which was clear - irrefutable proof - that it was Ellis's Hurricane. Unfortunately Ken Anscomb tended to keep things to himself, and so the fact that positive proof had been found to identify this Hurricane as that of Sergeant Ellis - and that the human the remains found must have been, therefore, those of that pilot - would not become known for some years.

Mark Kirby:-

In September 1992, I made an effort to re-locate the Ellis site using a Forster bomb locator. I received a signal and found the triangular shaped buckle of a leather flying helmet. Andy Saunders was already in contact with the pilot's cousin, Mr Peter Mortimer. He told us that Sergeant Ellis's parents, like so many others, would have given anything to see him given a decent burial. Although they were dead, the rest of the family remained keen to know the truth. I resolved there and then that if Sergeant Ellis remained buried at the site concerned, then he should be recovered. I met the landowner who agreed that if the family required it, then it should be done. Although I was fully aware of the PMA, I made no approach to the MOD as I knew what their answer would be: 'No'. Rather than let this happen, I decided to go in there and do it. We recovered Sergeant Ellis, fortunately with his identification numbers, but there were no personal effects. We telephoned the police, and upon the attendance of officers we explained the situation to them.

Peter Osborne (who was not involved in the recovery):-

The mystery still remains as to why the human remains found in 1940 were not identified at the time, because even then there was only one pilot missing on that date. Why, having found some parts of a body, were the AV Nicholls gang not induced to find the substantial remains which were eventually located in 1993? Why was the site not completely excavated in 1940 to firmly establish the aircraft's identity? To the best of my knowledge only one Browning machine gun has ever been found from the eight which would have equipped this Hurricane and these would have been identifiable by their numbers. The Intelligence Officer for 601 Squadron recorded in the squadron history that he was '... *getting tired of roaming around the countryside identifying the smashed remains of his former friends by the serial number of their aircraft's guns.*' Possibly the recovery teams were under pressure to attend numerous sites over a wide area and may have intended to return but did not. Suffice it to say we will probably never know the answers.

The reader may be wondering how Sergeant Ellis could have been buried as 'Unknown' if his body was later recovered and identified in 1993. The answer is simple. For legal purposes, only seven pounds in weight of a body has to be recovered to justify the coroner's interest, although that quantity must include an organ without which the organism would be unable to sustain life. The shattered bodies of airmen, therefore, could, for practical reasons, be legitimately buried incomplete only for the outstanding remains to be recovered many years later, as in this instance (see also Chapter Nine).

Sergeant JHM Ellis was buried with full military honours at Brookwood Military Cemetery on Friday, October 1st, 1993. Peter Osborne asks a pertinent question, however:-

Why did the recovery of this airmen have to be undertaken by individuals who were breaking the law rather than the MOD, which officially remains responsible for those pilots who are still 'missing'?

Mark Kirby has already explained why he chose to act as he did, adding:-

The police appeared sympathetic. I was not arrested or dealt with by them in any way other than to unofficially receive 'advice' regarding the future. There was very little publicity and the MOD, for whatever reason, took no action against me.

The MOD would perhaps argue that in this case it was not given the opportunity to review and act upon the facts available. Since 1986, as the MOD had recovered Sergeant Scott and co-operated with the MST in respect of Sergeant Caldwell, the evidence certainly suggests that an approach to the Ministry would have been appropriate prior to the recovery. Mark Kirby:-

At the time, given the previous history relating to the missing pilots, and the MOD's established policy, I doubted that the Ministry would respond positively and so I decided, rightly or wrongly, to go in there and make it happen.

Sergeant Ellis, therefore, represented the first pilot recovered by enthusiasts since 1986. It was the first such contravention of the PMA, and yet no action was taken. This is puzzling, even to Mark Kirby, and the lack of any retribution by the authorities contributed greatly to future events.

### Sergeant John Stanley Gilders: April 20th, 1994.

Without a doubt, however, the most significant of these between the PMA becoming law and the publication of this book occurred in 1994. Although concerning one of the Few, the fatal crash in question occurred several months after the Battle of Britain had officially concluded.

At 1210 hrs on February 21st, 1941, Flight Lieutenant John MacKenzie led his flight of 41 Squadron Spitfires off from Hornchurch to patrol the Ramsgate - Canterbury - Dungeness line. Interestingly, given the fact that Fighter Command did not emulate the *Luftwaffe Schwarm* (which consisted of two fighting pairs spread out in loose, line abreast formation) until several months later, MacKenzie arranged his fighters into three *pairs*, as opposed to the usual two vics of three. This squadron, however, was amongst Fighter Command's most experienced at this time and had been in action frequently throughout the summer and autumn of 1940.

*Proud father and son: Sgt J S Gilders.*
*(Via Mark Kirby)*

Fighter clashes over southern England were still taking place during the winter of 1941; only the previous day, Flight Lieutenant Peter Brown had led his flight of 41 Squadron on a patrol over Dover during which the Spitfires were badly bounced by *Stab* JG51, losing two pilots, Sergeants McAdam and Angus, in quick succession. On February 21st, 'bandits' were reported by Hornchurch Control, but went undetected by MacKenzie's Spitfires.

At 32,000 feet over the English Channel, just off Folkestone, Spitfire P7816, flown by Sergeant John Stanley Gilders, was seen to drop out of formation in a shallow dive. No response came from 'Gilly' on the R/T, and his aircraft was last seen disappearing into the haze some 25,000 feet below. The remainder of MacKenzie's flight landed at 1405 hrs, but Sergeant Gilders was reported missing.

*Sgt John 'Gilly' Gilders:*
*Spitfire pilot.*
*(Author via Beardsley)*

Due to the high altitude at which their patrol had been conducted, the 41 Squadron pilots were naturally using oxygen. The Spitfire's somewhat rudimentary system was prone to failure, however, often from icing and with fatal results due to pilots, starved of the life-sustaining gas, blacking out. Some regained consciousness in time to recover control of their aircraft; on October 29th, 1940, 19 Squadron's Pilot Officer Arthur Vokes had occasion to record the following in his log book:-

Blue 2 with Squadron Leader Lane DFC. Oxygen failure at 24,000 feet. Recovered at 6,000, phew!

There is little doubt that Sergeant Gilders, like the cases of Richard Riedel and Charles Barber (see Chapter Four), suffered the effects of anoxia due to the failure of his oxygen system.

As Flight Lieutenant MacKenzie had led the remainder of his flight back to Hornchurch, a police constable on duty near the main Ashford to Canterbury Road, near Chilham in Kent, saw a Spitfire emerge from cloud out of control. The aircraft crashed at Chilham Beeches, to the east of the River Stour, where it immediately exploded. A report was sent to the Air Ministry and consequently 49 MU attended the scene. Under difficult, water-logged conditions, the men recovered various items of wreckage, including confirmation that the Spitfire concerned was that flown by Sergeant Gilders. No human remains were reported, however, and it was therefore officially assumed that the pilot had baled out. As no reports were received regarding RAF pilots baling out over land, the Gilders family naturally hoped that John had baled out, unseen, over the sea and had been captured by the Germans. Sadly this was not to be, although on February 27th, the authorities wrote to Mr Gilders stating that his son's body had been found and was lying at RAF Hawkinge. This was actually a tragic mistake, as the pilot concerned was not Sergeant Gilders (but is presumed to have been either McAdam or Angus). The pain suffered by the Gilders family can only be imagined.

Mr Gilders was unable to accept his son's apparent disappearance. After a telephone conversation which took place that morning, the Air Ministry wrote to Mr Gilders on March 21st:-

The possibilities, as I see them at present, are either that the pilot baled out before the crash, and that his body has not been discovered; this, in a fairly thickly populated country is, I must admit, unlikely; or that violence of the impact, and possibly the explosion subsequently, were the cause of the disappearance. Unfortunately it does occur sometimes that there is a complete disappearance in this way.

When we have been able to complete our enquiries I will write again, and you will be given further news as it comes in. I think we can rule out the possibility of anyone trying to cover up a mistake or omission; there would be too much risk attached where so many units are involved. I am so sorry for this suspense to which you and Mrs Gilders are subject. I wish it could be avoided, and I should like to thank you for the helpful attitude you adopt towards us in spite of it.

On March 24th, the Air Ministry wrote to Mr Gilders providing information regarding the crash site investigation:-

The aircraft had exploded on impact and the engine was buried in a hole some 16 feet deep which was full of water. The pieces of the aircraft covered a large area and these were all collected and the aircraft identified from its number, P7816.

Although pieces of cockpit and centre section were collected no trace could be found of the pilot, his clothing, or parachute. Owing to the soft nature of the ground it took all day to dig out the engine and the officer concerned is convinced the pilot concerned was not in the wreckage.

The Air Ministry also put forward the view that if Sergeant Gilders had baled out, the weather data suggested that he would have been carried out to sea. This seemed a reasonable possibility given the report by 49 MU, assuming, of course, its accuracy. Mr Gilders was not convinced, and interviewed Flying Officer King, the officer in charge of the 49 MU recovery team which had attended the crash site. The grieving father was told in person that although the Spitfire had been discovered, no trace of the pilot had been found. This, Mr Gilders had to accept, but he remained bitter. On April 3rd he wrote again to the Air Ministry, taking up various issues connected with his son's situation, and in which he remarked:-

It would seem .... that my boy has not been found, and in such circumstances it does seem most strange to me that he should be posted as 'killed in action'. Only in this week's 'Flight' his name appears amongst the killed. Surely this should be rectified in the absence of anything to indicate he has actually lost his life?

It was certainly a pertinent point. In August, Mr Gilders corresponded with the Chief Constable of Kent who provided details from his officer's report which confirmed that, at the time of the crash, 'there was no firing or other sound to indicate aerial combat'. This prompted Mr Gilders to write again to the Air Ministry; in its response, the Ministry considered that 'the violence of the impact and possible explosion subsequently were the cause of the disappearance'. The letter concluded that due to the time factor, the Ministry considered it unlikely that Sergeant Gilders had been captured by the enemy. The final item of correspondence in Mr Gilders' file is a letter from the Chief Constable dated August 28th, 1941:-

> Whilst it is true that the hole made by the plane when it crashed became filled with water before the salvage people removed the debris, the police constable was on the scene within 10 minutes of the crash and the local sergeant within half an hour and both had an opportunity to examine the crater before the water filtered into it to any great extent, and they could find no trace of the pilot or his parachute.

And so John Gilders parents grieved until their deaths, tortured by a mystery and the question: *had* enough been done?

In 1970, the LAM excavated the crash site, recovering various items before discovering a wire cable leading to a substantial piece of wreckage stuck fast at some depth. John Tickner was amongst those present:-

> In those days, before records were available at the PRO, we just used to drive to a village and ask local elderly residents whether they could remember any aircraft crashes. When pointed in such a direction, we often had no idea at first as to whether the aircraft concerned was British or German, much less what type it was. In the case of the Chilham Beeches aircraft, parts found confirmed it to be a Spitfire, but we had no idea then that its pilot remained on board. Obviously having discovered the hawser, we were keen to go back, but the farmer said no.

After official records were made available, and as research therefore progressed, the connection was made between contemporary documentation and the Chilham Spitfire. The LAM's 1970 discovery, of course, somewhat negated the Air Ministry's claim that the crash and explosion had been so severe that both the aircraft and pilot had been obliterated. Enthusiasts thereafter naturally assumed that Sergeant Gilders remained buried there.

Mark Kirby:-

> I first met Steve Vizard and Andy Saunders in 1986, and I went with them to excavate the crash site near Charing, Kent, of Squadron Leader Harry Hogan's Hurricane (which he abandoned on September 18th, 1940). Nearby was the crash site of one of his flight commanders, Flight Lieutenant George Stoney, who was killed at Chilham on August 18th. As we walked up a flint track towards that crash site, Steve pointed out the Gilders crash site to me, which was near a stream. Some years later, in 1993, I returned to the Stoney site and was there approached by a local. I knew from Steve and Andy that the owner of the Gilders crash site was against a recovery, so I was interested when it came out during this conversation that the landowner had changed. The new owner, it transpired, was Sir John Swires, the owner of the Cathy Pacific airline and apparently quite a religious man. When I got home I called Andy and told him the news, but as, for a variety of reasons, he was unable to continue the project, I took it over.

*The recovery of Sgt Gilders. This unauthorised act provoked a furore resulting in Mark Kirby later receiving an Absolute Discharge at Ashford Magistrates' Court.*
*(Mark Kirby)*

With the experience of Sergeant Ellis behind me, I resolved that I would put the case to the family, and if they required John Gilders recovered then I would ensure that this was done. Consequently I drove up to see them, unannounced, with a view to putting the circumstances to them. I found that John's brother, Geoff, was in Holland, but Bolly, his Dutch wife, immediately called him and we spoke on the telephone. He was appreciative of my gesture, but made it clear that as the family had apparently had such a hard time in 1987, trying to persuade the landowner and MOD to co-operate, they no longer wished to pursue the matter. Geoff told me that his sister had been particularly upset at that time. Although I had already communicated with Sir John's estate manager and through him ascertained that he was horrified at the prospect of having 'inherited' an unofficial grave and therefore happy for a recovery to go ahead, in view of the family's reaction I had no intention of taking any further action. I drove home and thought that was that.

The following day I was surprised to receive a call from Geoff Gilders who told me that he had changed his mind, for his father's sake. Final approval, however, had to come from his sister, Mrs Margaret Lawson, the head of the family. I then had a most emotional conversation with her, upon conclusion of which Mrs Lawson said 'Just look after John'. I said I would, a promise I was to keep.

The family then showed me the pile of correspondence John's father had had with the various authorities between 1941-42. I was appalled by the content of some of these letters to a grieving father and this strengthened my resolve still further. It is difficult to understand why 49 MU confirmed that P7816 had crashed at Chilham Beeches, but claimed to have recovered the engine, finding no trace of the pilot.

On April 20th, 1994, Mark Kirby recovered Spitfire P7816 together with the remains of Sergeant Gilders:-

In view of 49 MU's report describing difficult digging conditions, and bearing in mind that the site was adjacent to a stream, we went in with a tracked machine capable of reaching a great depth. Nevertheless we expected the operation to take several days, and anticipated ramping the machine. Incredibly, the maximum depth at which wreckage was found was just five feet deep. The Spitfire's remains were found to be substantial, and included the engine which confirmed the LAM's previous discovery and totally discredited 49 MU's report. A finger-tip search recovered the remains of the pilot, and just three-and-a-half hours later it was all over. Fortunately we had recovered his identity card, which at first was just a mushy, mashed scrap of paper. This I took home and dried carefully, later handing it in to the police. This conclusively proved the pilot's identity: Sergeant John Gilders was no longer missing.

When news of the recovery was released, the RAF told *Kent Today*:-

The exhuming of bodies is not a hobby in this country. If it must be done, it should be done by professionals and within the strict constraints of the law.

There is no room for amateurs and incidents like this are taken very seriously indeed.

Mark Kirby's reported view was published in, amongst other newspapers, the *Mail on Sunday* (May 8th, 1994):-

They (49 MU) did not dig down very far, denying John Gilders a Christian burial and the family's opportunity to visit him and be by him. I just think that men who went missing should be found and given Christian burials. If I had applied to the Ministry for permission, it would have strangled me in red tape and then refused me access. I thought I'd do it and worry about the consequences later.

In enthusiast circles, rumour was rife; Mark Kirby:-

Regarding other personal effects, we found a tobacco pouch, a handkerchief and a cigarette lighter. Although I gave the identity card to the police, which was obviously vital evidence, I temporarily retained the other items as I wished to hand over these personally to the Gilders family. I was concerned that the authorities might lose them. I telephoned Geoff Gilders accordingly, and he agreed with my chosen course of action. When I was arrested and interviewed by Ashford CID, however, I had to hand these items over. It was never my intention to keep them, so my frustration can be appreciated regarding the stories going around, some of them even published in the press, such as me hiding John's identity tags in a barn; it is true that straight after the recovery all items, except the human remains which were subjected to the Home Office Sudden Death Procedure and therefore collected from the scene by an undertaker supervised by the police, were taken to Steve's farm and stored in his barn, so it is easy to see how such things become exaggerated. The remains of the Spitfire were seized during the police inquiry and, as I understand it, remain in the possession of RAF Innsworth.

Six months after being arrested and dealt with by the police, Mark Kirby received a summons for contravening the PMA. John Tickner:-

Having represented Mark in this case, I think there are several things which should be made clear. Firstly he pleaded guilty, on December 1st, 1994, our mitigation being the discredited 49 MU report, the feelings of John Gilders' deceased father, as confirmed by the surviving correspondence, and the family's wishes. The subsequent newspaper reports gave the impression that Mark received an Absolute Discharge only because he was acting on behalf of the family. That is not entirely true, as the Justices were provided all of the evidence and deliberated for two hours before returning their verdict.

On December 5th, 1994, the Inquest concerning the death of Sergeant John Stanley Gilders was held at Ashford. In his summing up, the Coroner, Mr Brian ND Smith, said in part (I have highlighted particular points of note):-

Well, ladies and gentlemen, as I have said on more than one occasion my task is to provide answers to the questions, who, when, where and how and having heard this afternoon's evidence I can say that I am satisfied as to identity, in other words that the human remains which were recovered on 20th April of this year were in fact those of Sgt. John Stanley Gilders. As to when, on what is circumstantial evidence, but the best that can be obtained, I am satisfied that the date of death, the date when Sgt. Gilders' aircraft was seen to dive to the earth, was 21st

February 1941 and I have every reason to suppose that he met his end in the course of that crash and on that day. As to where, I am satisfied that it was at the site excavated by Mr. Kirby at Chilham Beeches adjacent to the Ashford-Canterbury road at Chilham. As to the question how and therefore the verdict which I should record, there are occasions, and perhaps now fewer, when I might feel justified in recording a verdict of enemy action. It may not be appropriate in view of the length of time since the war ended, or that war ended, but having no evidence that enemy action was involved in the actual loss of control, I feel it appropriate to record a verdict of "Died on War Service", and so it will be that form of words which will ultimately appear in any Death Certificate.

Now there is, although the Coroners Rules having said that I and/or a jury should provide answers to those four questions, there is a further limb to that Rule which says that "neither the coroner nor the jury shall offer any opinion on any other matter". I take the view that I'm not offending against that Rule in offering perhaps some guidance in relation to the applicable law so far as it relates to coroners. I know there to have been criminal proceedings which have now ended in relation to the recovery of the Spitfire itself. I know it also to be the case that the Ministry of Defence from whom a licence is required for the recovery of military remains has a view that such a licence would not normally be granted where the military remains are likely to contain human remains or where there is unexploded ordnance.

**Now what I have to say in relation to human remains is that it does not lie within the power of the Ministry of Defence to grant or deny permission for human remains to be exhumed.** There is basically a general prohibition against the exhumation of human remains and the leading case of that, Foster v. Dodds says 'That a dead body by law belongs to no one and is therefore under the protection of the public. If it lies in consecrated ground the ecclesiastical law will interpose for its protection, but whether in ground consecrated or unconsecrated indignities offered to human remains and improperly and indecently disinterring them are the ground of an indictment'. That is not to say that human remains may not on occasion be exhumed, but there are three authorities who may have the power to grant or refuse exhumation. Basically if there has been a burial in consecrated ground then the person who has the authority to grant exhumation or permission for an exhumation is the Ordinary who generally is the Bishop of the diocese. If the exhumation is from any other burial ground then in all ordinary circumstances the person having the authority to grant a licence for an exhumation is the Home Secretary.

The third person to be involved or having involvement in exhumation is the coroner. The coroner may issue an order for exhumation if he is advised that there is a body in his jurisdiction and he intends to hold an inquest into the death of that body. That however is the extent to which a coroner has authority to grant permission for exhumation; only if it is his intention to hold an inquest. Obviously, I say the most common instance, one hopes it doesn't happen too often, but obviously one of the instances when this occurs is when following the burial of a body there is good reason to suppose that the cause of death was perhaps not that which was certified or earlier found and that further examination is necessary and for the purposes of holding an inquest. But since the law refers to the word buried which in my view is to be used in its intransitive form, in other words the fact of being buried and not necessarily through human agency, I would say that the presence of a body which is buried means that it cannot be exhumed except by the permission of one of those three authorities.

Now clearly if a body on the face of it is likely to have met its death in the circumstances which I hold Sgt. Gilders did, I would have to consider whether it was appropriate for me to hold an inquest. I would have to say that I would not in normal circumstances be influenced by, although I would take into account, the wishes of any surviving family and the like. What I would have to decide in my judicial discretion is whether there is reason for me to hold an inquest. If I decide that there is, then I would of necessity have to issue an order for exhumation. I hasten to say I speak only for my own jurisdiction, but I've no reason to suppose that my views are not generally adopted by coroners. I would also have to consider whether in giving permission for such exhumation I would attach conditions to it. What I'm thinking of is not only the manner of excavation but also the wisdom or otherwise of having in attendance a pathologist experienced in aircrash injuries, generally from RAF Halton, because it seems to me that there might be value in obtaining the evidence of such a qualified pathologist who has had the opportunity of seeing the remains in situ. **I would also expect the exhumation to be carried out decently and reverently and I say this because in fact having held inquests into a number of such deaths, I am aware of one occasion, most unfortunate, when the remains were discovered in a plastic supermarket bag which cannot possibly have been in existence at that time that death occurred. It is therefore apparent that there had been some earlier investigation and the concealment of the human remains. I do not, I hasten to say, say that this happened on this occasion, but it is something within my experience and something which in my view should be avoided for the future.**

So those are the words of guidance which I attempt to offer in relation to other matters. **As I say I do not ignore the provisions of the Protection of Military Remains Act but that is a matter for the Ministry of Defence in relation to aircraft, not to bodies.**

When news of the Inquest was published, I was at a loss to understand Mr Smith's comments concerning the MOD's power under the PMA. I was not surprised, however, to read of the 'supermarket bag' incident (see Chapter Four); again, the authorities need only one negative to vindicate their policies and here was a most distasteful one. On November 10th, 1997, Mr Smith kindly wrote to me regarding his summing up:-

My remarks were extempore and I have to acknowledge, following correspondence with the Ministry of Defence, that in one important respect, my statement of law was wrong. The Ministry **does** have power of human remains associated with the aircraft but there is a specific reference to the co-terminus powers conferred by any other enactment. This presumably includes coroners legislation.

As we have seen in Chapter Five, however, there are actually no coroners powers relevant to sites protected by the PMA. The sole authority, not withstanding the landowner's consent, is the Secretary of State, which is not to say that in the event of an official recovery the Department would not act in conjunction with the relevant coroner. Mr Smith's letter is further evidence that the interpretation of the PMA provided by Chapter Five is entirely accurate. Mr Smith continued:-

I acknowledge that for whatever reason my remarks were nevertheless sufficiently misinterpreted to paint me as being in favour of exhumation in such circumstances which has led to my being approached for support from elsewhere in the country which I am not prepared to give.

On Thursday, 11th May, 1995, during what was the week commemorating the 50th anniversary of Victory in Europe Day, Sergeant Gilders' funeral service was held in the Guards Chapel, Alexander Barracks, Pirbright. The Chaplain, David Osborne, said:-

> In a week that has seen so many moving and appropriate symbols of commemoration, we give thanks for the sacrifice of one young pilot.

> What we owe John and others like him we cannot repay.

*The RAF plot at Brookwood Military Cemetery.*
*(Author)*

Later that day Sergeant Gilders was buried at Brookwood Military Cemetery with full military honours, joining there many thousands of servicemen, including not only those from Britain and the Commonwealth but also Americans, Belgians, Czechs, Poles and Italians. Walking amongst the rows of headstones and crosses I find a deeply moving experience; at such places the enormity of sacrifice during the two world wars suddenly becomes a tangible and tragic reality. Like the Runnymede Memorial, a visit to Brookwood is strongly recommended.

Mark Kirby:-

> As in the case of Sergeant Ellis, in my opinion had I made an application to the MOD on behalf of the family previous events again indicate that in all liklihood the authorities would have refused and again dissuaded both the family and landowner. It was a case of, 'if we do this now, we can make it happen'. To me, nothing else matters but making the family happy.

> At the time, I was angry and concerned that after our positive experience regarding MOD co-operation, the Gilders incident would destroy the respect and liaison achieved. As I have said before, my profession prevents me from condoning anyone taking the law into their hands, and I still believe that there are other avenues of enquiry which *must* be exhausted before such an act is

*Time to reflect: Mark Kirby and partner,*
*Monica, at Sgt Gilders' funeral.*
*(Mark Kirby)*

even remotely justified; for the practical reasons Mark relates it can be understood, however, why he chose to act as he did. Given my different approach and good relations with the MOD, it is perhaps a pity that 'The Men of Kent' and I were in different orbits, as it were, at that time, as I believe it possible that had the facts been presented to the authorities and personalities of influence, in an appropriate manner, the desired end result may have been achieved within the law. Some may consider that optimistic supposition on my part, but certain past and future events do support this view. What Mark Kirby did achieve, in addition to the burial of John Gilders, was to provoke a media storm which has undoubtedly assisted in forcing matters to a head, as we shall see.

### Sergeant Stanislaw Duszinski: Inconclusive recoveries, 1973 (two) & 1996.

*Sgt S Duszinski.*
*(Polish Institute)*

In August 1996, the subject of missing pilots was made topical again through events occurring once more on Romney Marsh. They concerned a Polish pilot, Sergeant Stanislaw Duszinski. Again, we need to examine this story.

Stanislaw Duszinski was born into a Roman Catholic family at Oteoczyn, near Torun, in Poland, on October 28th, 1915. Having completed his elementary education in Alexandrow Kujawski, he became a non-commissioned officer cadet on September 1st, 1931. He passed out with good marks exactly three years later. Between July 20th and August 20th, 1936, he completed a gliding course prior to moving on to instruction in powered flight until August 15th, 1937. This he completed with distinction, as was his advanced flying course. By October 28th,

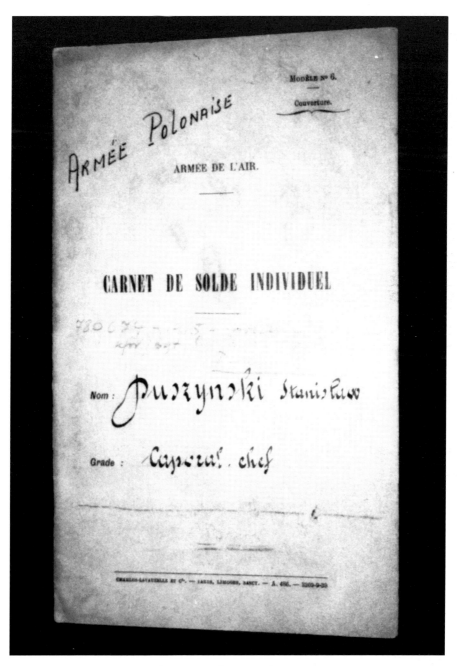

*Stanislaw Duszinski's French Air Force*
*Service Record.*
*(Author)*

1937, he was a fully-fledged pilot in the PAF. A flying instructor course at Radom kept him busy for another year, after which he specialised in fighter instruction. When war broke out on September 1st, 1939, he was ordered to defend Deblin airport. By September 17th the situation was clearly hopeless, and so Duszinski, who was fluent in both German and Russian, was ordered to supervise the escape of his training school's aircraft and pilots over the Roumanian border. Whilst interred at Babadag camp in that country, on October 3rd he was promoted to Platoon Leader. On October 14th, the Poles fled from Babadag, and were eventually able to leave Roumania for France on November 5th.

Stanislaw Duszinski arrived in France and joined the *Armee de L'Air* on December 16th, 1939. His French pay book and service record, now in my possession, indicates that by this time his flying hours amounted to 1,289. Like Franek Gruszka (see Chapter Three), Duszinski was a most experienced pilot. Along with other Polish pilots, when France fell Duszinski made his way to England, joining the RAF and learning to fly Hurricanes at No 6 OTU. Again like Franek Gruszka, he was amongst the first Polish fighter pilots posted to an RAF fighter squadron, in this case, on September 2nd, 1940, to No 238 based at St Eval in 10 Group. That station was situated on Cornwall's north-west coast, the Hurricane pilots being heavily committed with providing aerial protection for convoys. On September 10th, the squadron moved across to Middle Wallop, in Hampshire, and near the boundary between 10 and 11 Groups. The Wallop squadrons were frequently called upon to reinforce Air Vice-Marshal Park's fighters in the areas of Southampton and Portsmouth, and from September 7th onwards would often find themselves on patrol over London and the south-east. Gordon Batt was an NCO pilot with 238 throughout the Battle of Britain:-

I consider the most harrowing experience, whilst at readiness, laying in the flight hut, was hearing the 'phone ring, time and again, for just petty things. Just when you started to doze off, it would ring again: 'SCRAMBLE, ANGELS 15 PORTSMOUTH!' Then it was a case of panic and fear, but a strange mental security always took over immediately the wheels were up and the hood closed. All of this, however, was tempered with some 'high jinx'. I once dropped a Very flare cartridge down the chimney of said flight hut. The main part of the squadron was on a practice flight. Those left behind were rudely awakened, except one or two who were able to explain the pyrotechnic scene of exploding colour and flying coke issuing from the central stove!

On September 11th (the same day on which Pilot Officer Clarke of 504 Squadron was reported missing), just one day after arriving at Middle Wallop, 238 Squadron was scrambled and intercepted a formation of Ju 88s south of Tunbridge Wells, Kent. In the fierce combat resulting, Pilot Officer Tower-Perkins was shot down and baled out wounded, but neither Flight Lieutenant David Hughes or Sergeant Stanislaw Duszinski were ever seen again, alive at least. It was just nine days since the latter had joined 238 Squadron. Group Captain Jim Fenton:-

When I was shot down and wounded on August 8th, I did not think that the AOC 10 Group, Air Vice-Marshal Brand, would retain me as CO, but he did and I rejoined 238 on September 15th. By that time there had been many casualties. David Hughes had joined us on August 4th, but by my return was missing. Others, like Sergeant Duszinski, were also missing but I had never even met him, so little time had he been with the squadron. You are absolutely right, this change in tempo from the comparative quiet in the other group areas was quite a shock at first for new squadrons fighting over the 11 Group area.

As Gordon Batt says, 'these two pilots had been with us for such a brief length of time that now I cannot even remember them'.

David Hughes was the son of the Rev. A Price Hughes, superintendent minister at the King's Hall, Southall. Sadly, in May 1941, a proud father was to collect his son's posthumous DFC from Buckingham Palace. Fortunately his eldest son, Arthur, a bomber pilot, had been able to collect his own DFC the previous September.

Stanislaw Duszinski was destined to be amongst those missing pilots forgotten about until the 1970s. On January 13th, 1973, to be exact, the A&TRG excavated a crash site at Little Scotney Farm, near Lydd on Kent's Romney Marsh - only a few miles away from where Pilot Officer Clarke crashed at Newchurch, in fact. The aircraft was identified as Hurricane R2682: Sergeant Duszinski's. Although the pilot's parachute, a shoe, fragments of uniform and personal papers were found, human remains were not reported. David Buchanan, who had already recovered Pilot Officer Drake, was in charge of the operation and reported to the MOD 'the reasons why the pilot's remains could not be recovered'. As he explained to me in 1998:-

> After our excavation, I wrote to the MOD explaining what had been found and stating my belief that more substantial remains existed at a greater depth than that which we were able to reach due to the difficult conditions. In winter, Romney Marsh is like a quagmire, water spurts in from under the ground, which is why we were forced to abandon the site. About a month later, out of the blue, I received a visit one event from an RAF officer; his team of airmen remained outside in their van. The officer told me that he and his men had been tasked with recovering Sergeant Duszinski, and that they were to stay at Lydd Camp. I offered to meet them and identify the site, which I duly did. I also introduced them to the farmer and offered to fix up a digger for them locally. My further assistance was declined, however, and it was made quite clear that the RAF wished to get on with it and make its own arrangements.

> As I heard nothing further, I wrote to the MOD which responded that there were 'no further details'. Later I received a telephone call informing me that the RAF had abandoned the site for the same reason as we, and that nothing further had been found. The problem is that Romney Marsh is just that, a marsh which has been recovered from the sea. Once you dig down several feet into it, particularly during the winter, water rushes into the hole. You are then dealing with running sand. The biggest problem is that this is like quicksand, so objects buried can sink down many, many feet and so defy recovery even with the mechanical equipment available today.

> A couple of years on I decided to have another go myself, so I contacted the farmer and made the necessary arrangements. By coincidence, concerned with the recovery of missing airmen, the MOD had written to all farmers on whose land such sites existed, urging the farmers to verify aviation archaeologists' documentation prior to giving permission. In this case the farmer concerned responded that he had given me permission for a further dig. I then received a telephone call from the Tenterden Police asking me to contact the MOD; I was given both a London office and out of hours number. I made the call, and spoke to a civil servant who requested that I did not proceed as planned at the Duszinski site. He could not demand, as in those days what I was doing was not against the law, but nevertheless it seemed pertinent to co-operate with the Ministry. Consequently I never returned to the site.

In 1980, Winston Ramsey edited and published the inspirational publication *The Battle of Britain: Then & Now* (see bibliography), which, for the first time, placed in the public domain details of aircraft and personnel casualties and details regarding recoveries. Having seen therein details regarding the Duszinski crash site, a Mrs Jean Day wrote to the MOD urging the authorities to recover the pilot; on October 30th, 1980, the AHB responded (the italics are my own):-

> The Hurricane that is thought to contain the Polish pilot's remains crashed into very soft ground, and when attempts were made in 1973 to recover it - both by a private group and an official RAF recovery team - it was found impossible to excavate below a depth of 12 feet because of running sand. Since there was no means of telling just how much more work would need to be done, how long it would take, or how much it would cost, it was decided to proceed no further.
>
> May I now make one or two general points? in trying to decide our policy on recovering human remains, we are most anxious to respect the views of those most closely concerned, namely the next-of-kin and the comrades of those who died. While some certainly favour recovery, we have evidence to suggest that the majority are opposed to it: after this length of time they feel it better that crash sites should - like the wrecks of ships in which sailors are drowned - be the airmens' permanent resting places. Consequently the recent activities of some of the private groups have caused much resentment in certain quarters and we in the MOD have to try to take full account of both points of view. *Our problem is made worse by the fact that we do not know - and shall never know - how many wrecks remain to be found on land, and that until a particular crash site is fully investigated (an expensive and time consuming task) we can often not be certain whether human remains are there, whose they are, or even if they are identifiable.*

By coincidence, in 1980, the pilot's niece, Professor Teresa Kintzer, was a visiting professor at Aberdeen University. Whilst in the country Professor Kintzer also read about her uncle in *The Battle of Britain Then & Now*. Having returned to Poland, some years later on July 10th, 1988, the Professor wrote to the Polish Institute appealing for information regarding Stanislaw Duszinski:-

> My brother and I (his closest surviving relatives) would like to make a symbolic grave for our uncle here in Poland. Have you any object associated with him, e.g. a small part of his plane's wreckage, a document, a piece of his uniform or other personal effect, which we could put into this grave? To have such an object and this grave would mean a very great deal to us.
>
> In 1980, the brief duration of my stay in Britain did not allow me to continue my search and I was unable to do so in later years because of the political situation in Poland ..... my brother and I would be deeply grateful for anything that you can do to help us fill in this blank in our uncle's life history.

Over a decade later Andy Saunders, who was not in contact with the Duszinski family, put the case before the Consul General of the Republic of Poland; on December 18th, 1991, Dr Janusz Kochanowski wrote:-

> May I thank you sincerely for trying for years to unravel the mystery of the disappearance of Polish airman Stanislaw Duszinski who died as a hero in the Battle of Britain.

On the basis of your enquiries, the Polish Consulate General has made an official request to the British Government for the excavation of the plane and honourable burial of Mr Duszinski.

I am indebted to you for pursuing this matter and hope that with your help it will be brought to a successful conclusion.

Such a promising response was to take an unexpected turn the following year. The Consul General wrote again on September 11th, 1992 (ironically the 52nd anniversary of Duszinski's crash):-

Recently, The Consulate of the Republic of Poland has been advised by the family of Sergeant Duszinski to abandon the further steps to search for the remains.

I would like to express my sincere gratitude for your efforts and assistance in this matter.

Considering Professor Kintzer's letter, this does appear surprising.

Mark Kirby:-

I knew about the Duszinski story and in 1995 considered arranging a recovery, but abandoned this idea as I was not in touch with the family. The following year I met Mr Simon Ashworth who actually owned the adjacent land to that on which the Hurricane crashed. Mr Ashworth, who had already responded positively to Professor Kintzer's letter requesting soil from the crash site for internment in the family grave, gave me the family's address. I had already received permission for a recovery from the actual landowner, so made arrangements for a Polish speaking friend to telephone and seek their view. The family supported the idea of a recovery, and the farmer's 'window' gave me just two-three days to go ahead. We went straight in with a machine, digging down to 30 feet. The Forster bomb locator then detected a further 20 feet, meaning that we had gone down, to all intents and purposes, at least 50 feet. All we found were a few items of Hurricane, in a small isolated pocket some 12 - 15 feet deep, together with bits of plastic bin liner which must have been deposited during one of the previous excavations. No human remains were discovered but we experienced no difficulties digging in these summer conditions.

When Mr Ashworth saw the unauthorised excavation in progress, however, he was outraged, and called the police. Upon the attendance of officers, the quantity of recovered aircraft wreckage was seized. Naturally the recovery was halted, and the Kent Constabulary again had to consider charging Mark Kirby with contravening the PMA. John Tickner:-

Again I represented Mark, although to his credit he voluntarily attended Ashford Police Station and submitted himself for interview. I later carried out liaison with the Crown Prosecution Service (CPS), and when I had presented all of the facts, the case went no further.

The CPS has an oft used phrased, 'not in the public interest', and it is not surprising that this matter was so deemed. Had a case against Mark Kirby proceeded, considering the known facts, yet another scandal would have hit the headlines, out of which the MOD would undoubtedly have, yet again, emerged second best. After the Gilders incident, deliberately breaking the law again could be considered a foolhardy course of action by Mark Kirby; as John Tickner says, 'had a body been recovered and proceedings initiated, I think things would have gone badly for us in court'. Mark Kirby adds, however:-

> I believe passionately that these pilots should be recovered and I am not afraid to stand up and be counted. I was hoping that they would take me to court so that the story would come out.

*Steve Vizard & Mark Kirby pictured during their attempt to recover Sgt Duszinski in August 1996. The dry digging conditions can clearly be seen. (Mark Kirby)*

The MOD, having apparently sought the Duszinski family's view regarding a recovery in 1992, was naturally unhappy regarding Mark Kirby's excavation. It can only be assumed that the MOD and Mark contacted different branches of the same family, each of which held differing views on the subject and which led, therefore, to this incident. The MOD, however, tells me that its contact with the Duszinskis is not 'a matter for public record'.

Subsequent to Mark Kirby's excavation, an RAF team spent some time at the site but the recovery of Sergeant Duszinski's mortal remains was not reported as many had hoped. Both the MOD and David Buchanan have suggested the same possibility, that Romney Marsh is like a quicksand and that the Hurricane's remains and pilot could now be very many feet below the surface. Could this be the case?

One rumour prevalent in enthusiast circles concerns the burial of an unknown airman at Northiam in Kent; the date of death given is merely 'September 1940'. Could it be that Sergeant Duszinski was recovered but not identified at the time and buried in this grave (as in the manner of Sergeant Ellis and others)? Perhaps, therefore, insufficient human remains were left at the site to later be discovered. Evidence exists, however, to refute the connection between Northiam and Sergeant Duszinski, as certain records confirm that the remains concerned were washed up on the foreshore at Rye.

So what has happened to Sergeant Duszinski? I doubt that we shall ever know but one thing is certain: Stanislaw Duszinski is undoubtedly missing.

### Sergeant Dennis Noble: November 8th & 9th, 1996.

*Sgt D Noble.*
*(KBoBM)*

Over a year after Mark Kirby's Duszinski excavation, another aircraft recovery caused further controversy, although this case was actually within the law.

On November 8th & 9th, 1996, the excavation of a Hurricane took place at Woodhouse Road, Hove, in Sussex; the recovery was licensed by the MOD as the pilot, Sergeant Dennis Noble, was known to be buried at East Retford Cemetery in Nottinghamshire. It was indeed Sergeant Noble's Hurricane which was found, so the reader may be wondering why this incident is included here. The fact is that substantial human remains were discovered, and important issues therefore raised regarding what was an authorised recovery.

At 1030 hrs on August 30th, 1940, the first raiders were detected of an attack during which two further waves each crossed different sides of the Kent coast at half-hourly intervals. The third formation of enemy aircraft, Ju 88 bombers protected by Me 109s, came in over Hove where they were attacked by the Hurricanes of Tangmere's 43 Squadron. The unit's CO, Squadron Leader John 'Tubby' Badger, later reported:-

We sighted an enemy plane and rolled over hard to engage it. Sergeant Noble fell away and another plane came in to fill his place. He did not rejoin us and crashed. The German may have got a short burst in at Sergeant Noble's plane.

The Hurricane concerned, P3179, crashed at the junction of Portland and Woodhouse Road, Hove, at 1150 am. Later that day, Badger himself was shot down and fatally wounded, although he was to succumb to those injuries until June 30th, 1941; he had commanded 43 Squadron for 51 days and had received the DFC from his hospital bed on September 6th, 1940.

A recovery team attended the crash site of P3179, and, to all intents and purposes, recovered the pilot for burial and tidied the site. As previously stated, Sergeant Noble was buried, the pavement repaired, and, once more, there the matter would have rested if not for aviation archaeology and the progress of property developers.

In 1995, the Southern Counties Aviation Club (SCAC) discovered that a major property development was to take place the following year in the area of Sergeant Noble's crash site. There was a suggestion that the block of flats due to be built would be named after the pilot, and permission was given, by Hove Council and all those companies with services running through the footway, and the MOD, for a recovery.

Being undertaken in a built up area, it was not surprising that the eventual recovery attracted great curiosity and interest amongst local people. Sightseers were to get more than they bargained for, however, when a substantial amount of human remains were found. David Brocklehurst, Chairman of the KBoB, was working on the dig alongside the SCAC:-

As soon as we discovered human remains, we contacted the local police, who in turn informed the coroner and MOD. We were given permission to continue with the excavation so that all human remains present could be recovered. The remains were handled with the greatest respect, as all team members hold the Few in the highest esteem. They are, after all, our greatest heroes.

Yet again, not least due to having coincided with Remembrance, the story of another Battle of Britain pilot recovered in his aircraft was well covered by the media. On this occasion, the press had the added bonus of a mystery: how could the pilot have been buried in 1940? Sergeant Noble's cousin, Gwendoline, was traced, naturally being shocked and upset regarding the gruesome discovery. As in the case of Sergeant Ellis, however, the reason was quite simple and legally the authorities were beyond reproach. Furthermore we know that in this case the Hurricane concerned impacted at full power, plunging over 15 feet below the ground and producing a water filled crater: very difficult operating conditions indeed given the limitations of both resources and equipment available in 1940.

Some may question whether, in the interests of preventing such a disturbing discovery happening again, permission should be given in respect of *any* fatality, unless the pilot is known to have baled out and perhaps been killed due to a parachute malfunction. It has to be said that I am personally aware of at least one Spitfire in Kent where, if the site was interfered with, such a thing could happen; fortunately the landowner is aware of the situation and has refused all comers permission to excavate. There is nothing to prevent a licence being issued in this case, however, and of course circumstances regarding landowners do change. If ever that site is excavated, at least there are no close relatives around to be distressed: the pilot's sister died in 1997.

In the instance of Sergeant Noble, however, David Brocklehurst provides justification:-

If we had not recovered the aircraft, the remains of the pilot could have been disturbed at any time by workmen. The road may have been improved, drains installed or whatever, any of which could have led to the Hurricane being disturbed. I would suggest this to be a likely scenario given that a block of flats was shortly to be built adjacent to the crash site. Surely it is better that Sergeant Noble has now been recovered, albeit by accident, than having traffic and pedestrians passing over the site, and perhaps dogs fouling the pavement, so close to where one of our Battle of Britain heroes lay?

I doubt anyone would wish to argue with David's sentiments.

The inquest was subsequently held on December 18th, 1996, the Coroner, Mr Donald Gooding, delivering the verdict that Sergeant Noble had died as a result of enemy action whilst on active service. In his summing up, Mr Gooding put valour into perspective:-

These days we are regaled by talk of heroes and really I don't think that people know what they are talking about. These heroes get paid large sums of money for kicking soggy lumps of leather about. These are just one type of what today are called heroes. They are not heroes. Dennis Noble was a hero.

During the early 1940s, this country was in real trouble. We were being assaulted by land, sea and air. The battle was fought by very young men and boys who were in their teens or early twenties. Shortly afterwards, Winston Churchill made a speech in which he mentioned the Few. Dennis Noble was one of the Few.

It is as a tribute to him and his comrades that we hold this inquest.

In early 1997, Sergeant Dennis Noble was finally, and completely, laid to rest in the original Retford cemetery grave. He received a full military funeral attended by his few surviving relatives, RAF representatives and those responsible for the recovery. Legally, the integrity of these enthusiasts clearly remains intact.

To summarise, since the PMA, three more missing pilots have been recovered (not counting the case of Sergeant Noble, the circumstances of which are quite different), and the last resting places of at least two more disturbed with no conclusive outcome. Where, the reader may well ask, will it all end?

*Corner of a British town:*
*Woodhouse Road, Hove,*
*August 30th, 1940, &*
*November 8th, 1996.*
*(KBoBM)*

CHAPTER SEVEN

# Destiny Can Wait

The reader will now appreciate the circumstances around which the question of the *Missing Few* revolves:-

1. The MOD's policy is one of non-disturbance.
2. Under the provisions of the PMA, only the Secretary of State can authorise a recovery, not even a coroner having the right to intervene.
3. That regardless of the above, the landowner's permission has to be obtained; if negative then not even the Secretary of State can proceed.
4. The views of a pilot's family are not catered for in law. Furthermore, if a family 'authorised' a private individual to act on their behalf in such a matter, it could technically be considered that they were inciting the commission of an offence.

In May 1995, an article appeared in a UK aviation magazine concerning the Gilders case in particular, and the situation regarding missing pilots generally. Although written in good faith, the author was clearly confused not only regarding the PMA, but also the powers of HM Coroner. This was not surprising as he quoted the inaccurate statements of the Ashford Coroner, Mr Brian Smith (see Chapter Five), from the Gilders Inquest. Unfortunately, a letter was also quoted from the (then) Defence Secretary, Mr Malcolm Rifkind, which also incorrectly reported the Coroner's power (making reference to exhumations which, as we have already seen do *not* apply). In view of the foregoing, it was perhaps understandable that the emphasis of the article was one of sympathy towards 'private recoveries' (for want of a better expression). Needless to say my telephone line became constantly busy as enthusiasts from all over the country urged me to pen an appropriate response. At this point, for a variety of reasons largely connected with the sheer volume of work already being undertaken by this office, I was reluctant to get involved but eventually felt so strongly about the matter that I felt left with only one course of action.

On June 19th, 1995, I wrote comprehensively to the Minister of State for the Armed Forces, Mr Nicholas Soames MP, the grandson of Sir Winston Churchill himself. My letter encapsulated the saga of the *Missing Few*, the penultimate paragraph of which read:-

> We believe that the MOD should now be prepared to organise at this juncture an operation to recover all of those outstanding pilots where appropriate, if only to avoid further scandals and prevent the recovery of our heroes' remains by anyone other than the professionals of the RAF. We suggest that the families concerned should be contacted by the MOD and it explained to them that the aircraft and last resting places of their loved ones may have been discovered. As a precaution against unnecessarily raising expectations, it should be emphasised during the initial approach that ultimately nothing may be found. Being aware of all the facts, the family concerned could then decide what course of action to take. Should a family not want a site disturbed, then it could perhaps be consecrated as a true grave and a memorial erected, either on the spot or as close as is practicable, by the CWGC. As the whereabouts of the majority, if not all, of the families of those pilots concerned are known to enthusiasts, and given the fact that public opinion would no doubt offer wholehearted support, it does now seem a reasonable juncture at which the MOD could authorise such an operational project. Such a process would,

of course, be a complicated process involving both the civil police and various coroners, but nevertheless this is, we believe, the only way forward rather than the ad hoc and unauthorised recoveries which have punctuated the past.

Copies of the letter were distributed to the following:-

Michael Mates MP, the Chief of the Air Staff (CAS), the head of the MOD's Air Historical Branch (AHB), HQ Personnel and Training Centre RAF Innsworth, CWGC, The Royal British Legion, the RAFA, the PAFA, the BoBFA and the Battle of Britain Memorial Trust (BoBMT, founded by Wing Commander Geoffrey Page and responsible for erection of the Battle of Britain Memorial at Capel).

Of the foregoing, no response was received from the RAFA, PAFA or BoBMT.

Prior to considering the MOD's eventual response, those from the organisations reflecting sufficient courtesy to reply are of interest. The CWGC's Enquiries Section (June 22nd):-

The CWGC is not involved with the discovery or identification of remains but rather with the commemoration of war dead, either with a headstone marking the grave or, if there is no known grave, by name on one of our memorials to the missing.

When remains have been discovered and identified, the MOD notifies us and we arrange for a headstone to be erected over the grave.

I note your suggestion that the crash sites could be designated 'war graves' and that the Commission should erect a headstone/memorial on each one. Even if the MOD did designate these sites as 'war graves', it is unlikely that we would commemorate the casualties in the way you suggest as we only erect headstones in a cemetery, and they are already commemorated on a memorial to the missing.

I also note that you have also written to various sections of the RAF which are the service responsible for the identification of the remains of airmen, and I am sure that they will be able to assist you with your desire to stop unauthorised excavations at crash sites.

By this time, I had actually sought advice from the Canon Graham Lyle regarding consecrated ground. It appears that such ground cannot be used for any purpose, so in the case of a cash site being situated within a field used for agricultural purposes it would clearly be impractical. Nevertheless, the foregoing letter seemed to indicate the CWGC's level of support for and interest in our ideas: zero.

On June 23rd, the secretary of Michael Mates MP wrote explaining that he was absent abroad on parliamentary business and that I would 'receive a full reply on his return to the office at the beginning of July'. On July 7th, I received a letter from Mr Mates:-

Thank you for copying to me your correspondence with Nicholas Soames and I hope that he will be able to help you.

So much for a 'full reply'!

The CAS, Air Chief Marshal Sir Michael Graydon was far more obliging in his letter of July 6th:-

> Thank you for your letter dated June 19th, 1995, which invited my support for your campaign for the recovery of those 'missing' Royal Air Force Battle of Britain pilots whose remains are buried at, as yet, undisturbed sites in South-East England.
>
> I know that 'aviation archaeology' is a potentially emotive subject and that the concerns you touch on are shared by the more responsible individuals and societies that take an interest in this field. Similarly, I am also conscious that a number of those involved act in an unauthorised way and that this can cause deep, personal distress to others. Not least for this reason, the issue is sensitive, but as you rightly point out, there s unlikely to be a solution that finds favour with everyone. That aside, as you highlighted in your letter to the Minister of State for the Armed Forces, the Protection of Military Remains Act 1986 already provides some legal safeguard against unauthorised recovery of aircraft. Additionally there is a very carefully considered and well established Departmental policy on the subject, and any proposed changes would therefore need to be particularly convincing and may, indeed, require the consent of Parliament.
>
> Against this backdrop, I am sure you will appreciate that I am not, at present, in a position to offer substantive comment. However, I can provide reassurance that the matter is being reviewed and that a follow-up reply will be forwarded by my staff in due course.
>
> In the interim, thank you for raising your concerns and, of course, for your continued support of the Royal Air Force. The sentiment is much appreciated.

On July 10th, I received a second letter from the CWGC, in response to mine of June 26th requesting confirmation that Pilot Officer Clarke's memorial at Newchurch was entirely privately funded; this was found to be the case, but the letter concluded:-

> As I explained in my letter of June 22nd, the CWGC is not involved with the discovery or identification of remains, and again I can only suggest that you contact the RAF regarding your wish to stop unauthorised excavations at crash sites.

Am I too sensitive or was I justified in feeling that my correspondence was considered an irritation? On July 13th, I replied, making reference to two particular cases (of which more later): one of identification, the other regarding a pilot with *two* graves. On July 24th, the CWGC responded:-

> If you believe that you can identify any casualty buried as an unknown, you should submit documentary proof to the Commission who will consider the case.

That rather contradicted the CWGC's responses of both July 6th and 10th. Perhaps being a nuisance was starting to pay off!

On August 3rd, Mr Peter Henderson, Assistant to The Royal British Legion's Secretary General, responded:-

It is the view of The Royal British Legion that the remains of war dead, of whatever arm, whatever and however they are exhumed have to be properly consecrated. Much depends on the wishes of the next-of-kin, but it is often wisest for those missing airmen to be left to lie where they fell, and their names recorded as they are at Runnymede and on other memorials.

It is of paramount importance that they should not be disturbed by souvenir hunting enthusiasts, however high the aims of amateur aviation archaeologists. Known war graves are sacrosanct. Unless the CWGC, or the MOD/RAF, are conducting an official exhumation, crashed planes of 50 years ago are off-limits. It is our view that this should be the case.

On August 23rd, Mr Jonathon Iremonger, the Private Secretary to the CAS, wrote, having liaised with the Department:-

On the matter of Departmental policy on crash sites which may contain the remains of aircrew, we recognise the concerns that you and others have about their possible unauthorised disturbance. I have passed your further comments to CS (Sec) 2a at HQ PTC, who will be responding to the detailed proposals that you made in your letter to the Minister for the Armed Forces.

At the September 1995 reunion of the BoBFA, held annually at Bentley Priory, my letter was discussed by the Committee. The Honorary Secretary, Wing Commander Pat Hancock, responded:-

Your letters were discussed and members were in general agreement. We all felt that airmen who were posted 'missing' and were later found to have died in their crashed aircraft should be left where they fell unless close next-of-kin wished to make other arrangements. It is doubtful that many close next-of-kin survive after 55 years since the Battle of Britain. The individual owners of crash sites might also have views when human remains were found. It was hoped that sites would be marked by a small memorial to the individuals concerned. I was asked to thank you for your concern.

The response of the Association has to be considered, and it is noteworthy that the wishes of relatives are considered to be the prevalent factor.

On September 8th, the PUS, the Earl Howe (and not the Minister himself with whom I had hoped to find some empathy given the identity of his late grandfather) provided the long awaited response:-

As you are aware the Department has a long standing policy of non-disturbance of sites where military aircraft are believed to have crashed and a member of the crew is still listed as missing. In addition to this policy the Protection of Military Remains Act 1986 provides additional legal protection for such sites.

Your remarks have been given due consideration but, whilst I appreciate your intentions, I think there could be practical difficulties in adopting your suggestion, not least the problem of identifying the exact sites after so many years. Landowners would need to agree to the consecration of the site and the erection of a memorial on their property and, even if permission was given, it may not be possible for the public to be given freedom of access to the sites. Marking of sites could also lead to unscrupulous enthusiasts using metal detectors to search for aircraft wrecage, particularly where aircraft crashed on common land. It may also tempt unprincipled landowners to charge admission to view the memorial.

Taking all these concerns into account, I am satisfied that the current policy is well founded and that there is adequate legal protection of these sites which enables the police and the Crown Prosecution Service (CPS) to act should the law be broken. The policy allows for sympathetic consideration to be given to the requests from any relatives of the deceased aircrew but, naturally the Coroner is the sole authority for issue of an exhumation order.

With all due respect to his Lordship but considering the foregoing information contained in this book, can the reader even begin to appreciate my frustration upon receiving such a response? The PUS had clearly missed several vital points. Firstly, the sites concerned have already been located and relatives traced by enthusiasts. Secondly, no consideration had been given to the erection of memorials as close to sites as would be *practicable*. Thirdly - and this I found quite staggering - the role of the coroner had yet again been totally incorrectly quoted (see Chapter Five). Truly and positively significant, however, is his Lordship's confirmation that 'The policy allows for sympathetic consideration to be given to the requests from any relatives of the deceased aircrew...' In fact the MOD's performance to date shows precious little evidence of this. It should be borne in mind that *all* applications from relatives have been flatly refused; only two pilots have been recovered by the authorities: Flying Officer Gruszka after intervention by his former comrades, and Sergeant Scott after the Prince of Wales became involved. In view of this, and given the natural desire of most relatives to see their loved ones buried, it is easy to understand the frustration of enthusiasts and indeed why they have sought, on occasions, to take the law into their own hands.

Remaining with the subject of 'sympathetic consideration' to relatives by the MOD, I would refer to the following letter from M D Tidy, the AUS (Personnel) (Air), to the brother of Sergeant Scott and dated January 24th, 1992:-

Sir,

I am directed to inform you that your petition to the Queen about the fate of Battle of Britain aircrew listed as missing, and for whom there is no known grave, has been referred by Her Majesty to the Secretary of State for Defence.

I am further directed to advise you that where, because of the numbers involved, the pressure of events at the time and the problems of positively identifying the exact site of many wartime crashes the remains of a number of Battle of Britain casualties have not been recovered, it is current Ministry policy that the memory of the aircrew should be perpetuated through the memorial in St Clement Danes church in London.

This policy was widely supported during extensive consultations during 1981 with such bodies as the RAF Association, the Royal British Legion, SSAFA, the RAF Benevolent Fund and the War Widows Association, as well as various aircraft archaeological groups when the majority, but not the unanimous, view was that the aircraft wrecks themselves served as a fitting last resting place for the crews and there was strong opposition to the deliberate digging up of wrecks thought to contain human remains.

This is a most sensitive area where personal views are bound to differ but where the Secretary of State considers that the current Ministry of Defence policy continues to reflect the most appropriate balance between the different considerations involved. This does not, of course, necessarily preclude the situation as in the case of Sergeant Scott, where subsequent events have clearly enabled you and your sister's wishes finally to be met.

My own observations are that, firstly, the Runnymede Memorial would have been a far better example of official commemoration to quote (see Chapter Two), secondly that the first half of the final paragraph sounds like a definite 'side-step', and finally that although Sergeant Scott was indeed recovered, this was only *after* the intervention of the Prince of Wales, *not* merely upon application by the relatives mentioned.

On October 11th, 1995, the Head of CS (Sec) 2a, provided the Department's official response to my own various letters:-

Lord Howe has asked me to thank you for your letters of 13 and 23 September, concerning World War II aircrew still listed as missing, and to respond.

I am also responding to your letters of 19 and 28 June to both the Minister of State for the Armed Forces and this Secretariat, in which you made proposals, including a review of MOD policy on the non-disturbance of crash sites, which you followed up in your letter of 11 September. I realise that considerable time and thought has been put into these proposals but, as the Earl Howe, explained in his letter of 8 September, the MOD is satisfied that its current policy is both well founded and assures adequate protection.

Thank you for providing a copy of the response you have received from the BoBFA in which it is agreed that crash sites are fitting last places for aircrew killed in battle. I also note the view given on the erection of memorials. I can assure you that, as Earl Howe indicated in his letter, although careful consideration has been given to this, the difficulties presented (in addition to the exact location of the sites) prevent the Department from supporting such a proposal.

As regards the concerns you have expressed over the possible future activities of Mr Kirby, which you feel are reinforced by the recent article appearing in 'Aeroplane Monthly'. May I first clarify that the MOD has not been approached, either by Mr Kirby or any relatives, about the possible recovery of pilots mentioned in the article. As you are aware the Department gives sympathetic consideration to the views of the relatives of deceased aircrew and we would do so should we receive any approach from the relatives of these pilots. However, any decisions in such cases are made in close concert with the appropriate coroner and any recovery authorised as a result would be done under strict conditions, which may be imposed by both the MOD and the coroner.

I can further assure you that in all cases where we are alerted to a possible breach of the PMA we advise the MOD Police, who, of course, liaise with the civil police as appropriate.

Having repeatedly warned the MOD that unless positive action was taken in respect of the *Missing Few* there would definitely be further contravention of the PMA, I was not surprised when I heard about the August 1996 Duszinski excavation. On November 6th, I wrote again to the PUS, reiterating my previous proposals, receiving a response from the Earl Howe dated December 1st:-

Thank you for your letter of November 5 in which you raise, once again, the subject of unauthorised excavation of aircraft crash sites and their protection under the Protection of Military Remains Act 1986.

Recent developments concerning contravention of the Act had made it necessary for me to seek specialist advice and I am unable to give a full response at this time. I shall write giving a more detailed reply in due course.

Surely mounting an operation to recover the last missing pilot would be easier?

Wing Commander Hancock, to whom I had copied the Earl Howe's most recent letter, responded on December 15th:-

I was much impressed with the contents and hope that Lord Howe will take more action. I have sent a copy to my Chairman, Air Chief Marshal Sir Christopher Foxley-Norris, for his information.

When sending a complimentary copy of my sixth book, *Bader's Tangmere Spitfires*, to the AHB (RAF), I also provided copies of various correspondence concerning the *Missing Few*. On January 6th, 1997, the Head of the AHB, wrote back:-

As you know the MOD shares your concern about the activities of a minority of aviation archaeologists - a concern which I expressed publicly in the recent Meridian TV documentary.

You will be aware from the Earl Howe's letter of December 1st that the problem of giving adequate protection to sites is currently being given renewed consideration.

By March 4th, no further response had been forthcoming from the PUS, so I wrote again pressing the issue. To his Lordship's great credit, the following was penned on March 22nd:-

Thank you for your letter of 4 March on the subject of the 'Missing Few'. Since my last letter there has been no significant change. The subject of the protection of military remains is under review and I am obviously unable to give you a detailed response until that review has been completed. I will write again when I have further information.

I am sorry for the delay: the legal aspects are proving considerably more difficult than we first thought.

Now this was progress indeed. The very tone of his Lordship's letter suggested a certain amount of sympathy with our efforts. Shortly afterwards, however, the Conservatives lost the General Election which led to the appointment of a new, Labour, PUS. The change in government actually mattered very little to this project, in my opinion, as any correspondence would still be referred to the same civil servants to formulate a response. Since I commenced this campaign of correspondence, however, there have been major developments as the remainder of this book reports.

CHAPTER EIGHT

# The Missing Few

One question the reader may be considering is, 'how many of the Few remain missing but are believed to be buried at known crash sites?'

As we have seen, the family of Pilot Officer Clarke elected non-disturbance and commemorative arrangements near the crash site were made. The cases of Sergeants McNay and Duszinski apparently defy resolution; astonishingly, the remains of Sergeant Adair were destroyed. There are also other cases to consider.

### Pilot Officer Robert Henry Shaw: MIA September 3rd, 1940.

*Plt Off R H Shaw.*
*(Andy Saunders)*

The Kent County Council War Diary confirms that on September 3rd, 1940, there was a 'British fighter aircraft down in flames at 1042 hrs, near Park House, Chart Sutton'. At 1115 hrs a further report stated that 'Plane still burning fiercely - machine-gun bullets are exploding - no news yet of pilot'. Which aircraft was this?

An examination of Fighter Command operations for this particular day indicates that No 1 Squadron, based at Northolt, were bounced by Me 109s, probably of JG51, whilst on patrol over Kent. Two of the Hurricanes failed to return, P3044, flown by Flight Lieutenant Brian Hillcoat, and Pilot Officer Robert Shaw's P3782; both pilots were reported missing and remain so to this day. Squadron Leader Colin Birch remembers:-

At the time I was a Flying Officer and on the sortie in question flew as the third member of Flight Lieutenant Hillcoat's section. We were bounced by Me 109s with yellow-painted spiralling motifs of their airscrew fairing spinners. I stalled in a hefty 'g' turn and came to at 8/10,000 feet with no other aircraft in sight. I never saw either Hillcoat or Pilot Officer Shaw ever again.

Also flying was Pilot Officer Pat Hancock (now a retired Wing Commander and Honorary Secretary of the Battle of Britain Fighter Association {BoBFA}):-

After so long, I can only say that at the time I was convinced that I saw Robert Shaw in his parachute, drifting seawards.

Which pilot really had gone into the sea; Shaw or Hillcoat? It must be remembered that in 1940, British Air Sea Rescue (ASR) facilities were rudimentary, largely relying upon high speed RAF launches, civilian lifeboats and passing friendly vessels. Also, although German pilots were equipped with a flourescine dye, which coloured the water around them, our pilots had no such visual assistance when bobbing around in the murky Channel.

On September 29th, 1940, together with PC 265 Whyman of the Kent County Constabulary, personnel of the civilian contractors AV Nicholls attended the crash site at Park House. They discovered that the wrecked aircraft had already been removed by an RAF squad three days previously; Mr Nicholls subsequently made out his report to Squadron Leader Goodman of 49 MU, indicating the aircraft concerned to be Hurricane *P3782*: Pilot Officer Shaw's aircraft.

The pilot of P3782 was not recovered, however, and the aircraft is known to have buried itself deep into the ground at the edge of an apple orchard, adjacent to a small stream. An elderly couple living in a cottage nearby marked the site with a cross, and planted a small memorial garden. Sadly, after their death in the 1950s, the site became neglected until formation of the Headcorn branch of the Royal Air Force's Association (RAFA), which then assumed responsibility for the garden.

On Battle of Britain Sunday in 1970, a Memorial Service was held at Chart Sutton church before the garden was formally dedicated. A similar service has since been held annually at the garden, a popular local act of remembrance which includes a stirring fly past from a Battle of Britain Memorial Flight (BBMF) Spitfire or Hurricane.

Mark Kirby:-

> After the Gilders recovery I received a telephone call from the chap who looks after the memorial garden who told me that he was acting on behalf of the Shaw family. I was advised that they were quite happy with the current situation and would strongly object to any recovery. That being the case, we would not even consider interfering with the site. There are something like 19 members of the family who regularly attend the annual service, which I think is terrific.

**Sergeant Gerald Henry Edworthy: MIA September 3rd, 1940.**

Another casualty of September 3rd, 1940, was Sergeant Gerald Edworthy of 46 Squadron, operating out of Stapleford, who failed to return from combat with German fighters over the Essex coast. Information concerning enemy combat claims is scant, however (remembering that German time was one hour ahead of our own):-

JG51: four claims, 1130-1150 hrs, Thames Estuary.
JG27: five claims, 1120-1150 hrs, Thames Estuary.
JG26: nine claims, 1100 - 1130 hrs, Margate - Rochester.
III/JG26: 12 claims, 1120-1140 hrs, Southend - Chelmsford.
I/ZG26 and II/ZG26: no details, possibly between five - eight claims.

At 1035 hrs, a British fighter crashed near the River Crouch, and was engulfed by Redwood Creek. Given the fact that No 1 Squadron had been bounced over mid-Kent, some distance to the south-west, casualty records indicate that the only possible candidate for the Redwood crash is

*Sgt G Edworthy.*
*(Andy Saunders)*

Sergeant Edworthy; he remains missing to this day. In 1974, however, this site was discovered by the LAM; apparently a machine-gun access panel and various small items were recovered from the thick mud. Other enthusiasts re-excavated the site in 1981 but found nothing to confirm the identity of the aircraft concerned. Steve Vizard:-

The aircraft had exploded near the sea wall and all we could find was numerous fragments of the Hurricane. This was a shame as the pilot's sister, since deceased, was very keen that, if he could be found, her brother should be recovered.

Despite the families wishes and the efforts of enthusiasts, it appears as though Sergeant Edworthy will remain 'Missing in Action' for Evermore. There are others.

**Flight Lieutenant Percy Stevenson Weaver DFC: MIA August 31st, 1940.**

*Flt Lt P S Weaver DFC.*
*(Paul Weaver)*

Yet another example of the quality of such young men is Flight Lieutenant PS Weaver, reported missing on August 31st, 1940 (coincidentally 21 years exactly before I was born). Paul Weaver, the pilot's nephew comments:-

My uncle was born on September 18th, 1916. He was christened Percival Stevenson Weaver, Stevenson having been his mother's maiden name; as he did not like the name Percival, or 'Percy', he was called 'Steve'. His father, Ernest Norman Weaver, ran Weaver and Son, an old established business, in Broad Street, Bath, and the family lived at Lansdown House, Weston Village, Bath. Steve had two older brothers, George, who served with the Bristol Fire Service, and Norman (my father) who was in the West Somerset Yeomanry. There were also two sisters, Joan who sadly died young, and Phil.

Steve was educated at Fair Lea Preparatory School in Weston-Super-Mare, and, from 1929, at Dean Close School, Cheltenham. Whilst at school, due to his initials being PSW and there being a well known cartoon strip called 'Pip, Squeak and Wilfred', he acquired the nickname 'Squeak'. Academically he was to do well, and represented both his school and house in most sports, including hockey, swimming and shooting, the latter in competition at Bisley. He was also a bugler in the Officer Training Corps (OTC), there not being an Air Training Corps (ATC) at that time. He was apparently quite introverted and thoughtful, quiet but completely unflappable.

Whilst still at school he owned a motorbike on which he attempted to reach the School Corps Camp at Preston, but did not quite get there. He had to be fetched from the local railway station by Mr B. Maxwell Phair, the Dean Close master-in-charge of the camp, with whom he struck up a friendship. Subsequently Mr Phair lent Steve his 1930 Frazer Nash (HX 846), having first established that he was an excellent driver. The car had been used for racing, lapping Brooklands at 90 mph. Mr Phair became quite an influence on my uncle, and encouraged him to take an engineering career.

*Paul Weaver proudly displays the*
*Comet Racer model made by his*
*late uncle.*
*(KBoBM)*

In 1934, Steve went straight from school to an apprenticeship with De Havilland. He had been interested in aircraft since he and one of his sisters flew with Sir Alan Cobham's Air Circus. At De Havilland, one of his first jobs was to de-coke an engine of the Comet racer, the engines being dismantled for evaluation after winning the 1934 England to Australia Air Race. He made a model of one of the five Comets into which was put a piece of the carbon from his de-coking job.

He had a passion for fast vehicles and in 1935 bought a Model 90 Sunbeam motorcycle, followed by a 2 litre Lagonda (HW3792) and a Frazer Nash (BMP850). The latter was raced at Brooklands by Tony Law in 1935, so had quite a pedigree. A confirmed motoring enthusiast, he was a regular visitor to the Shelsley Walsh Hill Climb, Donnington Park circuit and Crystal Palace.

In October 1936 he left De Havilland in favour of a short service commission in the RAF. Naturally he wished to be a pilot, and successfully completed his flying training at No 8 Flying Training School (FTS), Montrose, thereafter first joining No 151 Squadron before being posted to 56 Squadron, also at North Weald, on September 13th, 1937.

At this point it is worth considering the training of a fighter pilot at this time. The procedure was that all operational training would actually be given on a squadron. This was contrary to the system which developed soon after war was declared whereby such instruction was provided by the OTUs; when the fighting began, squadrons were to find themselves far too busy to train new pilots up to 'combat ready' status. As Paul says, however:-

Before the war, 56 Squadron undertook much formation flying, mostly training for the Empire Air Days. This helped establish a rapport in the air so that pilots could predict each other's manoeuvres - very useful, I would imagine, in a combat situation. Of course pilots who arrived on the squadrons after the outbreak of war could not be given such experience.

The first squadron to receive the Hawker Hurricane was 111, which was given the job of evaluating the Merlin engine under service conditions. Throughout 1937/38, the squadron suffered several fatalities and, it is said, lost heart. Together with Rolls-Royce mechanics, the fitters of 56 Squadron made a major contribution. During this period before the war, on 56, each pilot had his personal Hurricane, fitter, rigger and mate. All damage had to be signed for and the aircraft were kept spotlessly clean - which must have been difficult due to the grass runways in existence at that time. Flying regulations were very strict; they had to telephone RAF Stanmore (Fighter Command HQ) for permission to use spare aircraft!

No 56 Squadron was a regular air force unit which had been amongst the Great War's most outstanding fighter squadrons. Even in 1937, when Pilot Officer Weaver joined 56, the memory of the squadron's august past was very much kept alive; Wing Commander 'Taffy' Higginson joined 56 Squadron as a regular NCO pilot on October 20th, 1937:-

In a room was displayed the uniform and Victoria Cross of McCudden, one of the Great War's most famous aces who had been a member of the squadron. Every new pilot was made to study the exhibition and salute upon leaving the room.

On September 3rd, 1939, Steve Weaver was enjoying leave with his family who were holidaying in the Lake District. In the middle of the night he was recalled to North Weald; later that morning the reason became obvious to all: Britain and France declared war on Nazi Germany.

Three days later saw the war's first aerial instance of 'Friendly Fire' when 56 Squadron was mistaken for Me 109s over Ipswich by 74 Squadron Spitfires. In the ensuing 'combat' the former unit lost two Hurricanes, one pilot being killed. It was a tragic mistake, but overall just one of numerous similar incidents which have punctuated military history ever since man first took up arms.

In early 1939, Weaver joined the North Weald Operations Room staff, being made Acting Squadron Leader and being paid accordingly. As 'Ops' Controller, his experience as a pilot of modern fighters was obviously a great advantage, but Steve himself was unhappy on the ground. He made representation to various senior officers, all apparently possessed of deaf ears, until Group Captain Victor Beamish reviewed the situation favourably and sent Weaver to fly with 56 Squadron's 'B' Flight during the early summer of 1940.

A little earlier that year 56 Squadron had participated in the Battle for France, flying daily patrols over the Continent from bases in No 11 Group; for four hectic days in mid-May, 'B' Flight actually operated from Vitry-en-Artois. During the French debacle 56 Squadron claimed a total of 35 aircraft destroyed. On May 31st, 1940, the squadron re-grouped at Digby, returning to North Weald on June 1st, from where it operated over France on a daily basis. Once Operation Dynamo was complete, together with the rest of Fighter Command, 56 Squadron awaited the onslaught on this island fortress. Frequently the squadron's pilots flew south-east from North Weald to Rochford, on the Essex coast, from which satellite airfield they would operate from before returning home at dusk.

Shortly after dawn on July 20th, 1940, Blue Section of 56 Squadron, comprising Flight Lieutenant 'Jumbo' Gracie, Flying Officer Weaver, and Pilot Officer Geoffrey Page, engaged a reconnaissance Ju 88, of 4(F)122. The enemy aircraft was shot down and forced-landed, in flames, at Cockett Wick Farm, St Osyth. The Hurricane pilots shared the victory, which was Weaver's first blood. 'Squeak' was actually to develop into a first class fighter pilot, whose claims can almost exclusively be cross-referenced with actual German aircraft down in the battle area.

On July 29th, Weaver claimed an Me 109 destroyed and on August 12th a Do 17. An Me 110 followed on August 13th, this being a machine of 3/ZG26 engaged on an escort sortie to Southend; the enemy aircraft exploded over Warden Bay, Sheppey, killing both crew members. Three days later, Sergeants Higginson and Whitehead shared the destruction of a Do 17 with Weaver, who by this time had been promoted to Acting Flight Lieutenant and made commander of 'A' Flight. This particular raider disintegrated over Whitstable Beach, the crew being buried as unknown in the local churchyard (see Chapter Ten). On August 18th, Weaver destroyed another 110 of 3/ZG26, this aircraft crashing at Bonnington (mystery surrounds the fate of this aircraft's crew who remain missing; some claim that they were buried in Lympne churchyard, but no trace of any such graves can be found today). On August 21st, a Do 17 of 8/KG2 was shared by Flight Lieutenant Weaver and Flying Officer Brooker, and on August 24th, Weaver forced an He 111 of 9/KG53 to ditch some 13 miles off Brightlingsea.

In early July, Squadron Leader GAL 'Minnie' Manton had been posted to command 56 Squadron; he recalls 'Squeak' Weaver:-

> From those hectic times I remember well one particular incident concerning him, probably because it occurred shortly after I had taken over the squadron following two-and-half years behind a desk at the Air Ministry. Every moment with 56 Squadron, therefore, was new and exciting for me. After only my first or second combat, I was returning to North Weald, trying to gather my wits, when another 56 Squadron Hurricane came alongside and formated on me. The pilot opened his hood, gave me a great grin, a thumbs up and then one finger to indicate that he had made a kill; it was 'Squeak'.

It seems that the quiet, introverted boy from Bath had found his calling.

At 1.30 pm on August 28th, Flight Lieutenant Weaver forced-landed at Eastchurch after his aircraft was damaged during an attack on a Do 17. Later that afternoon he was back in action, however, claiming an Me 109 destroyed over Dover. This was probably a machine of *Stab* I/JG3, flown by *Leutnant* Landry who baled out, being captured at Church Whitfield (but died on September 23rd of injuries sustained). The British Prime Minister himself, on an inspection of Dover Castle, saw this enemy aircraft shot down and personally visited the crash site. As he approached on foot, his bodyguard, Inspector WH Thompson, heard the great man remark 'I hope to God it isn't a British plane'.

By the end of August, the strain of combat was beginning to tell on 56 Squadron. By August 30th, the unit had lost 18 Hurricanes destroyed and six more damaged; one pilot had been killed, five were missing, and seven had been wounded. Although arrangements were in hand to withdraw 56 Squadron from the front line, there was more action to come for the exhausted pilots.

August 31st, 1940, was an extremely hard contested day for both sides as the *Luftwaffe* continued pounding No 11 Group's airfields. The first raid of the day started fighting its way over England shortly after 0800 hrs: 30 Do 17s of III/KG2 bound for Debden and those of II/KG2 heading for Duxford in what was planned as a simultaneous attack. The Debden raid was escorted by *Hauptmann* Horst Liensberger's Me 110s of V(Z)/LG1, II/KG2's escort being provided by *Hauptmann* Hans Schalk's III/ZG26. From mid-August onwards, *Reichsmarschall* Goering had ordered that the Me 109s would provide a close escort. Consequently practically all of *Luftflotte* 3's Me 109s were transferred to *Luftflotte* 2 and based in the Pas-de-Calais. This gave *Generalfeldmarschall* Albert Kesselring an overwhelming provision of escorts for attacks against south-eastern England. Even so the Me 109 only had fuel enough for 20 minutes flying time over England, so although now operating from the Pas-de-Calais, London remained the practical extremity of their range. Nevertheless, despite the northerly locations of the targets in question on August 31st, Major Adolf Galland's JG26 *Schlageter* was tasked with providing a *Geschwader* strength *Freie Jagd*; such sorties were unpopular and on one occasion Galland lost 12 fighters through lack of fuel: five forced-landed on the French coast, seven ditched in the dreaded *Kanal*.

This mighty *Valhalla* actually passed over the North Weald Sector en route to Debden and Duxford. At 0820 hrs, Flight Lieutenant Weaver led eight 56 Squadron Hurricanes off from their forward base at Rochester. The Hurricanes clawed for height over the Thames Estuary, where Galland's 109s hung dangerously at combat altitude; even against the 109s alone, the Hurricanes were outnumbered some 13:1. By 0840 hrs, II and III KG3 were streaming south-east, heading home with their Me 110 escorts. Weaver's Hurricanes were vectored to 15,000 feet and ordered to patrol Chelmsford. No 56 Squadron climbed away to the north, in an attempt to gain height away from the actual combat zone, before turning eastwards. Near Chelmsford, the Hurricane pilots sighted elements of KG3, slightly above with its fighter escort strung out behind. It was a time for instinctive action, and Weaver, without hesitation, led his penny-packet force on a collision course with destiny.

The 109s, enjoying the height advantage, pounced on the Hurricanes. It was all over in a matter of minutes; of the eight Hurricanes, four were destroyed: Pilot Officer Mounsdon, Flying Officer Westmacott and Sergeant Whitehead all baled out safely, but Flight Lieutenant Weaver was reported missing. In return, Flight Sergeant Higginson shot down *Leutnant* Heinz Ebeling, *Staffelkapitaen* of 9/JG26, who managed to glide his crippled Emil well beyond Dover before baling out; he was later rescued by the *Seenotdienst*.

Again, so hectic was the press, it is impossible to be certain regarding who-shot-down-who. However, from the evidence available, it appears the most likely candidates for the destruction of Weaver's Hurricane are *Feldwebel* Luders and *Unteroffizier* Dahmer, both of 6/JG26 and who each claimed Hurricanes over Brentwood (Luders at 0942 hrs and Dahmer three minutes later, German time relates).

The Essex County Council War Diary entry for 1009 hrs, August 31st, 1940, states:-

> Crashed aircraft report. British Spitfire found West Point, Osea Island. Pilot believed drowned at 0845.

Information continued to be received from the Eastern Report Centre; 1123 hrs:-

> Plane now identified as V7373, confirmed pilot drowned.

The Situation Report Form, timed 1655 hrs:-

> One British plane marked V7373 crashed at Osea Island River Blackwater, pilot drowned.

V7373 was actually a Hurricane, which survived the Battle of Britain and did not, therefore, feature in Fighter Command's casualties on this day. V737**8** was Flight Lieutenant Weaver's Hurricane. Yet again it seems as though a contemporary clerical error has much to answer for. Also, how was it 'confirmed' that the pilot had 'drowned'? A body was not recovered, and there are no 'unknown' burials which could possibly relate to this casualty. The family, however, were told that a sock was washed up with a 'Weaver' nametape.

After Flight Lieutenant Weaver's death, the squadron received notification that he had been awarded a well deserved DFC. The Operations Record Book recorded:-

> He had been given the DFC this very day and was a great loss to the squadron.

In 1995, Group Captain Manton recalled the sad news of the 24-year-old Weaver's death:-

Squeak went missing on the very day I left the squadron on posting to command RAF Manston, or at least what was left of it! They rang me from North Weald the next day to tell me the news, such was Flight Lieutenant Weaver's standing in the squadron.

Whilst most eulogies tend to go overboard, my recollections of Squeak Weaver are all clear and sincere. Of all the boisterous, reckless young men in the squadron he stood out. He was universally liked and because of his irrepressible good humour, enthusiasm for life and everything he did, and his fearless attitude to the battle, he became an absolute lynch pin in the squadron. His loss was, I know, felt most deeply at a time when we all tried to shrug off such things for obvious reasons.

The following day, the remnants of 56 Squadron were withdrawn to the quieter atmosphere of Boscombe Down in 10 Group. That a young man of Flight Lieutenant Weaver's quality was killed just the day before this withdrawal makes his death even more tragic. Had he survived, there can be little doubt that he would have gone on to become an even more successful fighter pilot and leader.

Officially, Flight Lieutenant Weaver remains missing. However, an analysis of Fighter Command losses on August 31st, 1940, and given the other evidence available (despite the incorrect recording of the serial number of his Hurricane), there can be no reasonable doubt that Weaver crashed at West Point, Osea Island. The important thing now is that the pilot's sister does *not* wish for his remains to be disturbed.

Flight Lieutenant PS Weaver DFC is remembered on the Runnymede Memorial and on the Weston-Super-Mare war memorial. It is my view that a more personal commemoration is also appropriate on Osea Island, an idea supported by the Weaver family and towards which we are now working (see Epilogue).

*Proud parents, with their daughter, at Buckingham Palace after receiving their son's posthumous DFC; Flt Lt Weaver was sadly reported 'Missing' on the very day this award was notified.*
*(Paul Weaver)*

**Flight Sergeant Eric Edward Williams: MIA October 15th, 1940.**

Currently, the most significant name, however, amongst the *Missing Few* is that of Flight Sergeant Eric Edward Williams, of 46 Squadron, who failed to return from combat with enemy fighters over the Thames Estuary on October 15th, 1940. The unit's Operations Record Book relates:-

Commencing at 1230 hrs, a patrol was carried out by the Squadron over Seven Oaks and Gravesend. While flying at a height of over 20,000 feet, they were vectored East and attacked from the sun by a flight of Me 109s, three of our aircraft were shot down. P/O Reid attacked and destroyed one of the enemy but the others made a successful escape. It is recorded with regret that P/O PS Gunning was killed when his aircraft crashed near Little Thurroch, Essex. F/Sgt EE Williams was missing from this patrol, but it was later confirmed that his machine had crashed near Gravesend and his death had occurred. Sgt Gooderham escaped from his aircraft by parachute. He was suffering from burns but was not detained in hospital.

On this date, Major Galland led JG26 on three escort missions to *Jabos* attacking London. During the morning sortie, *Unteroffizier* Scheidt destroyed a Spitfire of 92 Squadron over Maidstone, but during the afternoon I & II *Gruppe* clashed with Hurricanes over the Thames Estuary; four were destroyed without loss, the German claims being as follows:-

| | |
|---|---|
| *Unteroffizier* Scheidt, 1/JG26: | One Hurricane south of Gillingham, time u/k. |
| *Oberleutnant* Henrici, Sfl Kpt, 1/JG26: | As above, 1.55 pm (German times). |
| *Hauptmann* Adolph, Grpn Kdr, II/JG26: | One Hurricane, London, 2.10 pm. |
| *Oberleutnant* Grawatsch, St II/JG26: | As above, 2.12 pm. |

Any of the foregoing claims could concern Flight Sergeant Williams.

According to the Kent County Council War Diary on October 15th, 1940:-

At 1425 hrs one British plane down at Albion Parade, Map Ref: 090908. Pilot missing, plane burnt out, slight damage to wharf buildings.

Some fifteen minutes later, another Hurricane crashed near Gravesend, its pilot having baled out safely.

On March 25th, 1981, the AHB responded to an inquiry to David Smith, the enthusiast from Chatham, Kent (responsible for the recovery of Pilot Officer Doulton, see Chapter Four), concerning various Battle of Britain crashes; regarding Sergeant Williams, the civil servant concerned stated that:-

The Hurricane aircraft piloted by Flight Sergeant EE Williams was shot down at approximately 1300 hrs on the 15th October 1940. The aircraft crashed on to a wharf, about one mile east of Gravesend Ferry Station.

For times in various contemporary records to be at odds is not unusual, given the circumstances of their reporting, but the location given by the AHB tallies with Albion Wharf. It seems, therefore, that Flight Sergeant Williams and Hurricane V6550 crashed through the roof of a warehouse-like building at Barton's Timber Wharf. Interestingly, the 46 Squadron ORB confirms his death at Gravesend.

*Flt Sgt Eric Williams: the last of the* Missing Few?
*(Via Mark Kirby)*

The crash site was first located by Steve Vizard in 1981, and in 1990, David arranged a memorial nearby, in Gordon's Gardens, which was unveiled by the pilot's widow, Mrs Joan Eddleston (who came over from Canada for that purpose). Moved though she was, Mrs Eddleston remarked that it would have been better if her husband 'had been buried'.

*The widow of Flt Sgt Williams, Mrs Joan Eddleston (right), pictured at his memorial in Gordons Gardens, Gravesend, 1990. (Via Mark Kirby)*

It may be that this will come to pass, as our Epilogue relates, but the events leading up to this possibility require reporting.

During the course of my research for this book, it became clear that there were three views on the subject of missing pilots: the MOD's stance, that shared by Mark Kirby and his associates, that the only relevant view was that of the pilots' families and that if they required 'private recoveries' then these should go ahead come what may, and mine that such things should only be undertaken within the law and with the authorities involved.

In the interests of fairness, and to provide the reader with the full facts, in addition to contacting the MOD, I wrote to Mark Kirby on November 3rd, 1997, inviting his view for publication. I was not surprised, this being in the wake of Meridian's *Grave Robbers* television documentary (which featured the question of the missing and, as its title suggests, showed aviation archaeologists in a less than favourable light), to receive a response from John Tickner, the solicitor acting on behalf of Mark Kirby and friends. Further correspondence and faxes proved to all involved that mine was an honourable exercise, seeking to present the *facts comprehensively*, even though I disagreed vehemently with Mark Kirby's apparent approach. As this was ongoing, my long-standing friend and associate Andrew Long discovered via the Internet that things regarding the Gilders case were not, perhaps, as had been previously reported. Having considered this new information, although as a serving police officer I could never condone anyone either taking the law into their own hands or breaking it for whatever reason, I did start to sympathise with Mark Kirby's actions and suspected that there was much more to this than at first met the eye.

On December 16th, 1997, I received a telephone call from Steve Vizard whose name is synonymous with the recovery of Battle of Britain aircraft. Steve had also been featured in the *Grave Robbers* programme and was represented by Mr Tickner. Nevertheless, Steve was anxious, for a variety of reasons, to help with my book. We all, it seemed, agreed that the truth must now be told. Our conversation was lengthy, and upon conclusion I was surprised just how much we did have in common. I was even more surprised that we both agreed that, as a first choice, recoveries really should be undertaken by the authorities; we parted company, however, at the point where a refusal was forthcoming from the MOD, our respective views being as previously stated. One thing was clear, however: we were both extremely moved by the question of the missing pilots and, in our own ways, were prepared to do something about it. Far too many, it seems to me, have either sat on the fence or murmured spitefully in the shadows; here, however, was someone else prepared to stand up and be counted.

The following evening I received a call from Mark Kirby. As with Steve, we immediately 'hit it off'. It became immediately apparent to me that he was totally genuine. Although for professional reasons I could not condone what he had done, I began to admire the courage and passion Mark placed in his conviction. To say I was surprised was an understatement, which just goes to prove that you cannot believe all you either hear on the 'grapevine' or indeed read in the papers.

The next morning I was contacted by Andy Saunders, another enthusiast who, like Steve Vizard, has been involved with such matters since the interest first began. Andy had also been subjected to a degree of bad press in recent times and I now have no doubt that much of this is both inaccurate and unfair. Again our conversation was protracted, and again I found that we had a great deal more in common than ever I would have previously thought possible. On the basis of all this (although Andy Saunders himself was unable to attend) a meeting was arranged at John Tickner's house in Farningham, Kent, for Sunday, December 21st, 1997. Needless to say, I looked forward to it with great interest.

On that day thick fog clung to the motorway but my mood did not reflect the depressing weather. On the contrary, I was delighted that we were all going to sit around a table to try and achieve a common aim together. For over six hours, John Tickner, Steve Vizard, Mark Kirby, Andrew Long and myself went over the whole subject. Each recovery was discussed in detail, and, as Mark showed me various correspondence and photographs concerning Sergeant Gilders, there were tears in his eyes; here indeed was a genuine person, without a doubt. As Steve pointed out, if people stopped and thought about it, the collection of aircraft parts could not possibly have anything to do with it; in the event of a body being recovered, the aircraft parts were seized as evidence, so the enthusiasts had nothing to gain in that respect. He had a valid point, I had to admit. The evidence was also produced to prove that certain personal possessions of recovered pilots were only retained at the behest of relatives. All of this, of course, rather flew in the face of various rumours and allegations prevalent for so long in enthusiast circles.

By the meeting's end, we were all clearly on the same side and agreed that we should move forward together, placing before the MOD a test case, as the reader will see. So was born the Missing Pilots Research Team (MPRT). Only two weeks earlier, after 11 years, we had disolved the MST; they say that as one door closes another opens, and being a great believer in that everything happens for a reason, I have no doubt that this development was perhaps ultimately inevitable: even a question of destiny perhaps? Many enthusiasts, however, will undoubtedly be surprised to learn of this rather unexpected alliance, especially considering my previous strong views and writings on the subject. All I can say is, read this book and consider the evidence yourself. Only after that exercise can a truly informed opinion be claimed; after all it is fair to say that in such matters I am probably more informed than most, but until this first meeting not even I was *completely* informed

It was a new beginning reflecting a spirit of working together, within the law, and projecting a new image and approach. Would my point, that if handled correctly the MOD could be persuaded to co-operate, be proved? Only time would tell.

*What can be achieved: the KBoBM at Hawkinge,*
*inspiring words at an inspirational venue.*
*(Andrew Long)*

CHAPTER NINE

# The Bell Road Burials

his chapter deals with two particular cases identified (literally) during the course of my research and provides an example of how protracted, frustrating and complicated such an investigation can become.

### Pilot Officer John Wintringham Cutts: MIA September 4th, 1940.

The Kent County Council War Diary (a mine of information) records at 1403 hrs on September 4th, 1940: 'Spitfire down at Chart Sutton. Pilot baled out'. It was the first in a series of clerical errors which have led to one of the Few being denied a named headstone.

At lunchtime on September 4th, 70 He 111s and Do 17s, escorted by a staggering 200 Me 109s, crossed the Kent coast before splitting up to attack Canterbury, Faversham, Reigate, Redhill and Eastchurch. Nine squadrons of No 11 Group engaged, No 222's Hornchurch based Spitfires intercepting the Canterbury bound raiders. The Spitfires' approach was detected by the ever watchful 109s, which lost no time in meeting the threat. Over West Malling, Sergeant Ramshaw was shot down and killed, and Pilot Officer Carpenter was literally blown out of his cockpit; Pilot Officer John Wintringham Cutts and Spitfire X4278 remain missing, officially at least.

The records of 49 MU dated September 7th, 1940, confirm Spitfire X4278 to have come down at Chart Sutton, and indeed that the matter was again 'In hand'. The recovery of Pilot Officer Cutts was never announced, however.

Hornchurch, Setember 1st, 1940:<br>
Spitfire X4278 in the foreground, reported Missing<br>
in Action with its pilot, Plt Off J W Cutts, on September 4th.<br>
(KBoBM)

*Plt Off J W Cutts: a posthumous friendship?*
*(KBoBM)*

On September 28th, the burial of two unidentified airmen took place at Bell Road Cemetery, Sittingbourne, Kent. According to the Register of Burials, a Certified Extract from which I have, the airman buried in Plot W, grave 143, had died on 'September 14th', at 'Amberley Farm, Loose'. More errors.

In fact, on September 4th, the Chart Sutton Spitfire's pilot had not baled out, as stated by the Kent County Council War Diaries; neither had he died on 'September 14th' at 'Amberley Farm, Loose', as per the Register of Burials.

Loose is actually a suburb of Maidstone, some two miles north-west of Chart Sutton. There has never been an *Amberley Farm* at Loose, and throughout the entire Battle of Britain no aircraft appears to have crashed in that district. There is, however, an *Amberfield* Farm at Chart Sutton (so-called due to the distinctive colour of the flint found there), and a Spitfire crashed there on September 4th (as confirmed by 49 MU). The only Spitfire pilot remaining missing from action on the day in question is Pilot Officer Cutts. I would suggest that it was he who was buried as unknown in W143. In 1972, the crash site was the subject of a major excavation by the A&TRG, during which, amongst many other items, the complete propeller boss and blades were recovered. Although nothing bearing the aircraft's serial number was found, those items recovered did at least confirm it to be a Spitfire (and are now displayed at the KBoBM).

Battle of Britain Historical Society (BoBHS) member and former police officer Ted Sergison of Staplehurst, considers himself to be the unofficial custodian of the Amberfield Farm crash site. On October 1st, 1996, he wrote to me:-

> Over the past few years I have kept an eye on the crash site and know that several people have undertaken unauthorised digs there. The most recent, I am told, yielded at least one machine-gun, my information coming from a most reliable source. I actually attended the site shortly after one of these incidents and was horrified to see pieces of bone on the surface. These I identified as being from the vertebra. There were also traces of other bones which I could not identify. Before leaving I respectfully covered these remains with soil.
>
> As there is a public footpath around Amberfield the site is easily accessible and I have no doubt that it is only a matter of time before someone else comes along to 'have a dig' and at which time these human remains will surface again.

The enthusiast responsible for the unauthorised excavation told me that:-

> The landowner did not mind us going in there so we had a poke about. The weapon recovered was in extremely bad condition, and the main area of impact was just ash, very badly burnt indeed. Even a section of the windscreen, made of armoured glass, was found to be melted. We did not find any human remains, and I am genuinely surprised to hear that bone fragments have been found on the surface.

To my mind, two things arise out of this case. Firstly, the fact that the aircraft was so badly burned provides the reason why the pilot concerned, who I believe was buried at Bell Road in W143, was unidentified. This may explain why no human remains were reported after the A&TRG's major recovery in 1972.

Secondly, this seems to be an identical case in principal to that of Sergeant Caldwell in the Severn Estuary (see Chapter Six), and entirely suited to a clearance operation, landowner permitting, by the RAF. So long as any aircraft remains exist at this well known location, enthusiasts will periodically pick over the site. Furthermore, I find it rather disturbing that what appear to be human remains can occasionally be viewed adjacent to a public footpath; not something I would like either of my children to find, not to mention being a somewhat unfitting situation for one of Churchill's Few.

It is my firm belief that a clearance operation should be authorised by the MOD, and the site cleared of all aircraft parts and any human remains discovered. Furthermore, the unknown airman's in W143 should be named: Pilot Officer JW Cutts.

## Sergeant John Brimble: A tale of two graves.

*Sgt John Brimble (right), who has two graves.*
*(Andy Saunders)*

On September 14th, a Hurricane crashed at Chart Sutton, near Park House Farm. A Certified Extract from the Register of Burials concerning the second unknown airman interred at Bell Road on September 28th, in W49, reads: 'Died at Park House Farm, Chart Sutton'. The date of death is given as September 14th, 1940. Furthermore, the Death Certificate relating to this burial, again a Certified Copy of which I have, confirms these details.

The September 14th Chart Sutton Hurricane site was excavated in 1980 by the TAM (see Chapter Four), from which were recovered the mortal remains of Sergeant John Brimble. This appears to me to be a case almost identical to that concerning Pilot Officer Noble: sufficient remains were recovered at the time to justify a burial (albeit as unknown in this case), further parts of the body, together with identification, later being discovered in 1980. The remains recovered at that time were buried at Brookwood under a named headstone.

For one person to have *two* graves is unacceptable, and as the evidence is readily available I cannot understand why the authorities did not rectify this matter in 1980. Surely those remains at Bell Road in W49 should now be added to those of Sergeant Brimble now buried at Brookwood?

On October 3rd, 1996, I wrote to CS (Sec) 2a providing the information above regarding Pilot Officer Cutts, together with photo-copies of the original Bell Road Burial Register, and the Certified Extracts. On November 7th, the correspondence was acknowledged 'with interest'. The information regarding Sergeant Brimble was sent to the CWGC, but apparently this letter went astray; consequently I duplicated the work, the Commission's Enquiries Section responding on January 8th, 1997:-

Your letter has been passed to our records section and they are investigating the situation and we will contact you when a decision has been reached, this may take some time as the staff in that section have a heavy schedule of day to day work and this sort of research has to be fitted around it. Checking with MOD and other authorities is not something which can be done quickly.

By March 4th, I had received no response from the MOD excepting the brief acknowledgement; I wrote again, noting that the decision regarding Sergeant Caldwell had been made immediately, over the telephone in fact. On March 20th, the Department responded:-

I have not, so far, found any documented evidence to confirm that the aircraft which crashed at Amberfield Farm was the one flown by Pilot Officer Cutts. On the contrary there is speculation that his body lies beneath the RAFA Garden of Remembrance at Chart Sutton.

Should a decision be made to excavate the crash site, the agreement of the landowner would need to be sought. If the field is under crop, it is likely that he would wish to set the time for any proposed excavation.

Should you have any documentary evidence to support the belief that the body of Pilot Officer Cutts lies at Amberfield Farm, it would be helpful if you were to pass copies to this office.

I am sorry you feel this case should have been given more priority but, as you know, there have been a number of organisational changes at Innsworth since the case involving Sergeant Caldwell. You may not be aware that this section is now part of the Personnel Management Agency with responsibilities for current day RAF casualties as well as those who died during hostilities. Naturally, as this involves co-ordination of funeral arrangements, priority must be given to new cases as they occur.

I think *exasperated* would be a fair description of my feelings upon receiving that letter. We have already reviewed in this book sufficient evidence from official records to prove that Pilot Officer Shaw lies beneath the Garden of Remembrance; his aircraft was, of course, a *Hurricane*, parts of which have been found over the years, so why should the Department 'speculate' that Pilot Officer Cutts, a *Spitfire* pilot, actually crashed there? Furthermore, as previously indicated, parts of the Amberfield Spitfire are even on show at Hawkinge. The problem, it seems to me, is that frequently those in authority, and indeed specialist departments, know *less* than we enthusiasts; with all due respect to all concerned, that appears to be a fact.

On March 24th, I wrote to the MOD with the crux of these observations. The response came on April 14th:-

I am afraid a final decision on the excavation at Amberfield Farm has yet to be made but I have passed your letter to a higher authority for information. The pressures on the MOD's budget are such that requests for funding have to be prioritised. It can take some time to get financial approval.

By July 20th, I had heard nothing further from the CWGC regarding Sergeant Brimble, and so wrote again to the Enquiries Section:-

I write to remind the Commission that a response is still awaited regarding the cases of both Sergeant Brimble and Pilot Officer Cutts, full details and evidence regarding which I sent to you last November. That the former airman now has two graves I believe is of particular concern and the information supplied proves this to be the case without a doubt.

Whilst I appreciate that pressures of work often prevent swift responses to such issues, I feel that eight months is long enough for someone to have looked at this. I would be obliged, therefore, for anything you could do to expedite the situation and I look forward very much to hearing from you as soon as possible.

The Commission wrote back on July 25th:-

I must explain that the information was passed to the RAF Personnel Section at Innsworth and any decisions taken will be theirs not the Commission's.

When they decide what should be done then no doubt they will let us know but it is not up to the Commission to press the matter.

As soon as we are informed of their decisions then we will let you know what action we may need to take.

Incredible! Why not tell me that eight months previously? A telephone call to RAF Innsworth revealed no trace of the paperwork concerned.

I feel that the way the authorities have treated these matters is totally unacceptable. Their job has, after all, been done for them gratis by a civilian, at his own expense and initiative, who has obtained and provided copies of all vital documentation. I can fully understand how some enthusiasts have become so frustrated with the MOD that they have felt no option but to act outside the law. My reaction, however, was to send the following letter, on November 11th, 1997, together with a copy of this chapter and further copies of the relevant paperwork, to Mr Tony Blair, the current British Prime Minister and amongst the world's greatest exponents of 'People Power':-

November 11th, 1997

Dear Mr Blair,

I am writing in the hope that you can help me rectify matters regarding the burial of two Battle of Britain pilots, the crash site of one of which has been subjected to unauthorised interference and at which human remains are sometimes exposed. The Ministry Of Defence seem either unable or reluctant to make a decision regarding these cases, and after an appropriate time lapse I feel that I have no option but to bring the problem to your attention, so strongly do I feel about this. The circumstances of each case are comprehensively outlined in the draft of Chapter Nine from my forthcoming book, *Missing in Action: Resting in Peace?* (Ramrod Publications, release date May 1st, 1998) which I enclose for your information. I have also enclosed the following exhibits:-

DS1:     Photo-copy of the Bell Road Burial Register, relevant entries highlighted.

DS2:     Certified Extracts of above.

DS3:     Certified Copy of Death Certificate relating to the 'unknown' airman killed at Park House Farm, Chart Sutton, Kent, on September 14th, 1940.

DS4:     Sketch-plan of Spitfire crash site at Amberfield Farm, Chart Sutton, Kent.

In 1990, the Prince of Wales intervened on behalf of the family of a missing Spitfire pilot, Sergeant Scott, which led to the RAF recovering this airman who had been 'missing' for 50 years. For that reason I have also copied this letter and enclosures to His Royal Highness.

Also currently in question is the Ministry Of Defence's policy regarding the question of pilots reported missing in 1940 but who are now believed to remain buried with the wreckage of their fighters in southern England. Over the years a number have been recovered in an unauthorised manner by various enthusiasts, and recent events have proved that the Protection of Military Remains Act, 1986, provides little deterrent due to the level of fines possible under this statute. I had corresponded regarding this matter with the former Parliamentary Under-Secretary of State for Defence, the Earl Howe. I have also enclosed a copy of the last letter received from his Lordship and trust that the recent change in government will not mean that no reply will actually be forthcoming from the Department.

I look forward very much to hearing from you and hope that this letter and enclosures have been of interest.

Yours sincerely,
Dilip Sarkar

A copy file was also sent to St James's Palace. On November 14th, Captain Richard Larkin of the Welsh Guards, The Temporary Equerry To HRH The Prince of Wales, responded promptly:-

The Prince of Wales was most grateful for your letter of the 11th November 1997 asking for any assistance in the matter of the final resting places of Battle of Britain airmen. The chapter that you sent made good reading and the remarkably detailed research that you have done on the subject is as impressive as it is commendable.

However, as you can imagine, His Royal Highness has many demands on his time and despite close links with the Royal Air Force he will be unable to become personally involved on this occasion. His Royal Highness greatly appreciated you bringing this matter to his attention and has asked me to pass on to you his very best wishes.

Mr Blair's Correspondence Secretary, Mrs T Sampson, responded on December 5th:-

The Prime Minister has asked me to thank you for your recent letter and the enclosure.

Mr Blair hopes you will understand that, as the matter you raise is the responsibility of the Ministry of Defence, he has asked that the letter be forwarded to that Department so that they may reply to you direct on his behalf.

On December 24th, 1997, I received an encouraging telephone call from Mr Peter Edwards, Head of the Casualty Section at the RAF Personnel Management Agency and we agreed to meet early in the New Year (see Epilogue). On December 30th, I received a written response on behalf of the Air Secretary:-

Dear Mr Sarkar,

Thank you for your letter dated 11th November 1997 addressed to the Prime Minister and regarding the burial of Battle of Britain pilots and the Protection of Military Remains Act 1986. The subjects fall within my area of jurisdiction and, therefore, I have been asked to reply.

I understand that, in the past, you have corresponded with a number of individuals within the Ministry Of Defence and whilst, to outward appearances, little progress has been made in resolving the issues of concern to you, I can assure you that they have not been forgotten. You will already be aware of the wide ranging subjects my staff have to contend with and you will also understand that we cover historical aircraft occurrences for the whole of World War II. Given this scenario we cannot always give priority to the Battle of Britain era as you would wish us to do. That said, I will bring you up to date on the issues you have raised.

Regarding Battle of Britain pilots, and particularly the case of Pilot Officer Cutts, our primary difficulty has always been the fact that, **officially**, there is little documentary evidence to support your view as to his fate and current whereabouts. The only evidence pointing to Amberfield Farm and Bell Road Cemetery is circumstantial. Your own research has uncovered possible 'errors' in official documents (burial records) of the time. Unfortunately they **are** official records and we must abide by them, and so long as it is Department policy not to permit disturbance of sites where crew are still officially listed as 'missing', your beliefs must remain exactly that - beliefs. The only possible way forward from this impasse is for the Department to undertake a clearance of the site. At this stage of the proceedings I am unable to state if this will be possible, however, I shall ask my staff to review the evidence with this in mind.

The case of Sergeant Brimble is somewhat different. Suffice to say that the documentary evidence is sufficiently compelling to cause us to seek further advice from the Commonwealth

War Graves Commission.

The final issue, that of the protection of military aircraft crash sites under the 1986 Act, has been under review now for almost a year. Your most recent letter specifically draws attention to the level of fines possible. Since there has not yet been a successful prosecution where a fine was awarded, it is somewhat difficult to judge its deterrent merits. Our primary concern in reviewing the Act was in the wording of some of the clauses which, you may recall, caused the Crown Prosecution Service (CPS) to halt their last prosecution. That case resulted in a meeting between the Department and CPS and suggestions as to how the Act might be reworded to automatically include **all** unauthorised excavations, regardless of the status of the site and quantity of remains recovered. Our proposals are currently in the hands of the Ministry Of Defence Legal Adviser and we await the outcome of deliberations.

I trust the above information is of assistance to you. I have asked Mr Peter Edwards, with whom you spoke prior to Christmas, to contact you early in the New Year to progress matters further.

Naturally I was pleased to receive this written response, especially in relation to both Sergeant Brimble and the PMA. On January 6th, 1998, I wrote back:-

I am grateful for your letter of December 30th, which I obviously read with great interest. I would comment as follows:-

Firstly, the pressure under which your department works is understandable, but what else are we to think, other than that little is being done, when correspondence goes completely unac-knowledged? With all due respect, this is a justified critiscm which I am sure you will accept.

Whilst it is true that my main interest is in the Battle of Britain period, it is incorrect to state that I wish the Department to give related cases priority over other casualties. This is not so.

Regarding the case of Pilot Officer Cutts, there is further evidence other than that suggested by official records. Firstly, the Amberfield Farm site was the subject of a major recovery in 1972 which confirmed the site to be that of a Spitfire Mk IA (recovered artefacts now being displayed at the Kent Battle of Britain Museum). Previous correspondence with the MOD (Mrs D Sheldon refers) confirmed that within the Department there is speculation that Pilot Officer Cutts lies beneath the garden of Remembrance at Chart Sutton. This is **totally incorrect**, as confirmed by the official records of 49 MU (*The Battle of Britain Then & Now Mk V Edition*, page 410 refers) stating that Shaw's **Hurricane**, P3782, crashed at 'Park House Farm, Chart Sutton', that, of course, being the memorial garden's location. Furthermore, a colleague recently found a fragment of Hurricane lying on the garden's surface, so we can **definitely** rule out this being the last resting place of Pilot Officer Cutts. The confirmation of Shaw's aircraft serial number by 49 MU also means it is incorrect to speculate that Flight Lieutenant Hillcoat (P3044), like Shaw also missing on September 3rd, 1940, may lie under the memorial garden. Furthermore, if Spitfire losses are studied for the whole of September 1940, it is clear that X4278, the aircraft flown by Pilot Officer Cutts, is the only candidate for the Amberfield crash; a report by Squadron Leader Goodman, the CO of 49 MU, covering the period September 1st - November 29th, 1940, confirms, on September 7th, not only P7382 (Shaw's aircraft) down at Chart Sutton, but also that of Pilot Officer Cutts: Spitfire **X4278**; the recovery of both aircraft, he states, is 'In hand' (see extract from said report attached).

On the basis of the foregoing, I would suggest that in the absence of identification being discovered at the Amberfield site, the alternative evidence could not be stronger regarding my belief that the 'unknown' airman buried in plot W143 at Bell Road is Pilot Officer JW Cutts. Surely it would be most unreasonable of the Department, given the 'new' information from 49 MU, not to now accept this to be the case and respond accordingly?

I remain of the firm opinion that, to prevent any further unauthorised interference at the Amberfield Farm crash site, the Department should organise a clearance operation; if this then revealed identification, then that would obviously be a most welcome bonus. Needless to say, should the MOD's budget be an insurmountable problem, we would be prepared to undertake this work at our own expense and on the Department's behalf. In these days of privatisation, is such a proposal not worth considering, especially given our experience in the recovery of wartime aircraft?

I am pleased to hear that the case of Sergeant Brimble has been referred to the Commonwealth War Graves Commission, although the Commission was provided this information some considerable time ago; its response was to forward the information to the Department for a decision! Nevertheless, I do hope that the required end result will ultimately be achieved.

Your comments regarding the review of the Protection of Military Remains Act was most interesting and it is reassuring to know that the matter is in hand. The wording of the Act, relating to fines, concerns the 'statutory maximum' (fine), which at present is £5,000. To increase this, in terms of PMA contravention, would surely mean increasing the 'statutory maximum', which would clearly be impossible. It will be interesting to see what the legal experts ultimately decide.

As you say, Peter Edwards and I spoke, at length, on the telephone, and have agreed to meet later this month to discuss further the points raised above and other matters. I look forward to this opportunity, and of course if I am able to assist the Department in any way, at any time, please do not hesitate to contact me.

On January 16th, Andy Saunders and I discussed the Cutts case with positive result. Many years ago, Andy had been given the records of AV Nicholls & Co, the civilian sub-contractors assisting 49 MU in aircraft recoveries (see Chapter One). Amongst these papers was the following letter, dated September 19th, 1940, to Mr Nicholls from Squadron Leader Goodman:-

Confirming telephone instructions, herewith authority to collect the following aircraft and deliver to this Unit; for further delivery instructions:-

Hurricane. Spit End, Elmley, Isle of Sheppey.
Fighter. Harty Sidings, Sheppey.
Hurricane. Wellingbourne.
Spitfire X4278. Amberfield Farm, Chart Sutton.
Hurricane P7382. Park House Farm, Chart Sutton.

This was incredible, official confirmation that X4278 (Cutts) crashed at Amberfield Farm, and P7382 (Shaw) at Park House Farm, Chart Sutton. With this document, any (unreasonable and inaccurate) speculation that Cutts lay below the memorial garden was totally disproved. It is interesting that the report also mentions a Hurricane at Spit End; this was the aircraft of Flight Lieutenant Hugh Beresford who remained missing until 1979 (see Chapter Six).

Furthermore, Andy had the Death Certificate regarding the burial in W143, confirming that the remains had been 'found at Amberley Farm, Loose Rural District' on September 14th, 1940. The relevant point is that although 'Amberley' again appears, 'Loose Rural District' makes some sense of the reference to Loose in the Bell Road Burial Register. Although, as previously discussed, Loose is a suburb of Maidstone, Amberfield Farm is actually within its parish and rural district. In my opinion, the fact that Pilot Officer Cutts was lost 10 days before the body was found at 'Amberley' is not crucial as there appears to be, by a process of elimination, no other contender. The word 'found' is relevant, however, as this again confirms the Burial Register's inaccuracy; it states that the 'Amberley' death occurred 'on' September 14th, which is not necessarily correct. I would suggest that September 14th was the date on which 49 MU eventually arrived at this site, recovering the pilot's remains at that time, although I accept that without documentary confirmation, this is mere supposition no matter how well founded. Nevertheless I looked forward to putting all of these facts to the MOD, face-to-face, in due course. I was determined that the evidence and common sense would prevail.

CHAPTER TEN

# In the Heat of Battle

As we near the conclusion of this book, it may surprise the reader to learn of the sheer volume of existing ambiguities concerning unknown burials generally. As we have already seen, crucial mistakes were often made in the heat of battle. Believe it or not, there are further RAF Battle of Britain casualties with more than one grave, and these cases are currently being researched with a view to putting the evidence before the authorities. There are also other cases where an unknown burial can be connected with a particular crash site. One such case, that of 603 Squadron's Flight Lieutenant Rushmer (reported missing on September 5th, 1940), has only recently been resolved. During the 1970s, Andy Saunders connected the unknown airman buried at All Saints churchyard, Staplehurst, with this casualty and informed both the family and authorities accordingly. No conclusion was reached, however, and there the matter lay until Jean Liddicoat and Ted Sergison united forces (working independently of Andy) to push the matter further. In late 1997, the authorities accepted that the All Saints airman was Flight Lieutenant Rushmer and, at the time of writing, erection of a named headstone is awaited. Sadly, one of the pilot's sisters died shortly before release of this news, which raises another important issue: unless these matters are expedited, how many other close relatives will pass on whilst the fate of their loved ones remain a mystery?

**Squadron Leader Hilary Richard Lionel Hood: MIA September 5th, 1940.**

*Sqn Ldr 'Robin' Hood (left)
and Flt Lt Terry Webster
DFC.
(Via Philip Harvey)*

Over the years I have had the pleasure of communicating with numerous fellow enthusiasts from all over the world, and am frequently pleasantly surprised at the volume, depth and standard of research often undertaken by would-be amateur historians whose efforts are completely self-funded. Amongst these erstwhile researchers is Philip Harvey, who also feels passionately regarding cases concerning missing airmen. The following account by him proves my point, especially as the matter investigated by Philip also concerns the events of September 5th, 1940:-

The events leading to Squadron Leader HRL Hood DFC being officially listed as 'Missing' are complex; contemporary records are now incomplete, contradictory and vague. By assembling the facts available, supplemented by eye-witness accounts and tangible relics, a clearer picture emerges which could possibly explain Squadron Leader Hood's true fate.

At 1500 hrs on Thursday, 5th September 1940, Squadron Leader Hood led 12 Spitfires of 41 Squadron off from Hornchurch with orders to patrol Maidstone at 15,000 feet. Hood flew as Blue 1 of 'B' Flight, rearguard cover being provided by 'A' Flight, led by Flight Lieutenant Norman Ryder. The scramble was a hurried affair and, as the squadron still climbed away from Hornchurch, a large enemy formation was encountered flying up the Thames Estuary towards London: He 111s, Do 17s and Ju 88s escorted by Me 109s. Other Fighter Command squadrons had been vectored to intercept this raid; the Hurricanes of North Weald's 249 Squadron, Debden's 17 and 73 Squadrons, Northolt's 303 Squadron and Stapleford's 46 Squadron. 41 Squadron's Pilot Officer 'Wally' Wallens:

As usual I was flying Number 2 on 'Robin' Hood leading 'B' Flight and, being unable to gain height advantage and position in time, 'Robin' put us in line-astern and open echelon port and attacked head-on, a desperate manoeuvre that could age one very prematurely. Within seconds all hell broke loose and, as the action developed, 'B' Flight was overwhelmingly attacked by the 109s.

Only four Spitfires from 41 Squadron failed to return this engagement. Pilot Officer Tony Lovell had parachuted out of his burning aircraft over South Benfleet and returned to Hornchurch. Pilot Officer Wallens had forced-landed, near Orsett, with a cannon shell through his leg and had been taken to hospital. One Pilot was confirmed killed in action. His body was identified as that of Flight Lieutenant Webster DFC. Squadron Leader Hood was officially recorded as 'Missing.'

Another casualty of this interception and relevant to our investigation was Flight Lieutenant Reg Lovett DFC of 73 Squadron. That unit's Intelligence Report states that:

A & B flights took off from Castle Camps at 14.55 hrs with orders to orbit North of Gravesend. At 1510 approx. enemy formation sighted about 1 mile to south being engaged by A/A at 19,000 feet.. E/A flying westwards in 3 vics, in line astern. A Flight led by F/Lt Lovett DFC attacked the rearmost formation. Leader commenced quarter attack, but as E/A travelling very fast it developed into astern attack at 350 yards. Leader experienced considerable cross fire and was hit by MG fire on the port side. Closed to 300 yards, but hit on starboard leading edge by cannon shell, and in breaking away a Spitfire came upwards almost vertically and they collided. Leader baled out and landed near Rochford, uninjured after a delayed drop.

Throughout this engagement, numerous aircraft fell to the earth below, observed by many military, police and ARP personnel, in addition to the general public. The majority of aircraft fell in the Nevendon area of Essex, adjacent the A127, the main arterial road between London and Southend-on-Sea. The ARP telephone messages recorded:

At 15.30 approx. at Nevendon 0.25 mile SE Nevendon Hall. Machine Wrecked. Spitfire. Pilot baled out unhurt.

At 15.30 approx. Wickford. Fuselage, part body and one wing fell Cranfield Park Road 400 yards SW Tye Corner. Wing bears marking K, believed British.

Further details were recorded in the War Diaries of local military units. The aircraft losses noted in the ARP records were also present in these diaries, but the following additional information was noted:

312 Searchlight Battery RA: A wing apparently belonging to a British fighter was recovered at M177010. One British pilot picked up dead on the Arterial Road at M1710.

37th AA Brigade RA: Spitfire crashed in Nevendon M180101. The pilots parachute became entangled with the plane and he was killed.

John Watson was working at 'The Old Cricketers' garage in Nevendon:

I could see and hear aircraft very high. Something fell into the centre of the junction and Mr Ryder, the proprietor of the shop on the corner, ran out and picked up what turned out to be a 303 bullet. As I looked up I saw an aircraft coming down. Part of the wing of this aircraft was missing and it was accompanied by a Spitfire wing. I was certain that I saw a complete Spitfire with it's wing cut off, both tumbling down together. The wing came down in the direction of Wickford; the aircraft I believe may be the one which came down about 75 yards North of the present junction of Courtaulds Road and Archers Fields, on land now belonging to Essex Water and part of the treatment works. I could see a parachute coming down in the direction of North Benfleet.

As all this was going on, my attention was drawn to a Messerschmitt 109 which was also coming down in a perfect tail spin and on fire. I looked back just in time to see the British aircraft crash down nearby. As soon as I finished work, I was able to visit the crash site of the aircraft. The Hurricane had been badly damaged on hitting the ground and I was not able to get too close.

For many years, various publications suggested that Terry Webster and Robin Hood had collided, but it appears more likely, given the evidence from the 73 Squadron report, that Webster actually collided with Flight Lieutenant Lovett's Hurricane. Therefore, it seems reasonable to suggest that the Hurricane which crashed a quarter of a mile South East of Nevendon Hall/ Archers Fields was the aircraft vacated by the latter. This is corroborated by items recovered by Roland Wilson, on whose land the aircraft crashed. A Hurricane radio mast and Merlin II engine limitations plate were removed from the wreckage before the area was cordoned off by the authorities.

The fragmentary remains of the aircraft reported on the Northern side of the arterial road were found by numerous local people. Walter Smith found the seat of the Spitfire, used by the family as a makeshift chair for many years. Roland Wilson encountered the entire tail section of the Spitfire and, daunted by the size of his souvenir, satisfied himself by removing the rudder mass balance weight and stub aerial for his collection. More importantly, some weeks later, Roland discovered an unopened parachute pack in open fields North of where he had found the Spitfire tail section. The parachute was marked 'WEBSTER'. Roland handed over the parachute to Nevendon Police, who congratulated him for his honesty. This event was recorded briefly within the Brentwood & Southend-on-Sea Police diary:

17.35 30.9.40. Nevendon. Parachute and engine of a Spitfire which crashed 5.9.40 found in a field at Nevendon.

A day or so after the 5th September, 13-year old Sam Armfield and his younger sister, Brenda, were on their way through scrubland, known locally as 'The Police Bushes' on account of being opposite the A127 Police Houses. The youngsters were en-route to fish at a pond. In the wasteland they were astonished to encounter the virtually intact wreckage of a Spitfire which was lying on the surface and hidden by the tall bushes. The entire fuselage forward of the control panel was missing, but there was no other indication of battle damage. Sam recalls:

The Spitfire obviously couldn't be seen from the main road, otherwise soldiers or Home Guard would have been guarding the aircraft. I don't recall any signs of bullet or cannon holes and no blood or anything in the cockpit - we would have looked for that sort of thing. The tailwheel was clear of the ground and we all commented on what a good wheelbarrow wheel it would make. None of us could remove it. We all took turns to climb in the cockpit and pretend to fly it, but we were all reluctant to press the gun firing button on the control column. We were able to remove the gun inspection covers and discovered that all the ammunition had been exhausted and the webbing belts were slightly frayed from passing through the guns.

Brenda Armfield recalls that she discovered the severed port wing on the other side of the bushes, some eight feet away from the main wreckage. The wing had separated at the last inboard gun position and the Browning machine gun was exposed. Brenda used the small screw-driver from her sewing kit to take off the ammunition feed chute, which was already loose. The boys were jealous of her prize and made unsuccessful attempts to remove the gun itself.

Every evening after school the youngsters would rush home to play on the aircraft and make further attempts to remove various souvenirs. Although they told no adults about 'their' Spitfire, after about a week they arrived to find that the wreck had been removed. The engine of this aircraft appears to have fallen further West of the main crash location, near Great Wasketts Farm. Apparently, the Merlin was shattered and many fragments lay scattered about the impact spot. The engine was guarded by a member of the LDV, although Sam Armfield managed to obtain some souvenirs which have since been identified as being of Rolls-Royce Merlin origin.

Although the eye-witnesses have identified this aircraft as a Spitfire, the lack of battle damage confirms the fact that it could not have been Lovett's Hurricane which had been badly damaged by the enemy - 73 Squadron Intelligence Report refers. Only one Spitfire remains unaccounted for: Squadron Leader Hood's P9428 'EB - R'; this may well have been his aircraft.

It is quite possible that the Spitfire discovered by Sam Armfield was that referred to in the War Diary of the 37th AA Brigade RA, although it is unclear why the wreckage was not discovered by the authorities earlier. The report states that 'the pilots parachute became entangled with the plane' prior to his death. However, there appears to be no firm evidence to confirm the recovery of the body of the pilot from this particular aircraft, or it's subsequent burial. It is understood from the Pitsea undertaker, Mr Green (who was responsible that day for the recovery of a German Casualty, *Hauptmann* Fritz Ultsch) that the bodies of all airmen were initially taken to local mortuaries before being collected en-masse by Frank Rivett & Sons of Hornchurch. The bodies were then transferred to RAF Hornchurch for distribution and burial. The records of Frank Rivett & Sons were apparently destroyed during the blitz.

The absence of any records relating to local undertakers makes positive identification of the final resting place of this pilot difficult to establish. Allied airmen were generally buried in the graveyard at St Andrew's Church, Hornchurch, unless it was requested otherwise by the family of the deceased. *Luftwaffe* casualties were interred at Becontree Cemetery and it is here that an interesting anomaly has been noted. Within the Barking & Dagenham Burial Register, Entry No. 5176 records the burial of a Walter Heatz/Heatry on September 12th 1940 in grave B1:684 - the day after the burial of *Hauptmann* Fritz Ultsch. The GWGC have confirmed that they have no record of any relevant casualty and, consequently, the body has never been transferred to Cannock Chase. Further research is currently being undertaken to examine the possibility that this grave may actually be the final resting place of Squadron Leader Hilary Richard Lionel 'Robin' Hood DFC.

In conclusion, it is believed that whilst attacking the bombers head-on, 'B' Flight of 41 Squadron were bounced by JG54. The exact cause of Squadron Leader Hood's loss remains unconfirmed, although there is one combat claim by 1/JG54 which *may possibly* relate to this casualty. Hood appears to have baled out, but his parachute became entangled with his aircraft with fatal consequences. Spitfire P9428 then tumbled down, engine-less and minus its port wing, landing near the arterial road in Nevendon. Whatever injuries Squadron Leader Hood sustained whilst baling out will never be know, but it must be presumed that they were such that personal identification was impossible. As it has recently been accepted that Flight Lieutenant Rushmer lies in the 'Unknown' grave at Staplehurst, there are no other unidentified RAF casualties with this date of death. Could it be, therefore, that at some point between collection of the body and it's eventual burial, a mistake has been made leading to Hood's burial as a non-existent German airman? I doubt we will ever know, but from the evidence available, and fantastic as this theory sounds, it has to be considered a very distinct possibility.

We may never know the truth regarding Squadron Leader Hood's fate or indeed last resting place, but I am sure we are all agreed that this research is of the highest standard for which Philip should be commended. If more enthusiasts were moved to undertake constructive research work such as this, history would be well served.

Perhaps not surprisingly given the circumstances of both their deaths and burials, much ambiguity exists regarding *Luftwaffe* casualties. David Brocklehurst and I hope that certain matters can be resolved in time, and would refer the reader to the following Me 109 casualties as examples:-

### *Leutnant* **Erich von Fonderen, III/JG3.**

Reported missing on August 18th, 1940. Believed crashed near Bredhurst, Kent. No where is it stated which churchyard he is buried in.

### *Oberleutnant* **Rudolf Krafftschick, 1/JG27.**

Shot down on September 18th, 1940, and crashed at 1230 hrs in Squirrels Wood, Stockbury, near Sittingbourne, Kent. Although a post-war history of JG27 states that Krafftschick was captured, as his watch, cash and parachute release buckle were amongst items recovered by enthusiasts during the 1970s, this would appear incorrect. No human remains were ever reported, and there are no unknown German burials which are contenders for *Oberleutnant* Krafftschick. This *Emil* was a *Jabo*, however, and its SC250 bomb exploded on impact. Whether this would have obliterated any trace of human remains is a moot point, so perhaps the German authorities should be invited to re-excavate this site?

### *Unteroffizier* **Erich Clauser, 9/JG27.**

On September 20th, 1940, the *Luftwaffe* made its first *Jabo* attack against London. Several bombs were dropped on the capital, at random from high altitude, and several waves of Me 109s on *Freie Jagd* sorties swept over Kent. Released from the close bomber escort role, the *Jagdflieger* gave Fighter Command a salutary lesson reminder of just how dangerous they were. Four RAF pilots were killed, offset on the balance sheet against one enemy pilot: *Unteroffizier* Erich Clauser. The German had been shot down at 1210 hrs by 72 Squadron's Sergeant Rolls:-

> I was Red Two in a section told to intercept the enemy fighters. We took off at 1040 hrs and after having completed a patrol by ourselves were instructed to rejoin the rest of the squadron as the leading section. We did this and met the enemy near Canterbury. We were climbing up towards one batch of Me 109s. I soon found myself over Ashford and unable to see any of the squadron near me. I was flying along at 22,000 feet when I saw what appeared to be a Spitfire or a Hurricane diving down to 16-18,000 feet and then climbing again. I decided to have a look at it so got into a position so that I had the sun behind me and could see the machine clearly. As it came up in the climb I saw plainly that it was actually an Me 109 with a yellow nose and fin. I let it climb up again and waited, thinking perhaps it would dive again. It did so and then I dived out of the sun onto its tail and waited for it to climb before I pressed the tit to fire. I let it have about three seconds fire and the 109 did a stall turn to starboard and I followed it. I saw a large black piece break away from the side of the cockpit on the port side. I got it in my sights again as it turned and let it have another four second burst. This time I saw smoke and what appeared to be oil and water coming from underneath it. It turned to dive and as it did I let him have a final burst when the whole back of the cockpit dropped away and the rest dropped down towards cloud. This was at about 12,000 feet. I flew through the cloud and made for the aerodrome as I only had 10 gallons of petrol left. I watched the spot where the machine went in and it was near Wye, between a wood and lake so far as I could make out from my own position. I landed back with three gallons of petrol and a leaky glycol seal.

As the raiders left only *Unteroffizier* Clauser behind when they withdrew back across the *Kanal*, there is no doubt that he was Sergeant Rolls' victim that autumn morning. The Me 109 concerned crashed and burnt out at Ospringe, Kent. At the time, the pilot's remains were recovered but could not be identified. Consequently the remains were buried locally as an Unknown German Airman at St Peter & Paul churchyard. As Unteroffizier Erich Clauser was the only German airman missing over England this date, and given the evidence from Sergeant Rolls' combat report, surely the GWGC would have to name this headstone accordingly?

### *Unteroffizier* **Hans Bluder, 4/JG26.**

This pilot was lost during a *Geschwader* strength escort mission to *Jabos* attacking London on October 1st, 1940. Although some sources credit this loss to Squadron Leader Finlay and Pilot Officer Adams of 41 Squadron, JG26 expert Don Caldwell states that the 109s were bounced from above by a lone Polish Hurricane of 303 Squadron which shot down Hans Bluder. Again, this machine was a *Jabo* and is believed to have exploded upon impact. One report states that due to the explosion, 'little remains of the pilot were ever recovered'; what happened to those remains, however? Where were they buried? If somewhere as unknown, again, could the authorities be persuaded to accept that the remains concerned are those of *Unteroffizier* Bluder, the only German airman missing over England this date?

### *Unteroffizier* **Karl Geiswinkler, 6/JG53.**

Possibly another *Jabo* pilot, Geiswinkler was shot down by Sergeant Fokes of 92 Squadron at 1030 hrs on October 26th, 1940. The Me 109 crashed at Chalklet Farm, Pembury, near Tunbridge Wells, Kent. Again, the violence of the crash meant that the pilot could not be identified at the time. The body was buried as unknown in Tonbridge Cemetery, where it remains today. Unteroffizier Geiswinkler is the only Me 109 pilot missing over England this date; the other, *Oberfeldwebel* Oskar Strack, was shot down into the Channel. Is this another headstone that should be named?

Needless to say, there are others. Ambiguities also exist regarding a number of Me 110 casualties; the following are just two examples:-

### *Oberfeldwebel* **W Stange &** *Unteroffizier* **H Hesse, 3/ZG26.**

This *Zestorer* was shot down by Flight Lieutenant Steve Weaver (see Chapter Seven) of 56 Squadron at 1340 hrs on August 18th, 1940. The aircraft crashed at Bonnington, near Lympne in Kent. Photographs of the crash show it to have been of a surface nature, although the aircraft concerned was badly broken up. According to at least one source, the crew, who remain *Vermisst*, were buried as unknown at St Stephen's, Lympne. No headstone confirming such a burial exists in the churchyard today, so were Stange and Hesse moved to the *Soldatenfriedhof*? Has their grave been lost in the undergrowth at St Stephen's? What really did happen to them? Who cares now, I wonder?

### *Unteroffizier* **R Mai and** *Unteroffizier* **J Gebaur, 1/ZG26.**

Another casualty of August 18th, this Me 110 was shot down by Pilot Officer Flinders of 32 Squadron and crashed at 1345 hrs at Rough Common, Harbledown, Kent. The machine was also engaged by AA fire and exploded on impact. Records state that no trace of the crew was ever found, but David Brocklehurst's local enquiries revealed an eye-witness who recalled human remains being buried in a nearby back garden!

## The Seasalter & Whitstable Do 17s.

The crew from the Do 17 shot down at Whitstable are buried as unknown in the local churchyard. Two of the Seasalter crew are missing. The KBoBM have recovered the identification plate from the Whitstable aircraft and have recently been given that from the Seasalter crash. From these crucial pieces of evidence it is hoped that the crew lying at Whitstable churchyard can now be identified in the hope that a named headstone could be erected.

David also points out that although some sources record *Leutnant* Mollenbrok missing after the crash of a 3/KG3 Do 17 at Eastry on August 16th, in 1990 Herr Mollenbrok visited the KBoBM and was therefore very much alive 50 years later!

Some may wonder, even after so long, why any interest is being shown in German casualties. The reason is quite simply for the sake of history. Whatever the politics of these Teutons, they too were victims of what in Germany is now known as 'Hitler's War'. These matters require resolution just as much as those ambiguities concerning the Few. In respect of the German issues, it would be essential to gain access to the records of the AHB, which include burial returns for all German airmen interred in the UK. These reports list exactly what was buried and what personal possessions etc were recovered from the corpse beforehand. A morbid task, but a necessary one nonetheless.

The following letter from the German Embassy in London, received by Andy Saunders and dated February 26th, 1996, provides some indication of the likely reaction of the Germans to such matters:-

> Thanks to your endeavours it has been possible to establish the names and fates of German air crews and also to identify graves here in England...... I would like to take this opportunity to thank you for your valuable work and your contribution to Anglo-German reconciliation and friendship.
>
> V. Zimmer, Colonel, GAF.

A somewhat different reaction to that generally displayed by our own authorities, I think it fair to say.

EPILOGUE

# Back to the Future

It is an unexpected bonus for me that, as a result of the research project this book represents, many enthusiasts have freely given of their information, and, more importantly, we are all now talking and working together within the law. I started out with the *strongly* held view that recoveries should only be undertaken in an authorised manner and by Service personnel; although I remain inflexible regarding my belief in the former, having listened to the views of others, especially given the prevailing financial climate, a compromise may be possible regarding the latter.

We are all agreed that if relatives require a recovery then this must be done, and that the Secretary of State should therefore accordingly task the RAF, or indeed some other Service unit to either undertake or supervise such work. Our collective experience also indicates that on certain occasions it is necessary for all concerned to share resources and knowledge for the required conclusion to be achieved (case of Sergeant Caldwell refers, see Chapter Six). Personally, for obvious reasons, I draw the line at operating outside the law, and believe that sufficient pressure could legally be brought to bear to influence matters. Steve Vizard adds his view:-

> We are agreed that the emphasis of such an operation should be on the authorities, if at all possible and that, of course, is a matter for the MOD. If money is a problem, as we believe it is, there are enough of us to fund the recovery privately. We would be happy to do this, for *no* personal gain whatsoever, but because we feel so strongly about the question of missing airmen. To simplify matters, why does the MOD not task us accordingly, but have an official present to oversee and supervise, as indeed was the case with Pilot Officer Francis?

The enthusiasts concerned certainly have great experience regarding the recovery of wartime aircraft which could be placed at the MOD's disposal, and in the prevailing climate of privatisation, is such an idea really so extreme?

I was interested to receive the opinion of Mike Llewellyn, also involved with the interest since it began (see Chapter Three, Flying Officer Gruszka refers):-

> I still feel now as I did 30 years ago: it has never been the job of aviation enthusiasts and relic hunters to recover the RAF War Dead. Back then, like most normal folk I hope, we were disturbed by the thought of human remains and quite honestly would not, by choice, wished to have been involved.

Clearly all involved share a passion for the Battle of Britain, but are divided on the question of the *Missing Few*. This, of course, proves the MOD's point that no matter what decision is taken, it would be impossible to please everyone.

As previously indicated, on December 24th, 1997, I was delighted to speak on the telephone with Mr Peter Edwards, Head of the Casualty Section at the RAF Personnel Management Agency; he said:-

I can understand that this is an emotive issue, and of course, especially as an ex-RAF man, I am not personally without sympathetic feelings. The problem is, however, that our small section does not deal with just the Battle of Britain, regarding which you are principally concerned, but with service casualties as a whole. We have always felt that if we make an exception for one then the floodgates would be opened; the resources and cost involved in such an operation would be too horrendous to contemplate. We just do not have those resources. It is very difficult, therefore, to satisfy all parties.

By conclusion of our conversation, however, Mr Edwards had agreed to further consider the case of Pilot Officer Cutts (see Chapter Nine) and also to meet with me to review the case of Flight Sergeant Williams. At this juncture, therefore, let us examine the Williams case in greater detail.

In March 1995, Mrs Eddleston, the pilot's widow, received a letter from a former member of the defunct LAM, informing her that the Barton's Wharf site was shortly to be re-developed and requesting approval for his desire to recover the aircraft. The 80-year-old lady responded via another researcher, Terry Williams, who had been her point of contact for many years, requesting further information. Although Mrs Eddleston remained enthusiastic regarding a recovery, the attempt was unsuccessful (for reasons as will be explained). Had the Flight Sergeant been recovered in such an unauthorised manner, however, I would suggest that, in the wake of the Gilders furore, strong action is likely to have been taken against those concerned. On June 19th, 1995, however, Mrs Eddleston sent the following via Terry Williams:-

To whom it may concern.

I give my approval for Mark Kirby to locate and recover the body of Flight Sergeant Eric Edward Williams, Service No: 562960, killed in action on 15th October 1940 and whose plane is believed to have crashed at Barton's Timber Wharf, Gravesend, Kent.

As the reader is already aware, on December 21st, 1997, Andrew Long and myself met with Mark Kirby and Steve Vizard at the home of solicitor John Tickner. After that meeting a pleasantly surprising rapport and friendship rapidly developed between all concerned. On January 3rd, 1998, Andrew and I again made the long journey to Kent and joined Mark and Steve at Albion Walk. The weather was appalling, high winds and lashing rain, and we found Barton's Timber Wharf a derelict and desolate place located on the banks of the Thames Estuary. The building itself was hangar-like, and in a state of disrepair. Within, the thin concrete floor was broken in several areas where attempts had been made in 1995 to locate the Hurricane (using for reference a photograph of the original building showing the damaged roof). The problem is that metal detectors are useless due to the building's steel girders. Even the Forster bomb locator used by Steve and Mark, or the Aquascan Magnetometer preferred by myself, would be of no use given such conditions. The only possibility of locating the point of impact was if a ground penetrating radar, of the type used during the Cromwell Street murder inquiry, could be used. Steve had a contact, so it was decided that he should put the case forward with a view to securing such assistance. My job was to collate the evidence to put before the MOD later that month.

As we walked away down Albion Parade, through the derelict buildings of a once busy dockland, Mark Kirby summed up, quite simply, the way we all felt:-

It 'aint right is it, that poor old Eric should be left down there in such an 'orrible place?

*An appropriate resting place for one of the Few? The derelict
Barton's Timber Wharf, Albion Parade, Gravesend,
pictured in January 1998.
(Andrew Long)*

He was right; beneath the thin concrete floor of a ramshackle, derelict warehouse is not a fitting last resting place for one of the Few.

Whether the required end result is possible depends now upon the capabilities and availability of modern science, notwithstanding the co-operation of the MOD. The plan put forward is one of mutual co-operation, as with the Severn Estuary project, given that both sides have information, knowledge, expertise and contacts which, if brought together, could successfully resolve this 'sad, sad situation' (with apologies to Sir Elton John). The agreement I ultimately hope to reach with the MOD is that if the Hurricane can be located, it will be recovered. If this ever goes ahead, in addition to the satisfaction at having played a major part in arranging recovery of the last known missing Battle of Britain airman, for me personally there would be the satisfaction of having brought together many threads of this complex enthusiast sub-culture to work together and within the law. Most importantly of all, for the pilot's widow Mrs Joan Eddleston, it would be a dream come true. Perhaps by the publication of this book, the outcome will already be widely known; I hope so, either way.

Also, following the inaugural meeting of the MPRT on December 21st, 1997, it was decided that memorials should be arranged in respect of Flight Lieutenant Weaver, Sergeants Edworthy, MacNay, Duszinski and Adair. This, at least, will ensure that these heroes will never be forgotten. Pilot Officer Clarke and Flight Sergeant Williams already have such markers, so even if recovery of the latter is ultimately impossible, for whatever reason, at least this fine young man's sacrifice is commemorated in a more personal manner than mere inclusion on the Runnymede Memorial.

As ever the research for this book has been an adventure, but in this case a particularly enlightening one. I have been pleasantly surprised, nay astonished in certain cases, to receive terrific support and help from numerous enthusiasts, many of whom I had previously only heard of by name and, sometimes, poor reputation. All I have found to be warm and genuine enthusiasts, notwithstanding our continued differences of opinion regarding certain issues; it seems to me that far too many have murmured spitefully in the shadows, having taken heed of frequently inaccurate and exaggerated stories often stimulated by jealousy. It really is about time this nonsense stopped and we all united and worked together. Bill Bond, founder of the BoBHS, agrees with me that the time has come for an 'amnesty' and that all applicants, without exception, should at this juncture be welcomed into the Society. To increase the volume of our combined voices, I would therefore urge *all* enthusiasts to join the Society. For too long, in my opinion, the enthusiast movement has been fragmented and divided; indeed, as Mike Llewellyn says, even 30 years ago it lacked 'leadership and direction'. Is it not time, for the good of our heart-felt cause to see the Battle of Britain appropriately recorded and commemorated, for us to start afresh, to start working properly together and building a new basis of trust, honesty, professionalism and responsibility? Only *together* will we become a voice which must be listened to regarding matters pertaining to our passion for Battle of Britain history.

In conclusion, I hope that the reader has enjoyed a fascinating read, and is now, like me, *informed*; if that has been achieved, the production of this book has been justified. With so many enthusiasts now offering, on an unprecedented basis, assistance regarding recoveries and associated activities, we are already considering a further volume on this subject, concentrating more on the stories of particular casualties and excavations. In addition, the Continental situation requires clarification, and recoveries undertaken across the Channel also need to be reported upon; unfortunately the constraints of space meant that such a chapter had to be deleted from this book, so I look forward to expanding upon this material in the sequel volume. It goes without saying that I would welcome contact with any readers involved with the recovery (past or present) of (in particular) Battle of Britain aircraft, and I can always be contacted via Ramrod Publications.

Never forget: We *Will* Remember Them.

*The next generation: James Sarkar (then aged three years) astride the equally mud encrusted engine of Spitfire LZ996!*
*(Author)*

# STOP PRESS!

As some of the cases related in previous chapters were subject to ongoing enquiries when we went to press, this section is included at eleventh hour to update the reader on certain developments to date; these are, in fact, significant.

On Tuesday, 10th February, 1998, I at last attended RAF Innsworth for a meeting with Mr Peter Edwards, Head of the Main Casualty Section. We jointly reviewed evidence relating to the following cases:-

### Pilot Officer JW Cutts

It was accepted that there was no 'Amberley Farm, Loose', and that correctly the reference was to Amberfield Farm in the Loose Rural District. The 49 MU records previously provided confirmed Spitfire X4278 at Amberfield Farm (having crashed on September 4th, 1940). The Death Certificate stated that the 'Amberley Farm' body had been 'found' on September 14th, *not* that death had occurred that day. On this basis it was accepted that the 'unknown' remains buried in plot W143 at Bell Road, Sittingbourne, were indeed those of Pilot Officer Cutts.

The evidence was subsequently presented to the CWGC, by Peter, and likewise accepted. We now await news of the erection of a named headstone.

### Sergeant JJ Brimble

As the Death Certificate gives the actual date of death as September 14th, 1940, at Park House Farm, Chart Sutton, and burial of those remains confirmed in the Burial Register as 'Unknown' in plot W49, it was agreed that this must be Sergeant Brimble. As the site was excavated by Steve Vizard in 1980, and a further quantity of remains recovered which were identified and buried at Brookwood accordingly, it was also accepted that Sergeant Brimble did indeed have two graves. This scenario has also now been accepted by the CWGC and we await with interest how matters will progress. Unfortunately enquiries to trace the Brimble family, with which Steve Vizard and the authorities were in contact with in 1980, have proved negative.

### Pilot Officer RH Shaw

Given that Cutts crashed at Amberfield Farm, and Brimble at Park House, and because 49 MU also confirms the serial number of Shaw's Hurricane at Park House Farm, it had to be accepted that Shaw did crash at what is now the Memorial Garden. We are both agreed, however, that it is impossible to conclude, *given the evidence available*, that this pilot remains buried at the site (although I personally believe that this is the case), and therefore no progress can be made regard-

ing this location becoming an officially recognised grave. Nevertheless, at least it has been officially accepted that *Pilot Officer Shaw* crashed at this location, something never, in fact, in any
doubt. The Shaw family has been made aware of this development.

**Sergeant EE Williams**

All I can report is that this case remains 'under consideration' by the MOD; perhaps by publication of this book the outcome may be common knowledge. The day after my meeting with Peter
Edwards, however, I received a telephone call from Meridian Television informing me that on the
previous Sunday a camera crew had attended Barton's Timber Wharf to film an illegal recovery
attempt by two amateur enthusiasts. Although these individuals were unaware of our efforts be-
hind-the-scenes, conducted in a thoroughly responsible, professional and law abiding manner,
the incident highlighted my point that unless the MOD takes appropriate action, such *fiascos* will
persist. Fortunately nothing was found during this haphazard and misguided attempt, the motives
for which can only be considered highly questionable.

Returning to Innsworth, there is no doubt that both Peter and I found our face-to-face meeting
mutually productive. I received a guided tour of the Casualty Section and was much impressed
with everything I saw and everyone I spoke to (which included Mrs D Sheldon whose name will
be familiar to many enthusiasts). I certainly have some first-hand knowledge now regarding the
pressures under which this small section works, and indeed the wide-ranging tasks it undertakes.

I thoroughly commend Peter Edwards for his far-sightedness in entertaining what, at last, prom-
ises to be a new age of openness, honesty and mutual co-operation. I suspect, however, that there
are others within the Ministry who are, for whatever reason, opposed to this policy. It is that very
draconian attitude, however, which has, in the past, contributed significantly to this sorry situation, and has just as much to answer for as those enthusiasts who have acted in an irresponsible
manner. There is no doubt that Peter Edwards has saved the MOD from a veritable public relations disaster, given the writing of this book and publicity arising. Long may our new working
relationship with the MOD continue, and let us hope that this 'New Age' will see an end to many
of the problems which have so frequently punctuated the past. Communication, it has to be said,
is a wonderful thing, and I am confident that publication of this book will greatly assist the future.
Hopefully *Missing in Action: Resting in Peace?* will inspire others to behave in a more professional, responsible and law abiding manner.

It is appropriate, I think, to quote Mr Ian Cutts, nephew of Pilot Officer John Wintringham Cutts:-

Thank you for your letter with the quite extraordinary news that your research has at last proved
to the MOD that John Cutts is not 'Missing in Action'. From my own limited correspondence and
discussions with them I realise what a feat you have achieved to convince a Government Department after 57 years that they got things very wrong. At least John can now be finally laid to 'rest'
after all this time.

I hasten to point out, however, that it was not myself alone which made this possible, but ultimately a joint effort between enthusiasts and the Casualty Section. This proves my point that such
an approach can achieve the right result. Having read Chapter Nine, the reader will appreciate
what this particular development means to me personally; Pilot Officer John Cutts: Missing in
Action, now Resting in Peace without a question mark.

# APPENDIX
## Map of Crash Sites

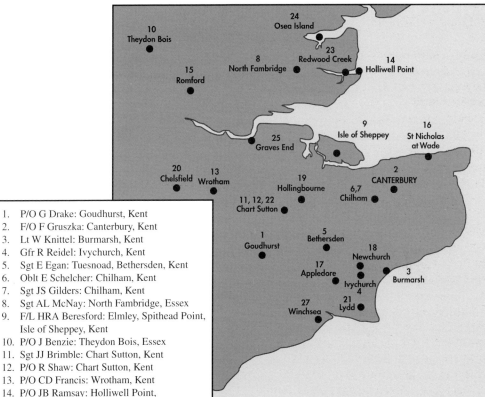

1. P/O G Drake: Goudhurst, Kent
2. F/O F Gruszka: Canterbury, Kent
3. Lt W Knittel: Burmarsh, Kent
4. Gfr R Reidel: Ivychurch, Kent
5. Sgt E Egan: Tuesnoad, Bethersden, Kent
6. Oblt E Schelcher: Chilham, Kent
7. Sgt JS Gilders: Chilham, Kent
8. Sgt AL McNay: North Fambridge, Essex
9. F/L HRA Beresford: Elmley, Spithead Point,
   Isle of Sheppey, Kent
10. P/O J Benzie: Theydon Bois, Essex
11. Sgt JJ Brimble: Chart Sutton, Kent
12. P/O R Shaw: Chart Sutton, Kent
13. P/O CD Francis: Wrotham, Kent
14. P/O JB Ramsay: Holliwell Point,
    Burnham-on-Crouch, Essex
15. F/O MD Doulton: Romford, Essex
16. Uffz F Buchner: St Nicholas-at-Wade, Kent
17. Lt H Strobl: Appledore, Kent
18. P/O A Clarke: Newchurch, Kent
19. Sgt E Scott: Hollingbourne, Kent
20. Sgt J Ellis: Chelsfield, Kent
21. Sgt S Duszinski: Lydd, Kent
22. P/O JW Cutts: Chart Sutton, Kent
23. Sgt G Edworthy: Redwood Creek,
    River Crouch, Essex
24. F/L PS Weaver DFC, Osea Island,
    River Blackwater, Essex
25. F/Sgt EE Williams: Gravesend, Kent
26. Sgt HH Adair: Cosham, near Portsmouth
27. P/O C Barber: Winchelsea, East Sussex
28. Obgfr H Schilling &
    Obfw K Herzog: Long Bredy, Dorset

# Acknowledgements

As ever, a number of people have kindly assisted with the research for this book.

Firstly, I must mention certain relatives of those 'Missing in Action', in particular Mrs Barbara Sykes (neice of Flying Officer F. Gruszka), Mr Paul Weaver (nephew of Flight Lieutenant PS Weaver DFC), Mrs Mary Cooper (sister of Sergeant PRC McIntosh), Mrs Jane Somerville (sister of Sergeant E Egan), Mrs Carol Doulton & Mr Paul Doulton (widow & son of Flying Officer MD Doulton); also Mrs Peta Jones (widow of Flight Lieutenant T Webster DFC), Mr Les Drinkwater (brother of Squadron Leader THD Drinkwater DFC), the late Mr John Rose (brother of Sergeant PG Rose), Mr Ian Cutts (nephew of Pilot Officer JW Cutts), Mr Robin Shaw (nephew of Pilot Officer RH Shaw), the late Mr Jack Lowson (brother of Pilot Officer V Lowson), Mr RM Griffiths (brother-in-law of Sergeant G Pearson) and the late sisters of Flying Officer F Surma: Elsbieta Morcinek and Otylia Paszek.

As always, it was a privilege to correspond with certain of the Few who all contributed their memories to whatever extent the passage of time permitted:-

Air Commodore EW Wright CBE DFC DFM
Air Commodore (the late) HA Fenton CBE DSO DFC
Group Captain (the late) GL Denholm DFC
Group Captain JH Hill CBE
Group Captain GAL Manton DSO DFC
Wing Commander NPW Hancock OBE DFC
Wing Commander J Poplawski VM KW DFC
Wing Commander TA Vigors DFC
Wing Commander FW Higginson OBE DFC DFM
Wing Commander PL Parrott DFC AFC
Wing Commander RW Foster DFC
Squadron Leader RA Beardsley DFC
Squadron Leader J Stokoe DFC
Squadron Leader ED Glaser DFC
Squadron Leader JI Hutchinson
Squadron Leader (the late) GHE Welford AE
Squadron Leader (the late) BH Drobinski VM KW DFC
Squadron Leader PDM Down
Squadron Leader CN Birch AFC
Flight Lieutenant RL Earp
Flight Lieutenant TG Pickering
Flight Lieutenant P Hairs MBE
Flight Lieutenant G Stevens
Flight Lieutenant LA Martel VM KW
Flight Lieutenant G Batt
Flight Lieutenant RT Holmes
Lieutenant-Commander (the late) JK Quill OBE AFC FRAeS
Mr PH Fox

I am indebted to the Keeper and Staff of the Public Record Office, and also extend appreciation to the MOD (in particular Mr P Edwards, Mrs D Sheldon and Mrs J Hawran), CWGC, Essex Record Office, Department for Kentish Studies, Kent County Council, Polish Institute, Imperial War Museum, Battle of Britain Fighter Association, Mr RAH Davies (HM Coroner for Hereford & Worcester), Mr Brian ND Smith (HM Coroner for Ashford & Shepway District) and his Officer, Mr Les White, Mr Roger Sykes (HM Coroner for Mid Kent & Medway District), PC Matthew Coumbe (Coroner's Officer for the City of Portsmouth and South East Hampshire), and Neville Cullingford of the Royal Observer Corps Museum.

The following friends and fellow enthusiasts ( not listed in any order) all assisted in various ways, and without their help this book would not have been possible:-

John Bale, David Brocklehurst, Colin Brown, Andy Saunders, Steve Vizard, Mark Kirby, Peter Osborne, Michael Payne, Mike Llewellyn, David Buchanan, Bill Bond, Ted Sergison, Jean Liddicoat, John Foreman, Norman Franks, Keith Dowel, Graham Cooke, Robert Amos, Andrew Long, Dennis Williams, Dave Smith, John Tickner, Philip Harvey, Ernie Hardy, Peter Bonell, Don Caldwell, Larry McHale, Allan White, Eugene Conway & Chris Goss.

We are again grateful to all at Aspect Design for making book production and business such an enjoyable experience; well done Allan, Sue, Simon and Paul!

I would also like to express appreciation to the surviving fighter pilots and other personalities who, often together with their wives, husbands or partners, turn out every year to our book launches and other events. In addition we thank Ramrod Publications' various helpers for their continued support. Without such friendships our operation would be impossible.

My wife, Anita, continues to provide an *essential* PA service, not to mention running Ramrod Publications and our hectic household. Our children, James and Hannah, require a special mention for tolerating a father who has two demanding jobs. The interest shown in the subject by Simon is also uplifting.

# Bibliography

For further recommended reading regarding the Battle of Britain, I would refer the reader to the extensive Bibliography in my previous book, *Bader's Duxford Fighters*.

For the specific purposes of this book, my references have included various documents preserved at the Public Record Office, Essex County Archive, Centre for Kentish Studies, and divers papers obtained from registry offices and various HM Coroners. I also referred to articles in numerous newspapers, and the following magazines: *Fly Past*, *After the Battle*, *RAF News*, *Aviation Archaeologist* and *Aeroplane Monthly*. In addition, I have quoted extensively from my own correspondence and that provided by others, and interviews with relatives, veterans and enthusiasts. The Protection of Military Remains Act, 1986, was essential reading and obtainable from HMSO together with other MOD documents relating to aircraft recovery.

To assist with the reconstruction of Battle of Britain events and combats, and the question of 'Missing' pilots, I would especially refer the reader to the following publications:-

*The Battle of Britain Then & Now Mk V*, Edited by Winston G Ramsay, After the Battle 1989.
*The Blitz Then & Now* (Volumes I & II), Edited by Winston G Ramsay, After the Battle 1989 & 1990.
*Battle Over Britain*, Francis K Mason, Aston Publications 1990.
*Men of the Battle of Britain*, Ken Wynn, Gliddon Books, 1989.
*Battle of Britain: The Forgotten Months*, John Foreman, Air Research Publications, 1988.
*The Hardest Day*, Alfred Price, MacDonald & Jane's Publishers Ltd., 1979.
*Bader's Duxford Fighters: The Big Wing Controversy*, Dilip Sarkar, Ramrod Publications, 1997.
*The Invisible Thread: A Spitfire's Tale*, Dilip Sarkar, Ramrod Publications, 1992.
*Angriff Westland*, Dilip Sarkar, Ramrod Publications, 1994.
*Through Peril to the Stars*, Dilip Sarkar, Ramrod Publications 1993.
*Spitfire Squadron*, Dilip Sarkar, Air Research Publications, 1990.
*One Hurricane, One Raid*, Geoff Rayner, Airlife, 1990.
*JG26 War Diary Volume One 1939-1942*, Donald Caldwell, Grub Street, 1996.

The following television programmes and video are also of interest:-

*Some Of Our Airmen Are No Longer Missing*, Nomad Productions, 1990 (video distributed by 'DD' Distribution).
*Missing: No Known Grave*, BBC 2 '40 Minute' documentary, first broadcast 1980.
*Grave Robbers*, Meridian TV documentary, first broadcast November 1996.